gas

written and researched by

Greg Ward

ROUGH
GUIDES

www.roughguides.com

Contents

The changing face of the Strip colour section following p.80

That's entertainment colour section following p.144

Aria • Crystals
CITYCENTER
• Mandarin
Oriental
Colour maps following p.208

3

Introduction to
Las Vegas

Shimmering from the desert haze of Nevada like a latter-day El Dorado, Las Vegas is the most dynamic, spectacular city on earth. At the start of the twentieth century, it didn't even exist; one decade into the 21st, it's home to two million people. A showcase for all that's most extravagant and exuberant about the modern United States, it attracts almost forty million visitors each year, anticipating their every appetite and indulging their every whim.

Las Vegas is not like other cities. No city has ever so brazenly valued its visitors above its residents. All its growth has been fuelled by tourism, but the tourists haven't spoiled the "real" city; there is no real city. Instead, the whole thing is completely self-referential; the legendary **Las Vegas Strip** boasts twenty of the world's 27 largest hotels not because visitors want to see the city, but because they want to see the hotels themselves. Most visitors never leave the Strip at all, except perhaps for a day-trip to the Grand Canyon, and many barely explore beyond their own hotel and its immediate neighbours.

Each of these monsters is much more than a mere hotel, and more too than the **casino** that invariably lies at its core. They're extraordinary places, self-contained fantasy lands of high camp and genuine excitement that can stretch as much as a mile from end to end. As well as luxurious accommodation, each holds half a dozen or more high-class restaurants, a lavish theatre or two, an array of swimming pools, several bars and nightclubs, and perhaps a roller-coaster or gallery or aquarium. But the whole is greater than the sum of its parts: it's entire ensemble that visitors flock to see, from the glorious Roman excess of *Caesars Palace* to the minimalist modernism of *Aria*.

First-time visitors tend to expect Las Vegas to be a repository of **kitsch**, but the casino owners are far too canny to be sentimental about the old days. Yes, there are a few Elvis impersonators around, but what characterizes the city far more is its endless quest for **novelty**. Long before they lose their sparkle, yesterday's showpieces are blasted into rubble, to make way for ever more extravagant replacements. The city's gaze is forever shifting towards what's newest. Currently, that means the **CityCenter** complex's attempt to redefine Las Vegas as a sophisticated contemporary metropolis, but there's always something even bigger and costlier in the pipeline.

Despite the enduring popular image of the casino business as being seedy and quasi-criminal, the days when the Mob controlled Las Vegas are far in the past. No longer is each casino in cut-throat competition with the rest; indeed most now belong to two massive corporations. **MGM Resorts International** owns a massive swathe of properties along the southern Strip, from *Mandalay Bay* all the way to *Bellagio*, while **Harrah's** claims a solid chunk of properties immediately north, centering on *Caesars Palace*. The rivalry between those two blocs is the biggest game in town, but there's still room for some good old-fashioned personal animosity as well, as seen in the endless one-upmanship between Steve Wynn of *Wynn Las Vegas* and Sheldon Adelson of the next-door Venetian.

On the face of it, Las Vegas is supremely democratic. However you may be dressed, however affluent or otherwise you may appear, you'll be welcomed in its stores, restaurants and above all its casinos. The one thing you almost

certainly won't get, however, is the **last laugh**; the whole experience continues to be rooted in the huge profits the casinos rake in from gamblers. Over eighty percent of visitors gamble, and they lose an average of around $500 each. On top of that, most visitors swiftly come to see that virtually any other activity works out cheaper than gambling, so they wind up spending their money on all sorts of other things as well. However, Las Vegas makes so certain that you have such a good time that you don't mind losing a bit of money along the

▲ Elvis impersonator

way; that's why they don't even call it "gambling" anymore, but "gaming."

Las Vegas being forever susceptible to boom-and-bust cycles, its latest era of soaring optimism – and room rates – was brought to an abrupt end by the recession that began in 2008. As a result, it's currently once more an exceptionally **cheap** destination. The fact that you can get a high-quality room on the Strip for well under $50, at least on weekdays, means there's less to gain than ever in spending your time in the ailing downtown, let alone elsewhere, and dining and entertainment prices too are more reasonable than they've been for years.

What to see

▲ Dancer in Studio 54

as Vegas is not a city that holds fascinating little-known neighbourhoods, where visitors can go off the beaten track to have more authentic experiences. Instead, although the urban sprawl stretches fifteen miles both east to west and north to south, only two areas hold any interest for visitors – the Strip and downtown.

The stretch of Las Vegas Boulevard known as the **Strip** begins at the *Stratosphere*, two miles south of downtown, and runs for another four miles south to

Las Vegas for free

The sole defining purpose of Las Vegas is to separate visitors from their money. However, the tradition of using elaborate **free attractions** to lure in passers-by is still going strong. You never have to pay for admission to any casino, and with their flamboyance, inventiveness and sheer scale the dozen largest make compelling spectacles in their own right. In addition, the following specific attractions are the best free shows in town:

Art at CityCenter A dazzling array of contemporary sculpture, by the likes of Henry Moore and Maya Lin, complements the urban modernism of this futuristic ensemble.

The Conservatory and Fountains at Bellagio Both indoors and out, you can always depend on *Bellagio* for old-fashioned, jaw-dropping ostentation.

The Fremont Street Experience When is a street not a street? When it's an "experience", thanks to its digital ceiling.

The Grand Canal at the Venetian Determined to out-Strip the Forum mall at *Caesars Palace*, the *Venetian* went bigger and better with this amazing indoor, upstairs replica of Venice, with a canal running right through the middle.

The Lions at the MGM Grand With a lion for its logo, the MGM did the obvious thing, and installed a real pride of lions to pad through a glass enclosure alongside the casino floor.

The Sirens of TI A real only-in-Vegas moment; having built two full-sized pirate ships, *Treasure Island* swiftly tired of all that yo-ho-ho-ing, and crewed them with lingerie-clad lovelies instead.

The Sphinx at Luxor Pass between the paws of a colossal Sphinx to enter a gigantic pyramid – there's only one place on earth that could happen.

The Volcano at the Mirage The original Stripfront not-just-for-kids nighttime extravaganza, now with a 21st-century revamp.

24hr Las Vegas

If ever a city was designed for round-the-clock living, it's Las Vegas. That's not living as in residing, or building a secure future, of course; it's living as in refusing to go to bed in case you miss something.

While the casinos no longer set out to make visitors lose track of time – all used to be dimly lit, devoid of apparent exits and clock-free – they still stay up all night. Stumble out of your room at 4am in search of a headache pill, or lurch through the front entrance at 6am as you return from a night out, and you're immediately assailed by the siren sound of shrieking slot machines. Bleary-eyed gamblers cluster around the green-baize tables, cocktail waitresses stalk the floors, and the 24hr coffee-shop is still going strong.

Mandalay Bay and the airport. Almost every building along the way is a casino, each frantically clamouring for the attention of the tourists who throng the road day and night. Officially, the Strip is not even in the city at all, but in Clark County; by no coincidence, it begins at the point where Las Vegas Boulevard leaves the city limits, meaning that the casino owners don't pay city taxes.

Downtown too is utterly dominated by casinos, albeit with each individual property being on a smaller scale. Its centrepiece, the **Fremont Street Experience**, is an extraordinary architectural conceit, in which four blocks have been roofed over to give it the feel of a theme park rather than a real city.

City residents, of course, can distinguish between several other Las Vegas neighbourhoods, but tourists are unlikely to see any of them. Broadly speaking, the northeast and northwest quadrants of the metropolis are its less affluent areas, while its most fashionable districts are fast-growing **Henderson** to the southeast and the newer **Summerlin** development to the west.

◄ Cupid's Wedding Chapel

When to go

Las Vegas is at the heart of the hottest, harshest **desert** in North America, and so receives less than four inches of rain (100mm) per year. Temperatures, however, vary enormously, with daytime maximums averaging over **100°F** (38°C) in July and August, and night-time minimums dropping below **freezing** in December and January. As the cliché goes, at least it's a dry heat, meaning that the lack of humidity often makes things more pleasant than they should be. That said, the **mid-summer** heat on the Strip is quite unbearable, making it impossible to walk any distance during the day, so the ideal times to visit are in **spring** between April and May and also during **autumn** between September and October. Hotel swimming pools tend to be closed between October and March inclusive.

The city is at its quietest, and room rates are therefore lowest, during the first few weeks of December and the last few weeks of January, and also during June and July, while Christmas and New Year are the busiest periods of all.

Average temperatures and rainfall

	Jan	Feb	Mar	Apr	May	Jun	Jul	Aug	Sep	Oct	Nov	Dec
Las Vegas												
Max/min (°C)	16/-2	20/1	22/4	27/8	32/12	37/17	40/20	39/19	35/14	29/9	22/2	17/-1
Max/min (°F)	60/29	67/34	72/39	81/45	89/52	99/61	103/68	102/66	95/57	84/47	71/36	61/30
Rainfall (mm)	15	18	15	4	6	2	11	12	8	6	8	10

things not to miss

It's not possible to see everything Las Vegas has to offer in one trip – and we don't suggest you try. What follows, in no particular order, is a selective taste of the city's highlights: eye-popping architecture, fabulous shows and majestic desert scenery. They're arranged in five colour-coded categories to help you find the very best things to see, do and experience. All highlights have a page reference to take you straight into the guide, where you can find out more.

01 Luxor Page **35** • This huge smoked-glass pyramid, complete with giant Sphinx and tongue-in-cheek Egyptian motifs, continues to lure in visitors of all ages.

02 **Fremont Street Experience** Page **85** • How do you persuade tourists it's safe to walk the downtown streets at night? Simple – you put a roof over the lot and turn the night sky into a movie screen.

03 **Cirque du Soleil** Page **147** • With an astonishing seven permanent shows on the Strip, and more on the way, the Canadian circus/theatre troupe has transformed Las Vegas's entertainment scene.

04 **Jubilee!** Page **149** • Las Vegas was weird long before it was postmodern; catch its last surviving ostrich-feathers-and-showtunes revue before an entertainment era ends forever.

05 **The Conservatory at Bellagio** Page **53** • Colourful beyond belief, the changing themed displays in *Bellagio*'s extraordinary indoor flower garden have a hallucinatory intensity.

06 **Zion National Park** Page **113** • If you want to see the Southwestern deserts at their best, on an easy overnight break from Las Vegas, forget the Grand Canyon and head to Utah's Zion instead.

08 **Mon Ami Gabi** Page **134** • Dining al fresco at *Paris*'s sidewalk bistro, right on the Strip beneath the Eiffel Tower, is quintessential Las Vegas.

07 **New York-New York** Page **39** • A loving recreation of the Big Apple in the heart of the Big Cheese, endlessly circled by the demented little yellow cabs of its Roller Coaster.

09 **Hoover Dam** Page **104** • If you wonder what on earth Las Vegas is doing, out here in the barren desert, then drive or fly out to see the dam that built the West, and the surreal waters of Lake Mead – then you'll realise it makes no sense at all.

10 **$500 on black** Page **162** • Can the simple spin of a roulette wheel change your life? It can; thanks to your donation, there'll be even more new casinos to gawk at, next time you come back.

11 **Grand Canal** Page **70** • There's more to see and do at the *Venetian* than perhaps any other casino in town, but it's the absurd Grand Canal, with its gondolas, bridges, squares and high-class shops and restaurants, that you'll be telling the folks back home about.

12 The Stratosphere thrill rides Page **82** • A thousand feet up from the Strip, the top of the *Stratosphere* features not one but four gut-wrenching thrill rides, including one in which you're expected just to jump off the edge.

13 Buffets Page **127** • Whether your tastes run towards the refinement of *Wynn Las Vegas* or the 1950s kitsch of the *Imperial Palace*, you can't leave Las Vegas without sampling at least one all-you-can-eat buffet.

14 The Forum Shops Page **172** • The shopping mall at *Caesars Palace* may be the busiest in the entire US, but its "living statues" and fake sky make it fun even for determined small spenders.

15 **The Havasupai Reservation** Page **111** • The turquoise waterfalls of this remote offshoot of the Grand Canyon, home to the Havasupai for a thousand years, feel as far removed from Las Vegas as it's possible to imagine.

16 **Gaudí Bar at Sunset Station** Page **144** • Quite why the lounge bar of a suburban casino should take the form of a surreal, mosaic-ceilinged tribute to Spanish architect Gaudí is just another of Las Vegas's eternally fascinating mysteries.

Basics

Basics

Getting there

For US and Canadian travellers who live too far from Las Vegas simply to drive there, and for international visitors, the obvious way to visit the city is to fly direct to McCarran International Airport, just off the south end of the Strip.

Flights from the US and Canada

Every major US airline flies to Las Vegas. Apart from the national carriers, the largest operator is **Southwest Airlines**, which offers nonstop flights between Las Vegas and a phenomenal number of cities – more than sixty, if you can be bothered to count them, ranging from Virginia Beach to Spokane. In addition, **Midwest** flies to Denver and Milwaukee; **JetBlue** has direct flights from New York (JFK) and Boston, and also from Burbank in California; **SkyWest** connects with Salt Lake City; and **WestJet** serves many Canadian destinations.

It's usually possible to find return **fares** to Las Vegas in midweek for little more than $100 from Los Angeles, $250 from Seattle, $350 from New York or CAN$350 from Toronto; prices rise significantly at weekends. Room rates in Las Vegas are so low these days that there's little benefit in booking your flight and accommodation together as a package; watch out, though, for special deals offered by the casinos themselves.

Flights from the UK and Ireland

The only direct, nonstop flights from Britain or Ireland to Las Vegas are the **Virgin Atlantic** services from London Gatwick (daily) and from Manchester (Thurs & Sun). With their convenient departure times and ten-hour journey duration these are by far the most appealing options, but typical round-trip fares range from around £500 in winter up to around £750 in summer.

Otherwise, all alternatives require at least one stop en route. From the UK, you can either fly nonstop to the West Coast and catch a connecting flight back to Las Vegas from there, or touch down on the East Coast and then fly west; time-wise, it makes little difference. If you'd rather keep your flying time to a minimum, it's also worth considering flying nonstop to California and driving

---

US entry regulations

Under the **visa waiver scheme**, passport-holders from Britain, Ireland, Australia, New Zealand and most European countries do not require visas for trips to the US, so long as they stay less than ninety days and have an onward or return ticket. However, anyone planning to use the visa waiver scheme is required to apply for **travel authorization** in advance, online. It's a very quick and straightforward process, via the website ⊕www.cbp.gov/xp/cgov/travel/. Fail to do so, however, and you may well be denied entry. Once you have authorization, you can simply fill in the visa waiver form that's handed out on incoming planes. Immigration control takes place at your point of arrival on US soil.

In addition, your passport must be **machine-readable**, with a barcode-style number. All children need to have their own individual passports. Holders of older non-readable passports should either obtain new ones or apply for visas prior to travel.

Prospective visitors from parts of the world not mentioned above need a valid passport and a non-immigrant visitor's visa. How you'll obtain a visa depends on what country you're in and your status when you apply, so call the nearest US embassy or consulate. For full details visit ⊕travel.state.gov.

to Las Vegas from there, taking advantage of the state's low car-rental rates.

From Ireland, you can either fly with Aer Lingus or Delta to various East-Coast destinations, and take a connecting flight to Las Vegas, or fly to London and take your pick of transatlantic routes.

Packages can work out cheaper than arranging the same trip yourself, especially for a short-term stay. All the transatlantic airlines listed on p.21 offer all-inclusive flight-and-accommodation deals via their websites, though be sure to check the current room rates at the specified hotel before you pay for a package.

Flights from Australia, New Zealand and South Africa

There are no direct flights from Australia or New Zealand or South Africa to Las Vegas, so you'll have to fly to one of the main US gateway airports and pick up onward connections – or a rental car – from there.

The cheapest route, and the one with the most frequent services from **Australia and New Zealand**, is to Los Angeles, which also has plenty of onward flights to Albuquerque, Las Vegas and Phoenix. Air New Zealand and Qantas/American fly to LA at least twice daily, while United flies once a day; other airlines that serve LA include Japan Airlines and Singapore Airlines. From **South Africa**, by far the cheapest route is usually to fly with Virgin from Johannesburg to London, and then from London to Las Vegas, which costs in the region of R10,000.

By car

Much the busiest **driving route** into Las Vegas is the **I-15** freeway from southern California. Traffic congestion, especially close to the state line, can mean that the 269-mile drive from LA takes as long as eight hours. Las Vegas Boulevard South, which becomes the Strip, begins to parallel I-15 well before it reaches the city, but the quickest way to reach your final destination

Six steps to a better kind of travel

At Rough Guides we are passionately committed to travel. We feel strongly that only through travelling do we truly come to understand the world we live in and the people we share it with – plus tourism has brought a great deal of **benefit** to developing economies around the world over the last few decades. But the extraordinary growth in tourism has also damaged some places irreparably, and of course **climate change** is exacerbated by most forms of transport, especially flying. This means that now more than ever it's important to **travel thoughtfully** and **responsibly**, with respect for the cultures you're visiting – not only to derive the most benefit from your trip but also to preserve the best bits of the planet for everyone to enjoy. At Rough Guides we feel there are six main areas in which you can make a difference:

• Consider what you're contributing to the **local economy**, and how much the services you use do the same, whether it's through employing local workers and guides or sourcing locally grown produce and local services.

• Consider the **environment** on holiday as well as at home. Water is scarce in many developing destinations, and the biodiversity of local flora and fauna can be adversely affected by tourism. Try to patronize businesses that take account of this.

• Travel with a purpose, not just to tick off experiences. Consider **spending longer** in a place, and getting to know it and its people.

• Give thought to how often you **fly**. Try to avoid short hops by air and more harmful night flights.

• Consider **alternatives to flying**, travelling instead by bus, train, boat and even by bike or on foot where possible.

• Make your trips "**climate neutral**" via a reputable carbon offset scheme. All Rough Guide flights are offset, and every year we donate money to a variety of charities devoted to combating the effects of climate change.

will almost certainly be to stay on the interstate as long as possible. I-15 also connects Las Vegas with Salt Lake City, 421 miles northeast.

From the major cities of Arizona, direct access is provided by **US-93**, which leaves I-40 at Kingman, a hundred miles southeast. It joins **US-95**, running north from Needles, California, outside Boulder City; together, the two become **I-515**, which crosses I-15 immediately northwest of downtown Las Vegas.

Four hundred miles northwest of Las Vegas, US-95 meets I-80 thirty miles east of Reno. Using that interstate is the fastest way to get between Las Vegas and San Francisco, but threading cross-country via Yosemite and Death Valley national parks is a much more scenic option.

Buses

Greyhound's long-distance **buses** to and from Los Angeles, Phoenix, Salt Lake City, Denver, Reno, San Diego, Bakersfield and other cities use a terminal alongside the *Plaza* hotel at 200 S Main St downtown. For schedules and fares, call ☏1-800/231-2222, or access ⓦwww.greyhound.com.

In addition, **LuxBus** (☏1-888/217-4066, ⓦwww.luxbusamerica.com) offers somewhat more expensive daily buses to Las Vegas from Los Angeles ($88 one-way, $120 return) and Anaheim ($68/$99).

Trains

Amtrak stopped running passenger **trains** to Las Vegas in 1997, and its downtown terminal was demolished. Constant rumours and proposals suggest that a new light-rail service between Los Angeles and Las Vegas will come into operation at some point during the next few years, with a projected journey time of 5hr 30min. Some level of subsidy from the casinos is anticipated; individual carriages may belong to specific casinos, and be equipped with slot machines to be switched on as soon the train crosses the Nevada state line.

Airlines

Aer Lingus ⓦwww.aerlingus.com
Air Canada ⓦwww.aircanada.com
Alaska Airlines ⓦwww.alaskaair.com
American Airlines ⓦwww.aa.com
British Airways ⓦwww.ba.com
Continental Airlines ⓦwww.continental.com
Delta Air Lines ⓦwww.delta.com
Hawaiian Airlines ⓦwww.hawaiianair.com
JetBlue ⓦwww.jetblue.com
Midwest Airlines ⓦwww.midwestairlines.com
Qantas Airways ⓦwww.qantas.com
Scenic Airlines ⓦwww.scenic.com
Skywest ⓦwww.skywest.com
Southwest ⓦwww.southwest.com
United Airlines ⓦwww.united.com
US Airways ⓦwww.usair.com
Virgin Atlantic ⓦwww.virgin-atlantic.com
Westjet ⓦwww.westjet.com

Arrival

The runways of Las Vegas' busy **McCarran International Airport** (☏702/261-5211, ⓦwww.mccarran.com) start barely a mile east of the southern end of the Strip. However, the main terminal is a three-mile drive from the Strip via Tropicana Avenue and Paradise Road, while downtown is roughly four miles distant. Although some hotels run free airport shuttle buses for their guests, most people just hop in a **taxi**. Theoretically, a cab ride from the airport to the southern end of the Strip will cost $15 and up, and more like $30 for the northern Strip or downtown, but traffic delays can easily force those fares up by another $10 or so.

Car rental is readily available (see p.22), while **Bell Trans** (☏702/739-7990, ⓦwww .bell-trans.com) runs minibuses from the airport to the Strip ($6.50) and downtown ($8), leaving from just outside the terminal. Making the journey by **public bus** ($3; ⓦ www.catride.com) is possible, but slow and laborious; if you must, take CAT service #108 from the airport to the *Sahara* monorail, or take #109 to downtown.

Getting around

If you're happy to see no more of Las Vegas than the Strip and perhaps downtown – and on a short visit, there's no great reason to venture any further – then it's perfectly possible to survive without a car. However, even the Strip is too long to explore comfortably on foot; walking more than a couple of blocks in summer is exhausting, so you can expect to make heavy use of taxis, shuttle buses and the monorail links. Ranging further afield, the metropolitan area is very large and spread out, with only intermittent public transport access, making driving the only practical way to explore, while the excursions detailed in chapters Seven and Eight require the use of your own vehicle.

Driving

Las Vegas is plagued by severe traffic problems, especially on the Strip. That said, so long as you're not in a hurry, driving along the Strip is an exhilarating sensory blast, and worth experiencing both by day and night. When speed is a priority, use I-15, even for short hops. The fastest east–west route tends to be Desert Inn Road, which passes under the Strip and over I-15, with connections to neither.

All the Strip casinos offer **free parking** to guests and non-guests alike, usually in huge garages at the back. The snag is that the walk from your car to wherever you actually want to go – your hotel room, for example – can be as much as a mile in places like *Caesars Palace* or the *MGM Grand*. If you're spending a day touring the Strip, you may prefer to go through the rigmarole of parking once only, somewhere central. **Valet parking**, usually available at the main casino entrance, can save a lot of stress; it's nominally free, although a tip of around $2 is all but obligatory.

Renting a car is worth considering if you're either staying off the Strip or are planning on any amount of exploring. Typical rates in Las Vegas, including taxes, start at around $40 per day, $200 per week. All the major chains have outlets at the airport, and nearly every hotel is affiliated with at least one car rental outfit.

Car rental companies

Alamo ⓦ www.alamo.com
Avis ⓦ www.avis.com
Budget ⓦ www.budget.com
Dollar ⓦ www.dollar.com
Enterprise ⓦ www.enterprise.com
Hertz ⓦ www.hertz.com
Holiday Autos ⓦ www.holidayautos.com
National ⓦ www.nationalcar.com
Thrifty ⓦ www.thrifty.com

Taxis

Every casino has a line of **taxis** waiting at its front entrance. Standard fares are $3.30 for the first mile and $2.40 for each additional mile, but the meter continues to run when you're caught in traffic, at the rate of $1 every two minutes. A $1.80 surcharge is added for trips to the airport; sample fares for the airport run are listed above. **Tip** the driver between fifteen and twenty percent.

To **call a cab**, contact ABC (☎702/736-8444; ⓦ www.lvcabs.com); Ace (☎702/736-8383; also on ⓦ www.lvcabs.com); or

Sightseeing tours

Las Vegas is not a city that lends itself to organized **sightseeing tours**. On foot, you'd have to walk too far; on a bus, you couldn't visit the Strip casinos that are the main focus of interest. What bus tours there are tend to head out from the city instead, mainly to the destinations described in Chapter 7. Gray Line, for example, charges $60 for a 4hr 30min trip to Hoover Dam, and $55 for a six-hour tour of the Strip and downtown at night (☎702/384-1234, ⊛www.grayline.com).

Operators who run tours to the **Grand Canyon** are listed on p.109. Among them, helicopter companies such as Papillon (☎702/736-7243 or 888/635-7272, ⊛www.papillon.com) and Maverick (☎702/261-0007 or 888/261-4414, ⊛www.maverick helicopter.com) also have scenic flights over Las Vegas itself, from around $60 for ten minutes.

Checker (☎702/873-2000; ⊛www.ycstrans .com).

The Monorail

The **Las Vegas Monorail** (Mon–Thurs 7am–2am, Fri–Sun 7am–3am; one-way trip $5, 1-day pass $12; ⊛www.lvmonorail.com), runs along the eastern side of the Strip from the *MGM Grand* to the *Sahara*, with a business-traveller-friendly detour off the Strip via the Convention Center and the *Hilton*. Though trumpeted when it opened in 2004 as the cure for local traffic problems, the Monorail doesn't connect the Strip to either the airport or downtown – thanks largely to political and commercial pressures – and has been a financial disaster. It's just possible it will close down altogether, but for the moment it remains more of a handy, high-priced occasional extra than a much-needed lifeline. Be warned, too, that for short hops along the Strip the Monorail can easily be slower than walking, because the actual stations tend to be located at the very back of the casinos.

In addition, separate **free monorail** systems, not connected with each other or the main line but in their own small-scale way much more useful, link *Mandalay Bay* with *Excalibur* via *Luxor*; the *Monte Carlo* with *Bellagio* via *CityCenter*; and the *Mirage* with *TI*.

Buses

CAT **buses** (flat fare $2 per ride; ☎702/228-7433, ⊛www.catride.com) serve the entire city from their hub at the **Bonneville Transit Center**, a few blocks south of Fremont Street at 101 E Bonneville Ave at Casino Center Boulevard. The most useful routes for visitors are two 24hr services – the **Deuce bus**, which runs from the Downtown Transportation Center all the way down the Strip as far as *Mandalay Bay*, and the faster **Gold Line**, which also runs down the Strip from downtown, though it makes fewer stops and bypasses the *Riviera* and *Stratosphere* by going via the Convention Center instead, and continues further south to the Town Square and Las Vegas Outlet Center shopping malls. Passengers using these two routes can buy a **two-hour pass** for $5 or an **all-day pass** for $7; if you only use the other city routes, which is not a very likely option, the passes cost $3 and $5 respectively.

The media

Despite their radically different standpoints on practically every topic, the two long-standing rival daily **newspapers** in Las Vegas, the *Las Vegas Review-Journal* (⊛www.lvrj.com) and the *Las Vegas Sun* (⊛www.lasvegassun.com), have recently merged to form a single rather bizarre hybrid, in which they're sold together but still bear separate mastheads. It's worth buying at least once during your stay, as the outer pages every day are devoted to a basic, current city guide. Otherwise, Friday's edition, which features the useful *Neon* listings supplement, is the best. The same conglomerate also owns the free *City Life* (Ⓦ www.lasvegascitylife.com), a nominally "alternative" weekly, published on Thursdays and the best source of up-to-date local listings.

In addition, any number of **freesheets and magazines** – usually bursting with discount vouchers, plus details of accommodation, buffets and the latest shows – provide local information.

Seasonal events

Although Las Vegas celebrates far fewer annual festivals than most American cities, almost every major event in the national calendar – from public holidays to sporting events – has a major impact on visitor levels, and thus on hotel room rates. The city's annual calendar is in many ways most useful for planning when *not* to visit. In particular, Las Vegas hosts several enormous **conventions**, each one capable of attracting up to 200,000 participants, and sending room rates soaring – partly due to the demand, but also because conventioneers tend not to gamble as much as tourists.

Mid-Jan Consumer Electronics Show
Mid-Feb Men's Apparel Guild (MAGIC) convention
Late Feb NASCAR Weekend/Winston Cup Ⓦ www.lvms.com. Racing at the Las Vegas Motor Speedway.

Early April National Association of Broadcasters convention
Late May to mid-July World Series of Poker Ⓦ www.wsop.com. Held at the Rio casino.
June CineVegas Ⓦ www.cinevegas.com. Popular little film festival, centered on the Palms casino, and attracting a considerable roster of A-list celebrities and filmmakers.
Mid-Aug Men's Apparel Guild (MAGIC) convention (again)
Early Nov Specialty Equipment Manufacturers Association (SEMA) convention
Early Dec National Finals Rodeo Ⓦ www.nfrexperience.com. Ten-day rodeo at Thomas & Mack Center.
Dec 31 New Year's Eve celebrations, festivities and concerts

Travelling with children

Despite the claims a few years back that Las Vegas was about to become a child-friendly destination, it never quite did. For a brief period the casinos competed to build theme parks and other attractions geared towards children, but it soon became clear that few visitors actually wanted to bring their kids, and those who did bring them didn't gamble enough.

While Las Vegas may primarily be an adult playground, there's plenty about it for kids to enjoy. In addition to the **Top Ten** attractions for kids listed on p.40, the sheer spectacle of the Strip mega-resorts is more likely to impress them than, say, the lacklustre

Children's Museum downtown (see p.90). And in summer, the **pools** at the bigger casinos are irresistible. Just be warned that almost all the time you spend in the city itself is likely to be in casino hotels, which require a huge amount of walking, within each property as well as from one to the next.

Note that it is not legal for under-21s to be in gambling areas (or to drink alcohol). In practice that usually means you can walk through the casino itself with your kids, but not stop for any reason. Properties such as *Bellagio* and *Wynn Las Vegas*, however, forbid under-18s, other than guests, to enter the building at all, and don't allow strollers; the children of non-guests can only enter to visit a specific show or restaurant. A city-wide **curfew** means that under-18s must be off the street by 10pm each night.

The big Strip casinos have stopped offering in-house **babysitters**, but all can put guests in touch with local agencies.

Finally, parents with kids in tow are often troubled by the in-your-face **sexualisation** of the Strip as a whole, and in particular the constant barrage of advertisements, fliers and street touts offering escort services, private dancers and the like.

Travel essentials

Costs

This book contains advice and specific information on prices for all Las Vegas activities and expenditures. By way of a general overview, North American travellers can expect to find prices in the city broadly similar to the rest of the US, with the exception of hotel costs, which are currently exceptionally low by national standards, and nightlife, from clubs to shows, which is expensive. Most visitors from Europe and Australasia feel that their money goes further in the US than it does at home.

If you want to keep your budget down, there's no need to rent a car to see the city itself. You should be able to find a room on the Strip for $50 or less on weekdays, more like $80 at weekends, while you can eat well for around $30 per day.

Crime and personal safety

No one could pretend that Las Vegas is crime-free. While you're very unlikely to be robbed or attacked in the casinos, on the Strip or on the major downtown streets – all are well lit and well policed – it's essential to watch out for pickpockets, and be careful not to display your cash. Always be on your guard when it comes to interactions with strangers. Never divulge your room number, and never accept food or drink unless you're sure of the source. Casino parking garages are also constantly patrolled, but be sure you know where the exits are before you park, and park as close to them as you can.

Electricity

The US electricity supply is 110 volts AC. Plugs are standard two-pins, so you'll need an adapter and voltage converter for your own electrical appliances if coming from a country with a different system.

Health

For **emergency** medical assistance, call ☎911. **Hospitals** with 24hr emergency rooms include the University Medical Center, 1800 W Charleston Blvd (☎702/383-2000, ⓦwww.umc-cares.org), and Sunrise Hospital, 3186 Maryland Parkway (☎702/731-8000, ⓦwww.sunrisehospital.com). Lesser problems can more easily be taken to the fully equipped Harmon Medical Center, 150 E

Rough Guides travel insurance

Rough Guides has teamed up with WorldNomads.com to offer great travel insurance deals. Policies are available to residents of over 150 countries, with cover for a wide range of adventure sports, 24hr emergency assistance, high levels of medical and evacuation cover and a stream of travel safety information. Roughguides.com users can take advantage of their policies online 24/7, from anywhere in the world – even if you're already travelling. And since plans often change when you're on the road, you can extend your policy and even claim online. Roughguides.com users who buy travel insurance with WorldNomads.com can also leave a positive footprint and donate to a community development project. For more information go to ⓦwww.roughguides.com/shop.

Harmon Ave (Mon–Fri 8am–5pm; ℡702/796-1116, ⓦwww.harmonmedicalcenter.com), or contact your hotel's front desk for assistance. **Pharmacies** on the Strip include the 24hr CVS Pharmacy, next to the *Monte Carlo* at 3758 Las Vegas Blvd S (℡702/262-9284) and Walgreens adjoining the *Palazzo* at 3339 Las Vegas Blvd S (℡702/369-8166).

Insurance

Because medical care in the US is expensive, all travellers visiting from overseas should be sure to buy some form of **travel insurance**. American and Canadian citizens should check they're not already covered by their homeowners' insurance or – in some cases – credit card policies. Most Canadians are covered for medical mishaps overseas by their provincial health plans.

Internet

All Las Vegas hotel-casinos offer internet access for their guests. Generally you have to pay, with the typical rate being an exorbitant $10 or more per day. At most properties, including all those owned by MGM Resorts, internet usage is included in the compulsory "resort fee" (see p.120); in Harrah's-owned hotels, it's optional. As a result, **free wi-fi** is much harder to find than you might expect. The only free wi-fi locations on the Strip when this book went to press were: the whole of the *Venetian* and the *Palazzo*; the Apple stores in the Forum and the Fashion Show Mall; the *Pizza Place* in *Wynn*; in and around the *Krispy Kreme* outlet in *Excalibur*; and around the *Coffee Bean* outlet in the Miracle Mile shops in *Planet Hollywood*. Elsewhere in the city, your best bet is coffee bars in general.

Money and banks

Although there's not a single bank on the Strip, there is still no easier city for getting cash or changing money: the casinos gladly convert almost any currency, day and night, and their walls are festooned with every conceivable ATM machine (most of which impose a service charge of around $2). Bear in mind that withdrawing cash with a credit card can incur punitive interest.

Phones

If you want to use your cellphone (mobile phone) in Las Vegas, you'll need to check with your phone provider whether it will work there, and what the call charges are.

Unless you have a tri-band or a 4-band phone, a mobile bought for use outside the US may not work inside the States (and vice versa), while many US phones only work within their local area code.

To save money on calls when you're on the road, it's well worth buying a **prepaid phone card**, available in various denominations from casino convenience stores, gas stations, supermarkets and other outlets. These offer

Calling home from abroad

Note that the initial zero is omitted from the area code when dialling the UK, Ireland, Australia and New Zealand from the US.

Australia 00 + 61
New Zealand 00 + 64
UK 00 + 44
Republic of Ireland 00 + 353
South Africa 00 + 27

sizeable savings on conventional phone rates – not least because they're normally accessed via a toll-free number that incurs no additional charge when called from a hotel room. Alternatively, if you have a smartphone you may want to use VOIP services such as Skype using a free wi-fi connection (see p.27).

Tax

Sales tax is currently set at 8.1 percent in Las Vegas. **Room tax** is charged at twelve percent on the Strip, and thirteen percent downtown.

Time

Las Vegas is on Pacific Standard Time, which is three hours behind Eastern Standard Time and eight hours behind Greenwich Mean Time, but moves its clocks forward by one hour to operate daylight saving between the first Sunday in April and the last Sunday in October.

Tipping

When in doubt, tip. The usual rate in restaurants or taxis is fifteen to twenty percent. In your hotel, for assistance with luggage, tip $1–2 per bag; for valet parking, $2; for maid service, $1–2 per day at the end of your stay; and for concrete help from a concierge, such as making a reservation, $5. You're also expected to tip dealers at the gaming tables a chip or two each time you win (and you can place bets on behalf of the dealer, if you choose). Bar staff, or cocktail waitresses bringing free drinks, normally expect $1–2 per drink.

Travellers with Disabilities

While all the major casinos offer designated rooms for the physically challenged – plus, of course, accessible gaming facilities – the buildings themselves are on such a vast scale that visiting Las Vegas can be an exhausting experience. The Convention and Visitors Authority runs an advice line at ☏702/892-7525; to arrange for a free disabled parking permit, call ☏702/229-6431.

Visitor Information

Although Las Vegas does have a **visitor centre** at the vast Convention Center, at 3150 Paradise Rd (Mon–Fri 8am–5pm; ☏1-877/847-4858, ⓦwww.vegasfreedom .com), it's not worth visiting. At half a mile east of the Strip it's too far to reach on foot, and its brochures hold little that you can't find more easily elsewhere. The casino where you're staying, for example, will have its own booking or concierge desk that can make reservations for shows, tours and the like, plus racks of brochures. Local newspapers and free magazines are detailed on p.24, while useful websites are listed below.

ⓦ**www.cheapovegas.com** Advice and information from a budget-oriented perspective.

ⓦ**www.eatinglv.com** Lively blog on the city's dining scene.

ⓦ**www.gayvegas.com** The best source for information on the city's gay scene.

ⓦ**www.lasvegasadvisor.com** Information and forums for Las Vegas visitors.

ⓦ**www.lasvegasgleaner.com** Progressive political blog.

ⓦ**www.lasvegassun.com** The best local newspaper site, with a searchable archive of every article for years.

ⓦ**www.lvol.com** Information, reservations and reviews for Las Vegas entertainment, including all the big shows.

ⓦ**www.lvrj.com** Website for the *Las Vegas Review-Journal*, with the latest details from the paper's Neon supplement.

ⓦ**www.ratevegas.com** Blog focusing on casino news, with a strong bias towards design and architecture.

ⓦ**www.vegastodayandtomorrow.com** All the latest news on forthcoming projects, as well as an archive of those that never got off the ground, and some amazing maps and statistics.

The City

The City

The South Strip

Broadly speaking, the Strip has been creeping steadily southward for over sixty years, the empty spaces at its southern end forever tempting developers with the twin advantages of room to build and proximity to the airport. When *Excalibur* opened just south of Tropicana Boulevard in 1990, it was seen as a daring move, but within a few years *Luxor* and *Mandalay Bay* had pushed yet further south. Exactly what constitutes the southernmost point of the Strip has become a moot point, as during the last few years new shopping malls and even casino resorts have appeared way to the south along Las Vegas Boulevard, but by any reckoning *Mandalay Bay* still counts as the first significant Strip landmark. Linked to its neighbours both by indoor passageways and an outdoor monorail, it's also as far south as any pedestrian sightseer would ever venture.

Of the six south-Strip casinos described in this chapter, all except the veteran *Tropicana* belong to the company now known as MGM Resorts International. The remaining five therefore tend to complement rather than to compete with each other. The *MGM Grand* and the hipper *Mandalay Bay* are renowned for their fine dining and nightlife; *New York-New York* and *Luxor* are better known for their eye-catching design; and *Excalibur* is the game-for-a-laugh family alternative.

How the Strip began

Seventy years ago, as Hwy-51, Las Vegas Boulevard was just a dusty desert thoroughfare, scattered with the occasional edge-of-town motel as it set off south toward California. Now, as a four-mile showcase of the most extravagant architecture on earth, it's a tourist destination in its own right, indeed second only to Orlando as the most popular in the US.

The boulevard was nicknamed "The Strip" because it reminded former LA police captain **Guy McAfee** of the Sunset Strip. McAfee moved to Las Vegas in 1938, after being obliged to resign because he controlled a string of illegal gambling joints, and took over the boulevard's first casino, the *Pair-O-Dice Club*. Over the next ten years, it was joined on the Strip by *El Rancho* in 1941, the *Last Frontier* in 1942, Bugsy Siegel's legendary *Flamingo* in 1946 and the *Thunderbird* in 1948.

For casino owners, much of the appeal of the nascent Strip was that it lay outside city limits in Clark County, where they could dominate what little political life there was, sparing themselves the scrutiny suffered by their rivals downtown. Their control of the county machine enabled them to resist repeated attempts to bring the Strip under the jurisdiction of the city authorities, and they've been free to pursue untrammelled development ever since.

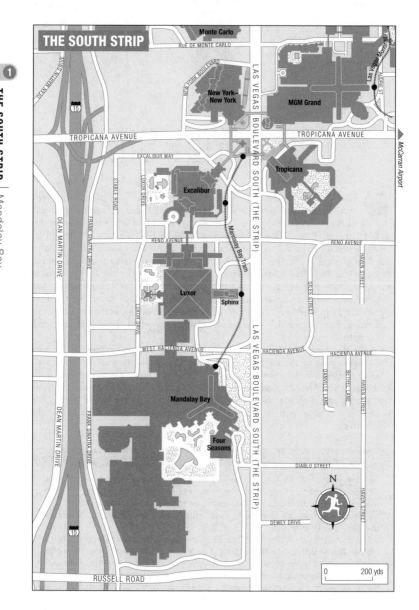

Mandalay Bay

3950 Las Vegas Blvd S ☎702/632-7777, ⓦmandalaybay.com. Hotel accommodation is reviewed on p.122; restaurants include Aureole (p.131), Border Grill (p.131) and Hussong's Cantina (p.131); bars and clubs include include Minus5 Ice Lounge (p.142), Red Square (p.143) and the House of Blues (p.146); and the shops at Mandalay Place are described on p.172.

Glowing like beacons as their gilded windows commandeer the sunset, the twin forty-storey sentinels of *Mandalay Bay* soar above the southern limits of the Strip. Opened in 1999, *Mandalay Bay* represented the next step in the upward progress of Circus Circus Enterprises, each of whose previous properties (from *Circus Circus* itself, to *Excalibur* and then *Luxor*) had been significantly more upmarket.

Now subsumed into the MGM empire, *Mandalay Bay* has successfully targeted a younger and more affluent generation of customers than its predecessors, with a hipper, rock'n'roll kind of emphasis that means its most direct competitors are the *Hard Rock* and the *Palms*. The second tower, *THEhotel*, added in 2004, is marketed as a distinct hotel, and has a separate entrance, but is to all intents an integral part of the property. *Mandalay Bay* has little to offer casual sightseers, beyond a soft-focus tropical feel in keeping with the vaguely romantic associations of its name. Its guests get to experience a full-on resort experience centred on a superb open-air pool complex – **The Beach** – complete with an "adult" (read, topless) pool known as Moorea Beach Club, a beachside gaming area, a scallop-shaped wave pool (not switched on all that often) and a "Lazy River" tubing ride.

When the *Hacienda* casino was built on this site back in 1955 – it was finally demolished by being blown up in 1996 – it stood well over a mile south of the Strip. An unbroken chain of casinos now stretches all the way here, but few pedestrians brave the long, discouraging slog to reach it outdoors; hence the rudimentary feel of the Strip-level entrance. Most visitors either arrive on the free monorail from *Excalibur* and *Luxor*, or on foot, via the indoor **Mandalay Place** mall (see p.172) that connects with *Luxor*.

It's at night that *Mandalay Bay* really comes alive. The twin cornerstones of the casino's strategy to lure hip customers are the dozen or so top-class, high-concept eateries that line its glitzy "**Restaurant Row**", and the **House of Blues** music venue. For major events, like boxing matches, *Mandalay Bay* also has its own 12,000-seat arena, while a separate theatre is usually home to a big-name musical – currently it's *The Lion King*. The crowds that spill out when the show's over tend to stick around into the small hours, grazing in the late-night lounges or gambling in the massive, ultra-modern Race and Sports Book.

Finally, windows from the main hotel lobby look out on an attractive tiled fountain, but oddly enough the pool beyond belongs not to *Mandalay Bay* but to the **Four Seasons** hotel – an entirely separate property, which has its own separate lobby and whose 424 guest rooms occupy the top five floors of the original *Mandalay Bay* tower.

The Welcome to Las Vegas sign

Long an iconic image in movies and tourist snaps alike, the "**Welcome to Fabulous Las Vegas**" sign stands in the centre of the Strip, just over half a mile south of *Mandalay Bay* – though it feels a hell of a lot further if you try to walk it in the heat of summer. Designed by Betty Willis in 1959, the sign celebrated its fiftieth birthday by being added to the National Register of Historic Places, while miniature replicas have become the city's best-selling souvenir. It has also finally acquired its own parking lot in the central median – only accessible to drivers heading south – so visitors eager to pose for pics no longer have to sprint through the traffic to reach it. On a pedantic note, the sign is actually four miles south of the official city line; at this point, you're still in Paradise, Nevada.

1

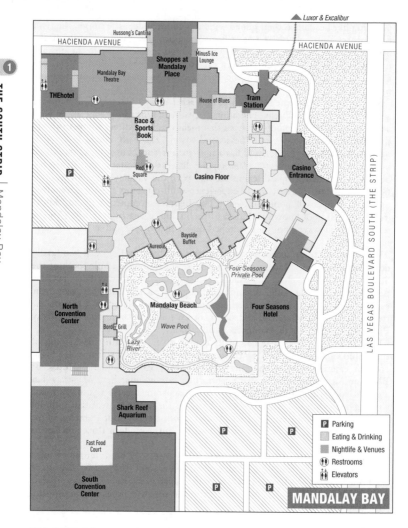

Luxor & Excalibur

HACIENDA AVENUE — Hussong's Cantina — HACIENDA AVENUE

Mandalay Bay Theatre

Shoppes at Mandalay Place

Minus5 Ice Lounge

THEhotel

House of Blues

Tram Station

Race & Sports Book

Red Square

Casino Floor

Casino Entrance

LAS VEGAS BOULEVARD SOUTH (THE STRIP)

Aureole

Bayside Buffet

Four Seasons Private Pool

North Convention Center

Mandalay Beach

Border Grill

Wave Pool

Four Seasons Hotel

Lazy River

Shark Reef Aquarium

Fast Food Court

South Convention Center

P Parking

Eating & Drinking

Nightlife & Venues

Restrooms

Elevators

MANDALAY BAY

Shark Reef

Mandalay Bay ☎ 702/632-4555, ⓦ sharkreef.com. Sun–Thurs 10am–8pm, Fri & Sat 10am–11pm; ages 13 and over $17, under-13s $11.

Mandalay Bay's one major attraction for sightseers, the **Shark Reef** aquarium, is a seriously long walk from the Strip-facing front of the property, far beyond the end of Restaurant Row. Even once you reach it, you may well be faced with a long queue; booking tickets online can save considerable time.

The emphasis in "North America's only predator-based aquarium" is more on eye-catching monsters than education, with video display panels rather than lengthy written captions next to each tank. The basic premise is that you're exploring a steamy, half-submerged temple complex, encountering yellow crocodiles, Komodo Dragons and (of course) sharks. Sharing these creatures' living quarters are some miserable-looking fish, many bearing large bite marks and missing portions of their anatomy. An excitable marine biologist provides a running commentary on the free "audio-wands," though for all his expertise he's somehow failed to spot that all the so-called "coral" on offer is actually a multi-colored mix'n'match plastic kit. Despite the substantial price, Shark Reef is nowhere near the scale of a major aquarium; many visitors scoot through in around twenty minutes.

Luxor

3900 Las Vegas Blvd S ☎ 702/262-4444, Ⓦ luxor.com. Hotel accommodation is reviewed on p.122; restaurants include Company Kitchen & Pub House (p.131); bars and clubs include Liquidity (p.142) and LAX (p.145).

When it opened in 1993, **Luxor** was heralded as the ultimate in-your-face Las Vegas casino. This stark, 350ft pyramid dominated the southern approach to the Strip, with the most powerful artificial light beam ever created shining straight into the sky from its apex, and its colossal Sphinx standing guard over not merely this one casino but all the splendours of the city. These days, however, it's surprisingly easy to forget that *Luxor* is even there. The entire exterior is so featureless that it's hard to get much sense of its vast scale, while being constructed out of black glass (technically it's a very dark bronze, but you'd never know) makes the pyramid even more inconspicuous, especially at night. It's flanked by two huge yet equally inconspicuous step-pyramids, which bring the total number of hotel rooms to 4407.

Luxor originally represented Las Vegas at its most exuberant; almost everything about it was Egyptian. Early guests used to sail to their rooms in barges along an artificial "Nile" (dropped following complaints that it was too slow); a full-size replica of King Tut's tomb lay buried upstairs; and every last corner was adorned with Pharaonic trimmings. Indeed, the Egyptian government announced in 2007 that it intended to sue for royalties. As it turned out, however, they were a little late; the decision had already been taken to strip *Luxor* of its Egyptian identity, and rebrand it as yet another "hip" casino resort. Fortunately that seems to be taking a long time to happen, and *Luxor* has so far lost little of its barmy charm.

The Sphinx

For the moment, *Luxor*'s original **Sphinx** still stares impassively out across the Strip, serving along with a white obelisk as a landmark for passing motorists. In theory, it's approached from the sidewalk via a palm-fringed avenue of ram-headed sphinxes, though the only pedestrians around are in fact *Luxor* guests briefly braving the sun for a photo opportunity. Most of *Luxor*'s foot traffic arrives along indoor mall-cum-corridors from its two neighbours, *Mandalay Bay* to the south and *Excalibur* to the north. Passengers disembarking from the free monorail that also links *Excalibur* and *Mandalay Bay* do however pass between the Sphinx's paws to enter the casino, while its body doubles as a *porte-cochère*, its vast belly sheltering dozens of vehicles at a time.

Inside Luxor

Visitors who enter directly from the Strip are greeted by a reconstruction of the temple of Abu Simbel, guarded by two huge seated statues. Only beyond that do the Pharaonic fripperies finally fizzle out. Where formerly *Luxor*'s various clubs and restaurants, along with its gaming areas, competed to outdo each other with Egyptian motifs, the main floor is now a dreary morass of minimalist-modern strip lighting and square columns. The emphasis these days has shifted more towards nightlife than dining, and insofar as any new theme exists, it's water: hence the central *Liquidity* bar, with its waterfall walls.

At least there's excitement in being inside a hollow pyramid. Only guests are permitted to ride the elevators to the top – those that follow the 39° slope of the pyramid are known as inclinators – and they don't in any case offer any views to speak of. Around the back of the pyramid, the large, attractively landscaped swimming pool – open to guests only, and very short on shade – is overlooked by more counterfeit colossi, as well of course as several thousand hotel rooms and a couple of huge car parks.

The Atrium Level

The best place to get an overall view of *Luxor*'s interior is the **Atrium Level**, immediately upstairs from the main casino floor. Above it towers what at 29 million cubic feet is said to be the world's largest atrium, with a steadily diminishing set of concentric tiered balconies providing access to sloping-walled, outward-facing hotel rooms. And if the obvious question springs to mind – yes, people do jump, in fact it was a 1996 suicide that prompted *Luxor*'s buffet to move downstairs.

Now home to the Bodies and Titanic exhibitions described below, the Atrium Level was originally intended to represent "the future," and its decor comes across as a weird hybrid of modern New York and medieval Cairo. Its small food court remains Egyptian-themed in every aspect, apart of course from the food itself.

Bodies...the Exhibition

Atrium Level, Luxor Ⓦ bodiestheexhibition.com. Daily 10am–10pm; $34, under-13s $23, audio tours $6 extra.

With its explicit warnings of the consequences of smoking, drinking and over-eating, **Bodies...the Exhibition** is by any standards a strange thing to find in a casino. These are indeed genuine **human corpses**, "plastinated" by an American company using techniques originally pioneered by maverick German anatomist Gunther Von Hagens.

Displays start gently enough, with assorted skeletons and bones, and even once you reach the entire specimens posed in everyday activities such as playing basketball, the colourful dyes used to make things clearer mean they look more like models or waxworks than actual dead people. However, before long you're faced with some serious home truths. There's a cross-section of a brain blackened by a debilitating stroke; a healthy liver is set alongside one damaged by alcohol-induced cirrhosis; and you're invited to discard any cigarettes you may be carrying as you inspect a smoker's tar-ruined lungs. Heads, complete with grimacing lips and sleepless eyes, are cut in half and labelled; genitals meticulously dissected and preserved; and entire digestive and circulatory systems laid out.

It takes most visitors around an hour to see the whole exhibition; even those expecting cheap thrills are swiftly sobered up. It's all unarguably fascinating, and the captions and educational intent – they call it an invitation to "become an informed participant in your own health care" – are faultless. Much of it could even be called beautiful, and many parents consider it appropriate to bring even young children here. What may be more of an issue for some visitors is the **provenance** of the bodies themselves. The company responsible says that these are "unclaimed" cadavers who died natural deaths and were released by the Chinese government; at the very least they were not willingly donated, and some have suggested they may have been prisoners or political detainees.

Titanic: The Artifact Exhibition

Atrium Level, Luxor ⓦtitanic-online.com. Daily 10am–10pm; $27, under-13s $20, audio tours $6 extra.

Plans to build an entire Titanic-themed resort across from the *Sahara* having struck their own iceberg – being synonymous with a world-famous disaster presumably didn't help – *Luxor's* Titanic exhibit provides a more serious opportunity to learn the story of the doomed liner. It centres on the so-called Big Piece, a genuine chunk of the ship's side that measures 26ft 6 inches by 12ft 6 inches, scattered with portholes and indented with just a few of its three million rivets. Most of the other artefacts salvaged from the wreck are essentially trivia, such as saucepans, discarded shoes and London bus tickets, but they're poignant nonetheless, and are complemented by assorted reconstructions. You can pose for photos on the Grand Staircase, while stepping out into the promenade deck on the dark, moonless, starlit night of April 14, 1912, is guaranteed to send a shiver up your spine.

A clever human touch is added by giving each visitor a "boarding pass" in the name of a particular passenger; you only find out at the end, from scanning the lists posted on the walls, whether your passenger survived. Allow roughly half an hour to see the whole thing.

Excalibur

3850 Las Vegas Blvd S ⓣ702/597-7777, ⓦexcalibur.com. Hotel accommodation is reviewed on p.121; the Tournament of Kings is reviewed on p.151.

The oldest and northernmost of the three interlinked MGM-owned casinos at the southern end of the Strip, the mocked-up medieval castle of **Excalibur** now makes a crude and unsophisticated neighbour for *Luxor* and *Mandalay Bay*, to which it's connected both by indoor passageways and an outdoor monorail. Hastily erected in 1990, in the hope of beating the then-new *Mirage* at its own game, it only cost half as much to build – and it shows. Its original owners, Circus Circus Enterprises, had earlier pioneered the concept of the child-oriented casino with the cheerfully downmarket *Circus Circus* itself (see p.78). *Excalibur* went a stage further by appearing to be both designed and assembled by children, with its oversized primary-coloured turrets drawn straight from a kindergarten art class, and its sharp angles and visible seams giving it the air of a cheap Christmas construction kit. The name "Excalibur", incidentally, was the winning entry in a public competition

At the planning stage, *Excalibur* architect Veldon Simpson – later also responsible for both the *MGM Grand* and *Luxor* – was dispatched to Europe to check out hundreds of genuine castles. The model he chose to follow was itself a playful, romantic fantasy. Neuschwanstein in Bavaria was built in the late nineteenth century by Mad King Ludwig, a devoted Wagner fan, who stuck the fairy-tale flourishes of a French château atop the redoubtable walls of a German fortress. If that sounds familiar, it's probably because Neuschwanstein was also the blueprint for Sleeping Beauty's Castle in Disney World.

Excalibur's immediate and continuing success has always been rooted in its appeal to low-budget tour groups, and its popularity with family vacationers remains undimmed, thanks to some of the best-value rooms on the Strip. The whole place has turned a bit more adult, though, with every square inch of the prominent bar/ diner *Dick's Last Resort* slathered in innuendos, and the Thunder From Down Under male strip revue in permanent residence.

Inside Excalibur

The pedestrian entrance to *Excalibur*, right at the intersection of Tropicana Avenue and the Strip, incorporates an elaborate station for the monorail system that ferries passengers to *Mandalay Bay*. The castle itself is then approached via lengthy walkways, on which almost no expense has been lavished.

Once inside, you're plunged as ever into the maelstrom of the casino floor, but it's easy enough to escape to the non-gaming areas, both above and below. Upstairs you'll find most of *Excalibur's* uninspiring assortment of restaurants, now marginally less child-oriented than they used to be, together with a bunch of "shoppes," a food court and assorted family-fun opportunities such as photo studios equipped with extensive wardrobes for dressing-up. The Canterbury Wedding Chapel caters to single travellers seized by the urge to settle down, and there's also a large outlet of the *Krispy Kreme* **donut** chain, where you can ogle the whole cooking process through plate-glass windows.

Downstairs in the **Fantasy Faire Midway**, the atmosphere is reminiscent of a traditional fairground, along the lines of *Circus Circus'* Midway (see p.79), filled with sideshows where kids can spend real money attempting to win plastic swords and other Arthurian memorabilia (Mon–Thurs 11am–11pm, Fri 11am–midnight, Sat 10am–midnight, Sun 10am–11pm). A large indoor arena hosts *King Arthur's Tournament*, a twice-nightly mixture of jousting, joshing and noshing.

The Tropicana

3801 Las Vegas Blvd S ⓣ702/739-2222, ⓦwww.troplv.com. Hotel accommodation is reviewed on p.123.

Formerly one of the great names of Las Vegas history, the *Tropicana* has spent the last couple of decades in the doldrums. It never managed to take advantage of the moment in the 1990s when its location, where the Strip meets Tropicana Avenue, became the city's hottest address. Said to be the busiest traffic intersection in the US, this spot holds the most hotel rooms of any crossroads in the world. The *Tropicana*, however, came to be seen as very much the poor relation of its mighty neighbours – the *MGM Grand*, *New York-New York* and *Excalibur* – all of which are owned by MGM. The "Trop" became a backwater, where visitors who didn't care for the new Las Vegas could drown their sorrows in a dingy, smoky, old-style gambling hall. As such, it was hit very hard by the recession, and collapsed into bankruptcy in 2008, without ever actually closing down.

Now owned by a heavyweight consortium, the *Tropicana* is finally bouncing back, with an ambitious and expensive revamp. So far, its former half-hearted Caribbean-village Strip facade has gone, while a much brighter new ceiling has replaced the century-old stained glass that previously hung above the main casino. They've also added a very high-tech Race and Sports Book. The ultimate aim is to give the property a **South Beach/Miami** theme, targeting it significantly towards Latino visitors from LA and elsewhere, with a general panoply of dazzling white, finished with abundant marble and gold. The *Tropicana* has always been renowned for its **pool**; Nikki Beach, a combined pool and nightclub, is expected to re-emerge as a real showpiece.

Las Vegas Mob Experience

For current opening hours and prices, see ⓦwww.lvme.com.

The *Tropicana's* great claim to fame was always the heavy **Mob** involvement in its early years. Originally bankrolled by the New Orleans Mafia in 1957, it was the focus of repeated FBI investigations into the "skimming" of casino profits that exposed unsavoury connections with the likes of Jimmy Hoffa's Teamsters Union, before several associates of the Kansas City Mob were finally jailed in 1981. That glorious tradition is celebrated in a new *Tropicana* attraction, the **Las Vegas Mob Experience**. As much theme park as museum, and a counterpoint to the city's own museum of organized crime (see p.87), it represents a "personal view" of the Mafia put together by the daughter of iconic boss Sam Giancana. In its eagerly anticipated culminating section, "Final Fate", each visitor is either "made" or "whacked".

New York-New York

3790 Las Vegas Blvd S Ⓣ702/740/6969, Ⓦnynyhotelcasino.com. Hotel accommodation is reviewed on p.123; restaurants include America (p.131) and Il Fornaio (p.131); bars and clubs include The Bar At Times Square (p.142) and Nine Fine Irishmen (p.143); the Cirque du Soleil show Zumanity is described on p.152.

The craze for creating counterfeit cities in Las Vegas was kicked off by the construction of **New York-New York**, which from the moment it was first unveiled in 1997 was hailed as a radical new departure. On the one hand, it looks utterly unlike the conventional idea of a "building", and yet on the other it's immediately recognizable as being an entire metropolis compressed into a single structure. The motives behind the creation of this miniature Manhattan were much the same as for the original; when space is at an absolute premium, the best way to build is upward.

Thanks to its exuberant attention to detail, *New York-New York* is a triumph, a must-see attraction that despite some recent watering-down remains the most perfectly realized of all the Strip's themed casinos. Surprisingly small once you get inside, with a mere two thousand hotel rooms, it's better known as a place to **drink** – both the *Nine Fine Irishmen* pub and the *Bar At Times Square* at street level are always crowded, while *Coyote Ugly* and *Pour 24* lure in passers-by heading between the *MGM Grand* and *Excalibur* bridges on the mezzanine level – than to **eat**. That said, the Italian *Il Fornaio* deli/restaurant is highly recommended (see p.131) and it's worth dropping in at the *America* diner (see p.131) to see the massive relief map of the US that dangles alarmingly from the ceiling.

The Statue of Liberty

From street level, *New York-New York* looks stunning, its twelve pastel skyscrapers silhouetted sharply against the blue desert sky. Apart from the proud **Statue of Liberty** (just over twice the size of the original) at the front, the mock skyline's various components are between a third and a half as big as their East Coast counterparts. Perhaps mercifully, the copycat towers never included the World Trade Center – strictly speaking, this is a facsimile of 1950s New York – so although the facade became an obvious site for memorials in the wake of September 11, 2001, it hasn't acquired any extra symbolic significance. Instead, the highest point is the 510ft, 47-storey **Empire State Building**. This squashed-up cityscape is not simply a static tableau. A fireboat jets arcs of water across a tiny New York Harbor, while up above, a Coney Island–style roller coaster loops and swoops around the skyline in full view – and earshot – of the Strip. Only the Brooklyn Bridge strikes a somewhat false note, just plonked down on the Strip sidewalk with nothing to span.

Greenwich Village and the casino

Walking into *New York-New York* from the Strip, past the large ESPN Zone sports bar, you find yourself in the **Greenwich Village** neighbourhood, which

Top Ten Strip attractions for kids

The following attractions are listed roughly in order of the ages for which they are most suitable, starting with M&M World for the youngest children.

comes complete not only with a fine array of genuine delis and fast-food outlets, interspersed with false storefronts and a fake subway station, but even fire hydrants, rubbish bins and postboxes, all sprayed with impressive (if firmly PG-rated) graffiti.

Beyond that, however, owners MGM, who took over the property in 2005, have taken a killjoy attitude to the former Central Park theme in its main gaming area, and made it just another generic casino. Appealing Art Deco touches that still survive include the elegant "Guys" and "Dolls" toilets, and the styling of the elevator lobbies, one of which is modelled on the Chrysler Building.

The Roller Coaster

New York-New York. Sun–Thurs 11am–11pm, Fri & Sat 10.30am–midnight; $14 first ride, $25 for an all-day Scream Pass.

To reach *New York-New York*'s most popular and eye-catching attraction, once known as the Manhattan Express but now imaginatively rechristened **The Roller Coaster**, head upstairs. You may have to wait for a while, snaking along the walkways of a mocked-up subway station, but once you've boarded its little yellow taxicabs, you hurtle very briefly above the casino floor, then race out into the open air on a juddering ride that reaches speeds of 65mph and spirals through some fearsomely tight rolls. Not an experience theme-park novices should undertake lightly, it's one of Las Vegas's very best thrill rides.

The Arcade

Most of the rest of the upper floor was when this book went to press still given over to the **Arcade**, a cornucopia of carnival sideshows, video games and other kids' attractions (daily 8.30am–2am; attractions individually priced). That has always seemed like an extravagant use of potentially profitable space, as well as an unnecessary duplication of the same owners' similar facility at *Excalibur* next door, so it may well have been replaced with something a bit more adult by the time you read this.

MGM Grand

40

3799 Las Vegas Blvd S ☏ 702/891-7777, Ⓦ mgmgrand.com. Hotel accommodation is reviewed on p.122; restaurants include Diego (p.132), Emeril's New Orleans Fish House (p.132), Grand Wok & Sushi Bar (p.132) Nobhill Tavern (p.132) and Rainforest

Cafe (p.132); bars and clubs include Tabú (p.143) and Studio 54 (p.145); the Crazy Horse Paris revue is reviewed on p.148; and the Cirque du Soleil show Kà is described on p.149.

Considering that it was built as the world's largest hotel and is still growing, the **MGM Grand** presents a remarkably small frontage to the Strip. Instead its colossal size only becomes apparent once you're inside, perhaps after you've been walking for twenty minutes and are still nowhere near where you want to go. The lack of a spectacular or even particularly noticeable facade – its one landmark feature is the 70ft bronze lion that roars at the exact intersection of Tropicana Avenue and Las Vegas Boulevard – contributes to the *Grand*'s oddly low profile. In reality, it's up there with the best Las Vegas has to offer, with a magnificent array of restaurants and shows, and some fine attractions too.

Spreading over 114 acres, the *MGM Grand* is larger than *Luxor* and *Excalibur* combined. All that now survives of its original 1993 identity, as a child-friendly celebration of MGM movies like the *Wizard of Oz*, is its all-pervasive

Kirk Kerkorian – The Wizard of MGM

Now well into his tenth decade, but still going strong as MGM's largest shareholder, the amazing **Kirk Kerkorian** has been a major Las Vegas player since the very earliest days of the Strip. That his name remains relatively unknown is due both to his own publicity-shy nature, and to his status as a quintessential wheeler and dealer, forever buying and selling his assets in a bewildering flurry of billions.

Born in California in 1917, to Armenian parents, Kerkorian never graduated from high school. Like Howard Hughes, his even more reclusive erstwhile rival, he made his fortune from aviation. During the 1940s, he operated a charter service that flew gamblers from LA to Las Vegas; Bugsy Siegel, then building the *Flamingo*, was a regular client.

In 1962, Kerkorian bought an eighty-acre tract of land across from the *Flamingo* for just under a million dollars. *Caesars Palace*, which was built on the site in 1966, paid him rent plus fifteen percent of its gross, and then bought him out in 1968. His total $8 million profit enabled him to build the largest hotel in the world – the *International*, now the *Las Vegas Hilton*, which opened in 1969 and became legendary as the venue for Elvis Presley's comeback.

Kerkorian's reputation as an asset stripper is inextricably tied up with his purchase of the **MGM movie studios** in 1969. Having first sold off most of its production facilities and memorabilia, he sold the movies themselves to Ted Turner, and has since sold and rebought the entire company twice more.

The first version of the **MGM Grand** hotel, once again the world's largest, opened in 1973. After it was devastated by a horrific 1980 fire in which 84 people died, however, it became what's now *Bally's*. Kerkorian sold everything except the MGM name, which he used again to build the current *MGM Grand* a decade later.

As MGM's majority shareholder, Kerkorian was the mastermind behind the buy-out of Steve Wynn's Mirage Resorts in 2000, and their joint acquisition of the Mandalay Resort Group four years later, which gave what's now MGM Resorts International total domination over the southern end of the Strip. The company is now entirely devoted to the hotel business, with plans to expand worldwide.

Even so, he remains very much his own man, seeing MGM as just part of his overall portfolio. As recently as 2007, he offered to buy CityCenter and *Bellagio* from MGM; that same year, he made his second serious attempt to buy car manufacturer Chrysler, having previously owned ten percent of General Motors. Only in 2009 did he finally reduce his MGM holdings to below fifty percent, and there's still no saying what may come next; if we could predict his next move, then maybe we'd be billionaires too.

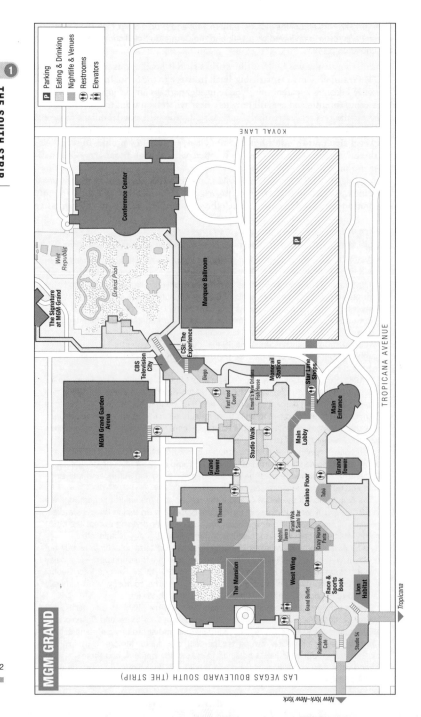

MGM GRAND

THE SIGN (THE STRIP)
LAS VEGAS BOULEVARD SOUTH

New York–New York ▶

Tropicana ▶

The Signature at MGM Grand

Conference Center

Wet Republic

Grand Pool

CBS Television City

Marquee Ballroom

CSI: The Experience

Diego

KOVAL LANE

P

MGM Grand Garden Arena

Fast Food Court

Emeril's New Orleans Fish House

Monorail Station

Star Lane Shops

Grand Tower

Studio Walk

Main Lobby

Main Entrance

Kà Theatre

Casino Floor

Grand Tower

The Mansion

Nobhill Tavern

Grand Wok & Sushi Bar

Tabú

TROPICANA AVENUE

West Wing

Crazy Horse Paris

Grand Buffet

Race & Sports Book

Rainforest Cafe

Lion Habitat

Studio 54

P Parking
  Eating & Drinking
  Nightlife & Venues
  Restrooms
  Elevators

Wicked-Witch-green colour. The entire site was previously occupied by the *Tropicana*'s golf course and the *Marina* hotel. In fact amazingly enough the *Marina* is still right here; the *MGM Grand* simply swallowed it up like a vast green slime monster, incorporating it into its record-breaking tally of five thousand rooms.

Inside the MGM Grand

One way in which the *Grand* copes with its sheer bulk, and potential for overcrowding, is by not having one obvious main entrance, thus dispersing the crowds. Pedestrian entrances are located to either side of the lion, both at street level and also on the second floor, at the end of walkways from the *Tropicana* and *New York-New York* respectively. Hotel guests and all other traffic use a separate entrance a hundred yards east along Tropicana Avenue, while Monorail passengers disembark at the back of the property, a very long walk from the hotel lobby.

Several high-profile attractions stand just indoors from the Strip, including the Lion Habitat described below, the *Studio 54* nightclub (see p.145), the buffet and a gleaming Race & Sports Book. Beyond that, the casino proper stretches off into infinity. Even though clubs, restaurants, and theatres stand to all sides of the gaming area, the *Grand*'s main concentration of restaurants line the so-called **Studio Walk** at the far end. This pedestrian passage leads past the Monorail Station to the seventeen-thousand-seat Arena, used for big-name rock concerts and boxing matches, and the *Grand*'s lavish **pool** complex, now featuring its own adult enclave, Wet Republic.

Although there's surprisingly little **shopping** at the *MGM Grand*, it's worth checking out **CBS Television City**, on Studio Walk near the monorail entrance (daily 10am–8.30pm). On first glance, it simply sells toys and gadgets related to current CBS programmes, but it's also a research facility where you can watch new shows and pilots for free – or even test the latest iPhones and Xboxes – in return for answering questions at the end.

Lion Habitat

MGM Grand. Daily 11am–7pm; free.

Shamelessly taking a leaf from the *Mirage* and its tigers, the *MGM Grand*'s **Lion Habitat** holds the world's only commuting lions. At any one time, two or three of the forty or so lions that the casino owns have made the 12-mile trip from their ranch home to spend half a day in this glass enclosure, beside the casino floor just off the Strip, lounging around a ruined temple gnawing at vitamin-enhanced horsemeat. Visitors can stroll through a glass tunnel as the lions pad, or snooze, directly overhead; the casino likes to say it's better than any zoo because they can't smell or hear you.

Paying $25 enables you to participate in the grotesque charade of having your photo taken with a cute little lion cub; oblivious to your presence, it's made to look wistful and winsome by having its milk bottle whisked away for a fraction of a second (daily except Tues 11am–5pm).

CSI: The Experience

MGM Grand ☎702/891-7006, ⓦcsiexhibit.com. Daily 10am–10pm, last admission 8.30pm. Ages 12 and over $30, $26 for repeat visits on same day; ages 4–11 $23/$20; family ticket $75.

The self-paced, interactive **CSI: The Experience** is definitely in the top rank of Las Vegas' paying attractions, especially for family groups. Closely based on the popular TV shows, it's sufficiently interesting and challenging that you don't need to be a fan to enjoy it, though if you are you'll no doubt get an extra frisson from the various on-screen interjections from the cast.

Each visitor chooses one of three cases to solve – a canny ploy that means you can visit again without repeating the experience. After inspecting a mocked-up crime scene, under strong pressure to spot every conceivable clue, you pass through to the crime lab, where assorted microscopes, film clips and other tools help you hone, and finally confirm, your suspicions as to the culprit.

The whole thing takes around an hour, ideally as part of a brainstorming family group. You'd have to be a bit wilful to get the case wrong – and you can expect stern words from Supervisor Gil Grissom if you do – but that doesn't detract from the fun.

Showcase Mall

3785 Las Vegas Blvd S ⓣ 702/597-3122.

Immediately north of the *MGM Grand*, the **Showcase Mall** is a rarity for the Strip, as a stand-alone modern development that's not a casino. As well as the Strip's only **cinema**, the eight-screen Showcase 8 (ⓣ 702/740-4511, ⓦ regmovies .com), it's home to the **GameWorks** arcade of video and virtual-reality games (Mon–Thurs & Sun 10am–midnight, Fri & Sat 10am–1am; pay per play, or $35 for unlimited play; ⓣ 702/432-4263, ⓦ gameworks.com).

Also part of the mall, **M&M World** (Mon–Thurs & Sun 9am–11pm, Fri & Sat 9am–midnight; ⓦ mymms.com) is a four-storey theme park-cum-store that's absolutely crammed with primary-coloured candies, both edible and in plush-toy form. Funnily enough, it gets to be more fun the higher you go, with a free 3-D movie show (starring "Red" and "Yellow") at the far end of a psychedelic revolving walkway.

CityCenter and around

Unveiled at the end of 2009, the **CityCenter** complex represents a bold attempt to reshape Las Vegas' urban landscape. Rather than simply adding another gimmicky casino, owners MGM set out to give the city an entire new neighbourhood instead. The thrilling new theme is that there is no theme; CityCenter is supposedly the kind of project that might be built in any city, or at least any city with $10 billion, burning a hole in its pocket. It's intended to mark the moment that Las Vegas stops thinking in straight lines, and steps away

CityCenter: from Genesis to Revelation

The overriding irony about CityCenter – the largest privately funded construction project in the history of the US – is, of course, that they'd never have built it if they'd known the **recession** was coming.

Although ground was broken in April 2006, the planning dates back considerably further. When what was then MGM-Mirage bought out the Mandalay Resort Group in 2004, attention focused on Mandalay's higher-profile properties like *Luxor* and *Mandalay Bay* itself. However, CEO **Jim Murren** had realised that gaining complete control of *Monte Carlo* – previously a joint venture with *Mandalay* – would enable MGM to develop the huge tracts of under-used land that lay behind it, between the Strip and the interstate. By showing that visitors could be enticed away from the Strip into a separate enclave, CityCenter would vastly increase the value of its underlying real estate.

The project only survived to completion thanks to large elements of luck. Along the way, MGM managed to persuade Dubai World to pay cash for a half-share in City-Center just months before Dubai World's own finances dried up, and MGM also had to sell *Treasure Island* for $775 million.

By the time CityCenter actually opened, the notion of adding seven thousand high-end rooms to Las Vegas' already bloated inventory, at a time when visitor numbers and expenditure were in decline, was self-evidently absurd. On top of that, the project was also predicated on attracting a new breed of urban sophisticates, drawn as much by art and architecture as by gambling, who would want to live in Las Vegas rather than merely visit, and buy enough condos to turn the Strip into a residential neighbourhood for the first time. If all that sounds like a recipe for disaster in the current economic climate, the sky hasn't fallen in yet. For the last couple of decades, Las Vegas has operated on the principle of "if you build it, they will come". CityCenter has not, however, delivered any bounce in visitor numbers; within a year of its opening accountants were valuing it at a mere quarter of what it cost to build. It remains anyone's guess whether it will provide proof that Las Vegas has finally come of age, or simply show that the casino giants are no better at gambling than the rest of us.

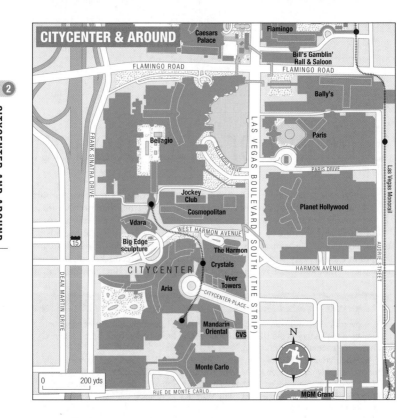

from building an endless progression of casinos, marching down the Strip, in favour of branching out to create new multi-purpose districts.

As well as a casino resort, **Aria**, and a high-end shopping mall, **Crystals**, City-Center consists of three non-gaming hotels – **Vdara**, the **Mandarin Oriental** and the unfinished **Harmon** – and a matching pair of condo towers, **Veer**, so named because each leans five eye-catching degrees off vertical in opposite directions. With each component designed by a different architect, they form not a single homogenous mass but a clashing cluster of futuristic skyscrapers.

CityCenter is not as large as the hype might suggest. Collectively, it covers about the same area as the *Venetian*; less than *Caesars Palace* or the *Mirage*. What's genuinely new is its commitment to cutting-edge **contemporary architecture**, coupled with a vigorous showcasing of large-scale **public art** (see box opposite). Casual sightseers will certainly find both *Aria* and *Crystals* worth exploring. Neither holds any specific paying attractions, but each is consistently breathtaking, not in the familiar Las Vegas sense but in provoking the sort of wonder you get from wandering the most dynamic urban spaces of, say, New York and Chicago. In addition, *Aria* especially holds a superb assortment of **restaurants**.

An unexpected consequence of CityCenter's arrival has been the extent to which the adjacent **Bellagio** and **Monte Carlo** casinos have been drawn into its ambit. City Center's Strip frontage, and in particular the two spur roads into the project, are too austere and exposed to encourage pedestrians, so for anyone walking along the Strip the best way to reach *Aria* is **indoors**, cutting through either *Bellagio* or the *Monte Carlo*. As a result, insofar as CityCenter is a "neighbourhood", then those two much more traditional MGM-owned properties form part of it too – which has the effect of diminishing the impact of CityCenter's modernism.

As for the elevated **monorail** that connects *Bellagio* to the *Monte Carlo* via *Aria*, it's fun to ride, but not as useful as it sounds – by the time you've walked to either terminus, you're nearly all the way to *Aria* itself. If you're **driving**, the only self-parking in CityCenter proper is in the *Aria* garage; everywhere else has valet parking only.

Monte Carlo

3770 Las Vegas Blvd S Ⓣ 702/730-7777, Ⓦ montecarlo.com. Hotel accommodation is reviewed on p.122 and the pub on p.143.

Never one of Las Vegas' showier properties, the sober, unassuming **Monte Carlo** has since the opening of CityCenter effectively turned its back on the Strip altogether. What used to be its front entrance is now largely obscured by *Diablo's Cantina*, a Mexican bar/restaurant, while its entire interior now amounts to little more than a corridor leading to and from the CityCenter monorail and *Aria* casino.

The Art of CityCenter

Using Las Vegas casinos as showcases for **fine art** is a relatively recent idea, and one with a chequered history. Steve Wynn, as so often, led the way, with Strip billboards proclaiming "Now Starring: Picasso and van Gogh" when his own collection was first displayed in *Bellagio*'s now-faded Gallery of Fine Art. The *Venetian* followed suit by opening two distinct Guggenheim museums, both of which have long since disappeared.

CityCenter has now upped the stakes by integrating stimulating contemporary artworks, especially in the form of monumental **sculpture**, into its overall design, as opposed to consigning them to paid-admission galleries. Not that the distinction between art and artifice is always obvious; huge sums have been lavished on commissioning and buying works by leading artists, but it's often hard to be sure whether a particular piece is a major work of art, a design feature put together by a commercial contractor, or even just a corporate logo.

Big names include **Claes Oldenburg**, who made the outsized steel-and-fibreglass typewriter eraser beside the *Mandarin Oriental*; **Henry Moore**, whose abstract *Reclining Connected Forms* (1969–74) fills the "pocket park" between *Aria* and *Crystals*; and **Maya Lin**, responsible for the gleaming 84ft *Colorado River*, cast in reclaimed silver, above *Aria*'s check-in desks. The colourful *Big Edge* installation, by **Nancy Rubins**, stands in the middle of the traffic circle between *Vdara* and *Aria*. Composed of hundreds of salvaged canoes, it's a larger version of her *Big Pleasure Point* at New York's Lincoln Center.

CityCenter's most intriguing and provocative artwork, however, is immediately below this spot, at *Aria's* underground "North Valet Pickup". The work of **Jenny Holzer**, *Vegas* is a 266ft-long, 18ft-high LED sign along which scroll such elliptical aphorisms as "the future is stupid". While Holzer has often been more overtly political, there's something deliciously subversive about the only electronic sign in a Las Vegas casino being an explicit challenge to the over-commercialized role of the written word in everyday life – and of course ironic about using it to lure lovers of conceptual art into a gambling den.

The Missing Link

Considering the harsh financial climate, it's perhaps surprising that only one element of CityCenter failed to open on time. The missing piece in the jigsaw is the **Harmon Hotel**, designed by the British architectural practice of **Norman Foster**.

The *Harmon* is the shiny rounded-end tower that stands closest to the Strip. If it looks a little stumpy, that's because it's only half the height it was supposed to be. Originally intended to soar 49 storeys, things went wrong for the *Harmon* in 2009, when it was discovered after its first fifteen floors had been constructed that incorrectly installed reinforced steel meant it would be unable to support its planned weight. The upper half was going to consist of residential condos, which might well have proved hard to sell anyway. Now, assuming the legal squabbles over the blame are ever settled, the *Harmon* will either simply be a hotel, or just be demolished altogether.

The great irony is that for the moment, although CityCenter set out to eschew traditional Las Vegas signage, the empty *Harmon* is nothing more than a gigantic billboard, with a huge display advertising *Viva Elvis!*

Ever since it was hastily erected in 1996, *Monte Carlo*'s nominal theme – it's supposedly modelled on the Place du Casino in Monte Carlo – has never amounted to much more than a few Rococo flourishes scattered along its Strip facade.

Always aimed squarely at middle-Americans looking for a touch of European class but unwilling to pay premium prices – this is where the Average Joes stayed in *Dodgeball*, for example – it now promotes itself with the dreary slogan "unpretentiously luxurious". While it's clearly decided to throw in its lot with CityCenter, quite how far that process will go will depend on the long-term success of CityCenter itself. Tantalizing rumours suggest that magician Lance Burton, whose 14-year run at the Monte Carlo ended in 2010, may be replaced by the Cirque du Soleil's latest project, a **Michael Jackson** show scheduled to open in 2012, though this may end up at Mandalay Bay instead.

For the moment, however, the *Monte Carlo* continues to offer middle-of-the-road dining and entertainment, and little else. Calling its main shopping and dining arcade the **Street of Dreams** can only be a tacit acknowledgement that it's liable to put you to sleep. The *Pub* here, incidentally, used to be the Strip's only brew-pub until CityCenter built over its brewing facilities; it's now an ordinary sports bar.

Crystals

3720 Las Vegas Blvd S ⓣ702/590-5299, ⓦcrystalsatcitycenter.com. Restaurants include Mastro's Ocean Club (see p.132); the nightclub Eve is reviewed on p.145. See also Shopping chapter, p.170.

For the sheer exuberance of its design, CityCenter's most memorable segment has to be the Strip-front **Crystals** mall. As a shopping destination, it defines itself as "extremely high-end", which is saying something in Las Vegas; only a tiny percentage of visitors could afford the prices in its exclusive boutiques. However, Crystals also serves the dual purpose of luring in passing sightseers with the prospect of a spectacular air-conditioned walkway through to *Aria*.

Crystal's spiky roofscape, and the angular planes of its stark white interior walls – the work of architect Daniel Libeskind – are complemented by its rich polished-wood floors and staircases, and the stones and crystals embedded throughout. A plethora of eccentric oddities provide sharp contrast, however. Most dramatic of all is the 70ft **Treehouse**, created by David Rockwell, who designed the Broadway show *Hairspray*. A sinuous three-storey lattice of curving wood, it accommodates the main dining room of *Mastro's Ocean Club* within its central bulb. That effect is echoed in the smaller-scale wooden follies that arch over diners in the more casual *Pods*, one of the mall's two Wolfgang Puck outlets.

Crystals has the feel of a stylish urban park – indeed, it was originally envisaged as being outdoors, before they decided to put a roof over it (hence the flamboyant planters and flowerbeds on its lowest level). Interspersed among them are two extravagant water features. One, **Halo**, consists of fifty glass columns, some rising from the floor and others sinking beneath it, all filled with whirling water that ceaselessly changes colour, level and direction. In the other, **Glacia**, pillars of ice both cloudy and clear emerge from a lake then melt back into it.

Of all CityCenter's components, Crystals may well prove the most vulnerable to economic downturn. It has yet to find occupants for all sixty of its retail outlets – a situation acknowledged by commissioning German graffiti artist DAIM to cover some of the endless white space on the third floor with a huge mural – and the dividing line between futuristic fantasyland and white-elephant folly is looking alarmingly thin.

Aria

3730 Las Vegas Blvd S ⊤ 702/590-7111, Ⓦ arialasvegas.com. Hotel accommodation is reviewed on p.121; restaurants include Julian Serrano (p.133) and The Buffet (p.128); the club Haze is described on p.145; and the Cirque du Soleil show Viva Elvis! is reviewed on p.151.

Despite CityCenter's longing to be seen as an entire district and not just another casino, its centrepiece, the 4004-room **Aria**, is...just another casino. The question is, is it anything more than that? It's certainly different to what's gone before, flaunting a new modernist aesthetic that makes its plush marble-clad predecessors seem suddenly old and tired. And yet there's only so far you can take minimalism when you also have a casino to run, filled with slot machines and gaming tables and all the glamorous accessories it takes to coax gamblers into spending more than they ever intended.

Approaching *Aria* directly from the Strip, your first impression will be of several curving glass skyscrapers, towering above a darker, low-slung central building that's arranged around a traffic circle. On closer inspection, all turn out to be connected to form a single structure. In the centre of the circle, a fountain spurts pulses of water, spotlit by coloured lights, which form intricate patterns. WET – the company also responsible for the balletic fountains at *Bellagio* – created the 270ft-long, 24ft-high "water wall" nearby, running along the outer side of the casino proper.

Inside Aria

The most immediately striking feature of *Aria*'s interior is the abundance of natural light. With its high glass ceiling, the main atrium especially is the kind of space you'd expect in a cosmopolitan arts centre or new airport rather than a casino-hotel.

Once in the actual **casino**, however, which takes up most of the ground-level floor space, you're plunged into the sort of artificially lit gloom that characterizes most Las Vegas casinos. At its core, as ever, lie rank upon rank of slot machines, but all sorts of stylish flourishes lurk around the edges. Look out for the open-sided **Poker Room** for example, delineated by columns made up of giant gilded playing cards; the mysterious cavernous recesses of the high-stakes Baccarat area; or the

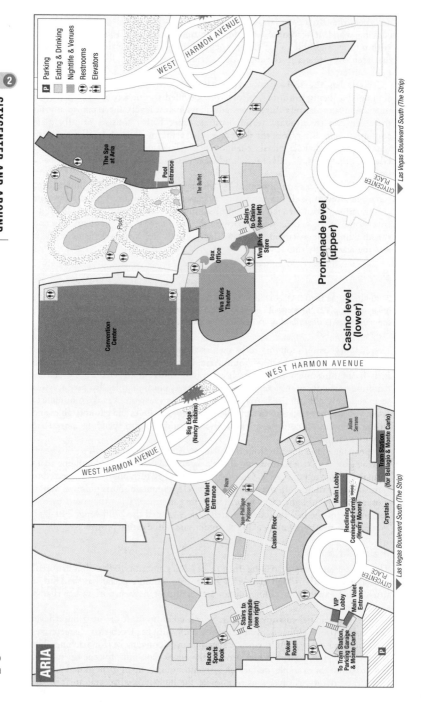

ARIA

Parking
Eating & Drinking
Nightlife & Venues
Restrooms
Elevators

Promenade level (upper)

Casino level (lower)

WEST HARMON AVENUE

The Spa at Aria

Pool

Pool Entrance

The Buffet

Stairs to Casino (see left)

Viva Elvis Store

Box Office

Viva Elvis Theater

Convention Center

CITYCENTER PLACE

Las Vegas Boulevard South (The Strip)

WEST HARMON AVENUE

Big Edge (Nancy Rubins)

Haze

North Valet Entrance

Jean-Phillipe Patisserie

Casino Floor

Julian Serrano

Main Lobby

Reclining Connected Forms (Henry Moore)

Crystals

Tram Station (for Bellagio & Monte Carlo)

VIP Lobby

Main Valet Entrance

Stairs to Promenade (see right)

Race & Sports Book

Poker Room

To Tram Station, Parking Garage & Monte Carlo

CITYCENTER PLACE

Las Vegas Boulevard South (The Strip)

exuberant curves of the adjoining *Bar Moderno* and *Jean-Philippe Patisserie*.

In contrast to the labyrinthine tangle downstairs, *Aria*'s upper floor is very easy to negotiate. It's entirely gaming-free, with long broad hallways that lead to the **Viva Elvis!** theatre and shop; the lavish **Spa**; the *Buffet* and yet more high-class restaurants; several balconies overlooking the action below; and *Aria*'s glorious guest-only **pool** complex. Presumably the management would prefer it not to be quite so peaceful and crowd-free; that may change when and if *Aria* develops its **shopping** component, which at opening was the property's most obvious deficiency compared to its rivals.

Vdara

2600 W Harmon Ave, ⓣ 702/590-2111, ⓦ vdara.com. Hotel accommodation is reviewed on p.123.

Bracketing Aria with its crisp towering arc, the **Vdara** all-suite hotel serves mainly as a corridor between Bellagio and the rest of CityCenter. It has however achieved notoriety for the so-called "Death Ray" produced by its curving mirrored facade, which focuses an intense, shifting beam of heat onto hapless sunbathers beside its pool. For visitors, there's little reason to break your stride, though the *Silk Road* restaurant is well worth a stop, and fans of modernist painting will enjoy Frank Stella's *Damascus Gate Variation I*, behind the check-in desk.

Bellagio

3600 Las Vegas Blvd S ⓣ 702/693-7111, ⓦ bellagio.com. Hotel accommodation is reviewed on p.52; restaurants include Michael Mina (p.133), Noodles (p.133), Olives (p.133) and The Buffet (p.128); bars and clubs include Caramel (p.142) and The Bank (p.145); the Cirque du Soleil show O is reviewed on p.150; and the shops of Via Bellagio are also described on p.173.

The highest-earning and most profitable casino in Las Vegas, **Bellagio** is a commanding presence on the Strip, arrayed in stately elegance around an artificial lake where splendid fountains perform balletic pirouettes to adoring crowds.

The Cosmopolitan Alternative

The one anomalous worm in the (Big) apple that is CityCenter – the **Cosmopolitan**, the only property in the vicinity *not* owned by MGM – had yet to open when this book went to press. Anywhere else in the world, a three-thousand-room casino hotel consisting of two fifty-storey skyscrapers might seem rather large. Here in Las Vegas, squeezed into less than ten acres next door to *Bellagio*, it's seen as a plucky little David pitted against a mass of Goliaths.

The *Cosmopolitan* was erected on what used to be the parking lot of the long-established *Jockey Club*, which meant it had first to dig out its own underground parking facility. It's owned, somewhat unwillingly, by Deutsche Bank, which found itself having to complete its construction after its original developers defaulted on their loans, and no one wanted to take the project over.

Rumours abound that sooner rather than later the *Cosmopolitan* will be swallowed up by MGM to become part of CityCenter. For the moment, however, Deutsche Bank has announced plans to create a luxury casino resort much like its many neighbours, with a huge ground-floor gaming area opening immediately onto the Strip, and a dozen or so big-name restaurants. The main defining feature of the hotel above is that all rooms will have balconies – otherwise unheard of in Las Vegas – and thus offer unparalleled views, with the twin blocks rising to the height of the Eiffel Tower opposite. For the latest details, visit ⓦ www.cosmopolitanlasvegas.com.

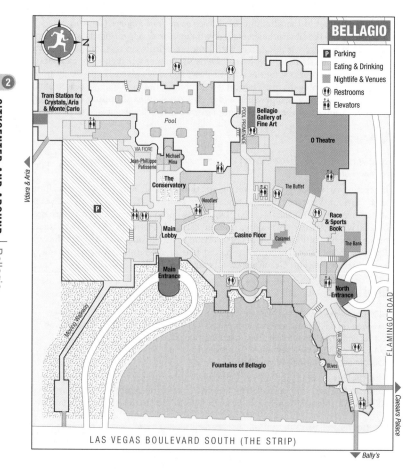

And yet, as it approaches adolescence, it finds itself in a peculiar position. Not only is it starting to fade, but it feels a trifle neglected by owners MGM Resorts International, whose attention is taken up instead with its brand-new sibling, CityCenter. More foot traffic than ever is passing through, but after years as a destination in its own right *Bellagio* has become a pedestrian walkway to and from CityCenter. What's more, the austere modernism of CityCenter so clearly represents a rejection of this kind of old-world opulence that *Bellagio* is having to accept that it's no longer so much the Belle of the ball as a blast from the past.

To get the full benefit of *Bellagio*'s facilities, which include a luxurious spa and beauty salon, and six superb swimming pools, you need to stay at the hotel. For any visitor to Las Vegas, however, the property as a whole makes an essential port of call. Even once you're done swooning over the general air of decadent luxury, there's still plenty to enjoy, including the stellar Cirque du Soleil show *O*, and the dozen or so top-quality restaurants, not to mention one of the best buffets in town.

The fountains of Bellagio

A graceful curve of blue and cream pastels, *Bellagio*'s main hotel block stands aloof from the Strip behind an eight-acre replica of Italy's Lake Como. The mere presence of so much water in the desert announces the wealth at *Bellagio*'s disposal, but the point is rubbed in every half-hour during the afternoon, and every fifteen minutes in the evening, when hundreds of submerged fountains erupt in Busby-Berkeley water ballets, choreographed with booming music and coloured lights. At the foot of the hotel, the lake is bordered by a reproduction of a small Italian village. Several of the structures here are restaurants, which offer lakeshore terrace dining. Each of the windows you see in the facade above, incidentally, is actually two storeys high and two rooms wide; it's a trick to make the building look smaller and closer than it really is.

Inside Bellagio

Hotel guests sweep up to *Bellagio* along a grand, tree-lined waterfront drive, to enter a sumptuous lobby that's deliberately distinct from the casino. A pedestrian walkway, starting opposite *Planet Hollywood*, arrives close by. Within the lobby, mosaic butterflies and insects writhe across the floor, while the ceiling is filled by a brooding sort of semi-chandelier of glass flowers, made by sculptor Dale Chihuly. It's all said to be hand-blown, but "overblown" would be closer to the mark. Even the area behind the check-in desks is themed; to reach the executive offices, disguised as a Venetian villa, the clerks have to make their way through a fully fledged Roman garden.

Most pedestrians, however, approach *Bellagio* from its northeast corner, crossing the bridges from *Caesars Palace* or *Bally's* where Flamingo Road meets the Strip. Mosaic-floored revolving doors grant admittance to **Via Bellagio**, a plush paisley-carpeted corridor of designer boutiques interspersed with restaurants that's described on p.173.

The Conservatory

Bellagio's real showpiece, the opulent **Conservatory**, lies just beyond the hotel lobby. Beneath a Belle Epoque canopy of copper-framed glass, a network of flowerbeds is replanted every six to eight weeks with ornate seasonal displays. A

Bellagio: from New Kid to Grande Dame

As president of Mirage Resorts, back in the mid-1990s, **Steve Wynn** set his sights very high indeed. He wanted not merely to build the best hotel in Las Vegas – he'd just done that, with the *Mirage* – but the best hotel there has ever been.

Bellagio therefore set out to surpass what's regarded as the greatest hotel in history, the *Ritz* in Paris, built in 1898. Originally the resort was going to be laid out around a French beach and be called Beau Rivage; then it was decided to replicate the Italian lakeside village of Bellagio instead. Not surprisingly, it proved hard to blend the understated elegance of provincial Italy with the Belle Époque flourishes of *fin-de-siècle* Paris, particularly when you also had to squeeze a state-of-the-art casino into the resultant mélange. Nonetheless, as soon as it opened in 1998, *Bellagio* was hailed as a quantum leap ahead of all its competitors. Ever since then, however, its successors have been raising the bar. First the *Venetian* proved that you can be this classy without being quite so elitist; then Wynn himself, with the money he made when Mirage Resorts was bought by MGM in 2000, gave *Wynn Las Vegas* and *Encore* a younger, hipper edge; and now MGM in turn have redefined Las Vegas style with *CityCenter*.

tremendous amount of imagination and whimsy goes into each redesign, combining abundant living plants with, for example, giant-sized watering cans and colossal multi-coloured bees and butterflies in spring, or a cornucopia of harvest fruits in autumn. Individual spotlights can be trained on each flower, so the place is at its most spectacular at night. Long considered a must-see attraction, the Conservatory now stands on the through route to the CityCenter monorail, and is more crowded with sightseers than ever.

Bellagio Gallery of Fine Art

Sun–Tues & Thurs 10am–6pm, Wed, Fri & Sat 10am–9pm; ☎702/693-7871; $15.

When Bellagio first opened, the **Bellagio Gallery of Fine Art**, reached via another avenue of shops and cafés at the rear of the casino, housed Steve Wynn's personal portfolio of Picassos and Monets. Seen (by Wynn more than anyone else) as a daring bid to introduce high culture to the Las Vegas scene, it has floundered ever since, and currently stages mostly lacklustre temporary exhibitions. Even at the best of times, it only has room for thirty or so paintings, so the high entrance fee is seldom worth paying.

The Central Strip: Caesars Palace and around

The central section of the Strip remains the heart of Las Vegas. Bugsy Siegel's legendary *Flamingo* ruled the roost here from 1946 to 1966, when it was joined by *Caesars Palace*, and mighty casino-resorts now cram into every available inch of space. No longer, however, are they cut-throat rivals.

Instead, the entire central swathe of properties, on both sides of the Strip, is now owned by the same company. And what no one would have predicted even ten years ago is that it's humdrum, unremarkable Harrah's that has managed bit by bit to buy up all its neighbours. Besides *Harrah's* itself, its portfolio currently includes *Caesars Palace*, the *Imperial Palace*, the *Flamingo*, *Bally's*, *Paris* and *Planet Hollywood* (as well as the nearby off-Strip *Rio*, covered in chapter 6).

Not only that, but despite its old-fashioned image Harrah's has achieved its success by a stealthy, under-the-radar strategy of using cutting-edge technology to target its low-rolling but reliable middle-aged middle-American customers ever more precisely, while its rivals were chasing such chimeras as the notion of Las Vegas as a child-friendly destination.

This part of the Strip was the first portion to attract significant foot traffic. Although at first casinos fought to keep pedestrians from wandering from casino to casino, they've had to bow to the inevitable, and feed the process instead by building over their parking lots and pushing ever closer to the street. Harrah's has taken that process to its logical conclusion by consolidating a large block of adjacent casinos together and encouraging guests to see them as a single entity.

That said, Harrah's has so far shown little desire to change the individual identities of any of the casinos it has bought, let alone to build any new ones. As a result, they remain distinct, with *Caesars Palace* still very much the pick of the bunch for sightseers, followed by *Paris*.

Planet Hollywood

3667 Las Vegas Blvd S ⓣ 702/785-5555, ⓦ planethollywoodresort.com. Hotel accommodation is reviewed on p.123; restaurants include Koi (p.134), Lombardi's Romagna Mia (p.134) and Todai Seafood Buffet (p.134); shows include The Amazing Johnathan (p.148) and V – The Ultimate Variety Show (p.151); the Miracle Mile Shops are also described on p.172.

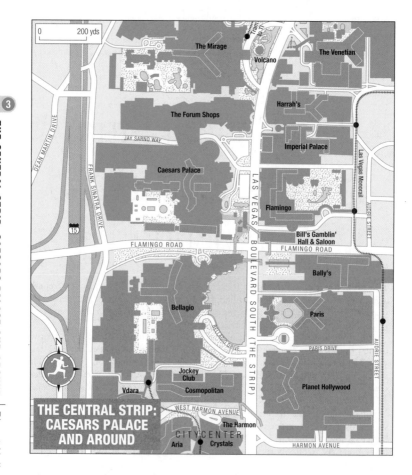

Planet Hollywood is the latest incarnation of a casino that has been plagued by one disaster after another. From 1966 until 1998, this site was occupied by the legendary **Aladdin**, best known as the venue for the 1966 wedding of **Elvis** and Priscilla. After the original *Aladdin* was imploded, it was replaced by an entirely rebuilt version that opened in 2000, just in time for its *Arabian Nights* Middle-Eastern theme to be rendered inappropriate by the events of 9/11. It subsided into bankruptcy and was bought out by Planet Hollywood in 2004 (although confusingly the *Planet Hollywood* dining chain is a separate entity, which explains why Las Vegas' *Planet Hollywood* restaurant is in *Caesars Palace* and not in, say, *Planet Hollywood*). They kept the *Aladdin*'s doors open while progressively transforming the place from the inside out, and only finally changed its name in 2007. In 2010 they went broke in turn, and the casino is now along with most of its neighbours part of the Harrah's empire.

Harrah's is not expected to make major changes in the immediate future, which leaves *Planet Hollywood* as something of a second-tier property in its ranks. The main casino interior has been given a complete makeover since the *Aladdin* days, very much geared towards the kind of younger crowd who go to *Mandalay Bay* and the *Hard Rock*. They call the decor "Hollywood Hip", which means lots of strip lighting and neon towers and giant screens, and a soundtrack of self-consciously hip rock music. Part of the gaming area, designated as the Pleasure Pit, features female dealers wearing "chic lingerie".

Planet Hollywood's **exterior**, on the other hand, has always been neglected and strangely inconspicuous. The building had been here nearly ten years before someone thought of adding a big sign saying "Casino Entrance". Now, finally, they've created a more imposing approach, and started added Strip-view balconies to the facade.

Despite being wrapped in an elaborate figure-of-eight around the casino and its theatre, the lengthy **Miracle Mile** shopping mall is owned and run by separate management. Formerly the *Desert Passage*, this too used to have a Middle-Eastern theme, but here much of the theme survives, especially further back from the Strip. In its Merchants Harbor segment, the faux-sky clouds over to unleash "thunderstorms" every half-hour. For a full description of its stores – typically more affordable than in other casino malls – see p.172.

Paris

3655 Las Vegas Blvd S ☎ 877/603-4386, Ⓦ parislasvegas.com. Hotel accommodation is reviewed on p.123; restaurants include Les Artistes Steakhouse (p.134), Mon Ami Gabi (p.134) and Le Village Buffet (p.130).

The last Strip casino to open in the twentieth century – September 1999, to be precise – Paris was the handiwork of the same team that designed New York–New York. Operating under similar spatial constraints, they made the most of Paris's smallish site by planting three legs of its centrepiece Eiffel Tower replica smack in the middle of the casino floor, and allowing it to straddle the Arc de Triomphe and the Opera. In this case, however, it's somewhat of a shame; feeling squashed up and claustrophobic is part of the fun of Manhattan, but Paris should surely be a bit more spacious and elegant.

The Eiffel Tower Experience

Paris. Daily 9.30am–midnight; $10 daytime, $15 evening, $22 for both in same day.

The Strip-front exterior of *Paris* is a well-realized miniature, incorporating a welcome strolling- and picture-taking area focused around the fourth leg of the Eiffel Tower, a sparkling fountain, a handful of trees and a colourful replica Montgolfier balloon. The Eiffel Tower itself – strictly speaking, the **Eiffel Tower Experience** – is also, of course, an extravagant sign in the finest Las Vegas tradition. Standing 540ft tall, it's half the size of the 1889 original, and made of welded steel rather than wrought iron, with fake rivets added for cosmetic effect. Some components, most obviously the elevators, had to be built at full size in order for people to use them, so it's not a perfect scale model. Oddly enough, for all its presence on the Strip, it can barely be seen from elsewhere in the city, or even from the air. Nevertheless, taking the ninety-second ride straight through the roof and up to the summit – for which you might have to wait in line for up to thirty minutes – offers amazing views, at their best after dark, and most specifically across to *Bellagio*'s water ballet. There's also a very expensive dinner-only restaurant, *La Tour Eiffel*, on its first level, seventeen storeys high and reached by separate elevators.

Inside Paris

Inside, the joyful wealth of detail ranges from top-notch French restaurants, authentic bakeries and pastry shops, to toy stores where the *Sesame Street* dolls talk in French. As any true Parisian could have warned you, the cobbled alleyways wreak havoc on high heels, strollers and wheeled suitcases, but no one seems too concerned. Notices everywhere are written in cod-French – "Les Show Tickets" – and in theory, every member of staff (or "citizen of Paris") has a twenty-word French vocabulary, which is splendidly inadequate to cope with any genuine situation.

An air of French glamour wafts appealingly over the gaming tables, which are covered by metalwork canopies modelled on the metro stations of Paris, and the appeal of all that fabulous French food is unlikely to pall. *Paris*'s original intention of programming predominantly French entertainment, on the other hand, has failed to pay off, and its 1200-seat theatre currently features such attractions as a long-term residency by Barry Manilow, or Cheap Trick performing as Sergeant Pepper's Lonely Hearts Club Band.

Bally's

3645 Las Vegas Blvd S Ⓣ 877/603-4390, Ⓦ ballyslasvegas.com. Hotel accommodation is reviewed on p.123 and the show Jubilee! on p.149.

Though long since outclassed by its mighty neighbours, the casino now known as **Bally's** was thirty years ago the most famous, and infamous, hotel in the world. This is the original *MGM Grand*, which opened in 1973. Setting out to prove that there was far more money to be made in the casino business than in producing movies, entrepreneur **Kirk Kerkorian** (see p.41) had sold off almost the entire assets of MGM Studios in order to build the biggest hotel that had ever existed. Named after the 1932 movie *Grand Hotel*, the *MGM Grand* did indeed generate vast profits. However, it was devastated in November 1980 by the worst hotel fire in history, when faulty wiring in the deli caused a blaze that killed 84 people and injured over seven hundred more. The *MGM Grand* reopened in identical shape within eight months, but four years later Kerkorian sold it to *Bally's*, the pinball- and slot-machine manufacturers, who had just had a tremendous cash windfall from the worldwide success of their Pac-Man machines. The name *Bally's* has for some reason survived repeated takeovers by other companies, most recently Harrah's; Kerkorian, meanwhile, retained the *MGM Grand* name for his own future use.

The fact that *Bally's* is actually one of the Strip's dullest buildings, consisting of little more than two monolithic rectangular towers, has been disguised by turning the whole thing into a giant neon sign. Not only the towers, but also the tubular walkway that carries pedestrians into the casino, shift constantly through a spectrum of four garish colours. The walkway moves so slowly, however, that you'll probably have tired of the light show long before you reach the end. This whole area used to be the hotel car park, famous as the spot where the parachuting Elvises landed in 1992's *Honeymoon in Vegas*.

Should the economy ever pick up, it's widely predicted that Harrah's will demolish *Bally's* and replace it with something much closer to the Strip. For the moment, you enter *Bally's* to find just a run-of-the-mill casino, with poor restaurants; the one spark of life is provided by the long-running *Jubilee!* show, the last surviving throwback to Las Vegas' feathers-and-tassels era. Most visitors simply head straight through, either following the connecting corridor to *Paris* next door, or making for the Monorail station, right at the back of the property. Free shuttle buses to the *Rio* leave every half-hour from *Bally's* Flamingo Road entrance (daily 10am–1am).

Caesars Palace

3570 Las Vegas Blvd S ⓣ 866/227-5938, Ⓦ www.caesarspalace.com. Hotel accommo-
dation is reviewed on p.121; restaurants include Beijing Noodle No. 9 (p.134), Mesa
Grill (p.135), The Palm (p.135) and Serendipity 3 (p.135); bars and clubs include
Cleopatra's Barge (p.142), Seahorse Lounge (p.143) and Pure (p.145); the Forum
Shops are described on p.172.

Despite approaching its fiftieth birthday – making it virtually prehistoric by Las
Vegas standards – **Caesars Palace** remains the most famous name in the casino
business. In the last few years, it has comprehensively overhauled itself to meet the
challenge of upstart rivals like *Bellagio* and the *Venetian*, to become once again a
must-see for every visitor.

When Las Vegas's definitive themed casino was unveiled, in August 1966, it had
cost less than $25 million to build – less than the volcano at the *Mirage*. The brain-
child of entrepreneur **Jay Sarno**, who had previously owned a Palo Alto motel in
partnership with Doris Day, it was the first Vegas casino to be financed through
loans from the pension fund of Jimmy Hoffa's Teamsters' Union.

A powerful Mob presence at *Caesars* was barely concealed from the word go, and
became even more apparent after Sarno sold out in 1969. However, Caesars has
been under sanitized corporate control since the early 1980s, and under a succession of unimaginative owners it had fallen way behind the pack by the time it was
acquired by the Harrah's empire in 2005.

Caesars was originally designed to be approached by car. In those days, its
distance from the highway was not a drawback, but made it seem even more
majestic. Over the years, the intervening space became filled, initially by fountains,
formal gardens and statuary, and then by *Caesars* itself. At its northern end, the
hugely successful **Forum** mall first snaked out to reach the Strip, and now towers
three storeys above it. To the south, across from *Bellagio* and the *Flamingo*, Caesars
has constructed the open-air Roman Plaza, with the large stand-alone *Serendipity
3* restaurant (see p.135).

Inside Caesars Palace

Although there's a little less togas-and-sandals high camp in the interior of *Caesars*
than there used to be, half-naked Roman centurions and Cleopatra-cropped
cocktail waitresses still scuttle through night and day. In terms of hotel rooms,
Caesars remains relatively "small", but the casino proper – the hub around which
everything else revolves – is a bewildering labyrinth, vast enough that it can take
half an hour's brisk walk to get from one end to the other. And that's if you know
the place well; with its low ceilings, low lights and lack of signs, it's designed to be
as disorienting as possible, and you're all too likely to be distracted by the appearance of an armour-clad Roman legionary standing guard atop a bank of slot
machines.

At the very front of the property, but only accessible via the casino, the four-
thousand-seat **Colosseum** proudly maintains *Caesars'* reputation as the biggest
name in Las Vegas entertainment. It was built specifically for **Celine Dion** in
2003; she still appears regularly, while it has also housed long-term residencies by
Cher, Bette Midler and Elton John.

One side passage from the casino connects with the **Appian Way**, a shopping
mall where a replica of Michelangelo's *David* stands beneath the central dome.
Another obliges you to squeeze between the golden prow of *Cleopatra's Barge* (a
floating nightclub and bar). Keep on heading back behind the scenes, and you'll
find yourself in the actual hotel, which is every bit as huge again. Large plate-glass
windows look out over the sumptuous and ever-expanding **Garden of the Gods**

THE CENTRAL STRIP: CAESARS PALACE AND AROUND | Caesars Palace

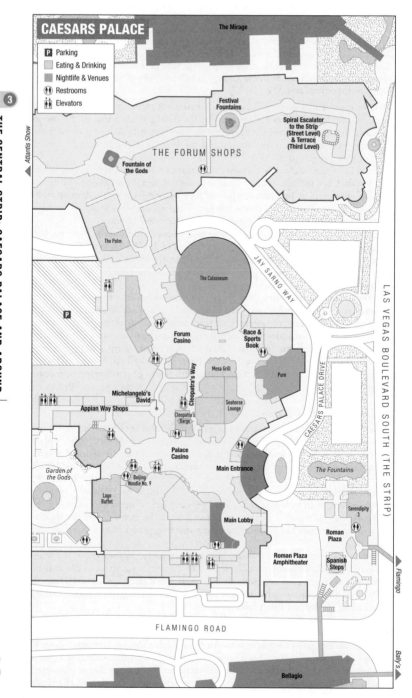

CAESARS PALACE

P Parking
  Eating & Drinking
  Nightlife & Venues
  Restrooms
  Elevators

The Mirage

Festival Fountains

Spiral Escalator to the Strip (Street Level) & Terrace (Third Level)

THE FORUM SHOPS

Fountain of the Gods

The Palm

The Colosseum

JAY SARNO WAY

P

Forum Casino

Race & Sports Book

Mesa Grill

Pure

Michelangelo's David

Cleopatra's Way

Seahorse Lounge

Appian Way Shops

Cleopatra's Barge

LAS VEGAS BOULEVARD SOUTH (THE STRIP)

Palace Casino

Main Entrance

CAESARS PALACE DRIVE

The Fountains

Garden of the Gods

Beijing Noodle No. 9

Lago Buffet

Main Lobby

Serendipity 3

Roman Plaza

Roman Plaza Amphitheater

Spanish Steps

Flamingo

Atlantis Show

FLAMINGO ROAD

Bally's

Bellagio

pool area, built using Carrara marble and modelled after the baths of Pompeii. The lavish high-roller "villas" in the new poolside Octavius Tower rent for $40,000 per night, plus a minimum expenditure of $5000 on food and drink.

The Forum Shops

3500 Las Vegas Blvd S ⓣ 702/893-4800, ⓦ forumshops.com. Sun–Thurs 10am–11pm, Fri & Sat 10am–midnight. Restaurants in the Forum Shops are reviewed on p.135 onwards. For a full description of the actual shops, see p.172.

A high proportion of visitors to *Caesars* are here to explore the stores and restaurants in the adjoining, seamlessly connected **Forum**. For twenty years now, crowds have gathered to gawk at the complex play of lights that transforms its blue-domed, cloud-strewn ceiling between dawn and dusk every hour, and enhancements and extensions have been added at regular intervals. The mall itself is now three storeys tall, but you may have to hurry to see the gloriously kitsch animatronic "living statues" which inhabit its various fountains; they do seem to be falling out of favour, and disappearing into the netherworld at an alarming rate.

Bill's Gamblin' Hall & Saloon

3595 Las Vegas Blvd S ⓣ 702/737-2100, ⓦ billslasvegas.com. Hotel accommodation is reviewed on p.121.

Slotted in between so many behemoths, the tiny, 200-room **Bill's Gamblin' Hall** – the smallest casino on the Strip – feels like a throwback to a long-lost Las Vegas. Its main distinguishing feature is a classic piece of old Vegas neon, the hourglass-shaped sign above its front entrance. Until 2007, when it was bought by Harrah's and renamed, this was the *Barbary Coast*. Don't expect to see "Bill" himself; the Bill in question is Bill Harrah, founder of Harrah's, who died in 1978.

Despite appearances, *Bill's Gamblin' Hall* is not in fact an independent entity; it's run by the staff from the nearby *Imperial Palace*. With its doors always thrown open wide, and clattering tables and slots just inside, it's kept ticking along nicely by walk-in gamblers weary of ogling its outsized neighbours – and by punters eager to watch "Big Elvis", who delivers his spirited renditions of the King's repertoire in the lounge (Mon–Fri 3pm, 5pm & 6.30pm; free). Elsewhere, the interior is filled with brass and glass, including "the world's largest Tiffany-style glass mural," but amenities are minimal. You can't help suspecting that one of these quiet nights, *Bill's* will disappear altogether, to make way for some new expansion plan.

The Flamingo

3555 Las Vegas Blvd S ⓣ 702/733-3111 or 800/732-2111, ⓦ flamingolasvegas.com. Hotel accommodation is reviewed on p.124.

Though neither brick nor bloodstain remains of Bugsy Siegel's original resort, the very name of the **Flamingo** is dripping with Las Vegas legend. Popular myth regards it as having been the first of the great Strip casinos. In fact, *El Rancho Vegas* and the *Last Frontier* had already blazed the trail by the time it opened in 1946, and the *Flamingo* when it started out – with barely a hundred hotel rooms – was much more a consummately stylish Forties motel than a foretaste of the neon extravaganzas of the Fifties. What it did offer, however, was the ambition to look beyond its bleak desert setting in both theme and ambience, not to mention a glamorous hint of underworld menace.

In a sense, Siegel's 1947 murder (see box below) was the perfect advertising gimmick to launch the *Flamingo*. It turned out that Las Vegas punters actually liked to feel that they were rubbing shoulders with murderous gangsters. Countless changes of ownership were required before the Mob presence was finally shaken off – the ubiquitous Kirk Kerkorian owned it for a while – and the *Flamingo* now belongs to Harrah's.

Today, it stakes its patch opposite *Caesars* with a magnificent cascade of neon, centered on a bulbous unfurling flower of light. As recently as 1990, this was the largest hotel in the world; now it pitches itself (not entirely convincingly) as a sophisticated upmarket resort, an elder statesman too secure of its status to need to compete head-on with brash modern competitors. In truth, you can get a better sense of its middle-American, middle-aged target audience from the ongoing presence of **Donny and Marie Osmond** in its main showroom, and the crowds in *Jimmy Buffet's Margaritaville*, open on one side to the Strip.

Inside the Flamingo

In the casino proper, only a continuing design predilection for the kind of pinks and oranges seldom seen outside Barbie's boudoir – take a peek at the guest elevators, for example – bears witness to the *Flamingo*'s racy past. There are no particular attractions inside, but it's worth stepping into the elaborate landscaped gardens at the back. Closest to the casino, the **Wildlife Habitat** abounds in flamingos both real and plastic, and also holds a few African penguins, unique among their kind in having adapted to hot climates. Beyond that lies a lovely complex of pools, lagoons, water slides and palm-shaded walkways.

In an unusual twist, the *Flamingo* caters to customers who hanker for the old days by offering lower-stakes gaming and cheap eats in what looks like a separate casino next door, the nominally Irish-themed **O'Sheas**.

Don't call me Bugsy

Benjamin Siegel started out as a New York mobster, co-founder with Meyer Lansky of the infamous Murder, Inc syndicate. By his own admission, he killed around twenty men; the FBI reckoned the total was more than thirty. His quick-fire temper, displayed in his tendency to "go bugs", earned him his famous nickname – though heaven help anyone who used it to his face.

Siegel headed west in the early 1940s in the hope of making it as a movie star; failing that, he settled for making it with movie stars. Las Vegas initially beckoned as a good base for running a horse-racing betting racket, but the casino business swiftly caught his eye. Hearing about the cash-flow problems of LA restaurateur Billy Wilkerson, who was building a new casino a mile beyond the *Last Frontier*, he put together a million-dollar package that enabled him to squeeze Wilkerson out and take control.

Construction materials were expensive and in short supply after the war, and Siegel soon found himself in trouble. There are tales of contractors delivering supplies to the site by day, stealing them back at night, and then delivering them again the next day, not so much to defraud Bugsy as to avoid his wrath at their failure to get hold of any more. Desperate to start repaying the additional $5 million he'd been forced to borrow, Siegel opened the incomplete *Flamingo* too early, only to have to close down after two weeks even deeper in debt. Although the hotel swiftly reopened, and was soon running at a profit, Siegel's backers had lost patience, and he was shot dead at his girlfriend's home in Beverly Hills in June 1947. Literally within minutes, new Mob-appointed managers announced themselves at the *Flamingo*.

The Imperial Palace

3535 Las Vegas Blvd S ⓣ 702/731-3311, ⓦ imperialpalace.com. Hotel accommodation is reviewed on p.122, the Emperor's Buffet on p.129 and the Human Nature show on p.148.

Despite its small and ultra-tacky exterior, which looks less like the facade of a major casino than that of a rundown used-car dealership – which is oddly appropriate, since that's exactly what its **Auto Collections** section is – the **Imperial Palace** is among Las Vegas' largest hotels. Every square inch of the twelve-acre site that stretches away from its slender frontage on the Strip is pressed into use. It has even built over its driveway, to create a separate building sandwiched between the Strip and the front doors that's currently occupied by the raucous *Rockhouse* nightclub and all-day daiquiri bar.

The emphasis inside the *Imperial Palace* remains squarely on gambling. As well as having a splendidly old-fashioned, theatre-like **Race Book**, rising in tiers above a central pit on the second and third floors, it also has a special, very central section of the casino floor where the table games are conducted by celebrity lookalike "dealertainers" – they even include Stevie Wonder, despite the obvious pitfalls.

Auto Collections

Imperial Palace ⓣ 702794-3174, ⓦ autocollections.com. Daily 10am–6pm; $9, or free with coupon from casino, website or listings magazines.

Former *Imperial Palace* owner Ralph Engelstad, who died in 2001, had a predilection for dictators (he was once fined $1.5 million by the Nevada Gaming Control Board for holding a party to celebrate Hitler's birthday) and a passion for **cars**. He indulged both in the **Auto Collections**, which can still be visited on the fifth floor of the parking garage at the rear. The collection is now as much showroom as museum; almost all of Engelstad's personal favourites have long gone, but there's a wide selection of beautiful and extraordinarily expensive vintage vehicles for sale. Exactly what you'll see can't be predicted, as the stock turns over regularly; at the time of going to press, however, the oldest car on show was a gorgeous pastel-blue Mercedes tourer from 1914.

King's Ransom Museum

Imperial Palace ⓣ 516/382-4414, ⓦ thekingsransom.com. Daily 11am–7pm; $12.

Tucked away behind the buffet, near the back of the *Imperial Palace*'s third floor, the **King's Ransom Museum** holds a small collection of **Elvis** memorabilia. Not nearly as extensive as Las Vegas' much-missed *Elvis-A-Rama* museum, which closed down a few years back, it consists of assorted stage and movie costumes, jewellery, guns and other "law enforcement items", all padded out with photos, cuttings and film footage.

Harrah's

3475 Las Vegas Blvd S ⓣ 702/369-5000, ⓦ www.harrahsvegas.com. Hotel accommodation is reviewed on p.122; the Improv comedy club is reviewed on p.149; Legends In Concert on p.149; and the Mac King magic show on p.150.

It's perhaps the greatest irony of the hip, new Las Vegas, which makes such a show of updating itself to lure in the affluent younger generation, that staid old **Harrah's** so consistently outperformed its high-profile neighbours for so long that it was eventually able to buy most of them.

Even so, it remains easy to walk past *Harrah's* namesake casino without noticing it's there. The only aspect likely to attract your attention is the large plaza that adjoins the *Imperial Palace* at its southern end. Still one of the few open-air public spaces on the Strip, it mollifies passers-by irritated at having to detour around the hotel's parking tunnel with free live performances on its Carnaval Court stage, and also holds souvenir, sandwich and cocktail kiosks, plus a *Ghirardelli Soda Fountain and Chocolate Shop*.

Behind its frontage, festooned with trumpeting golden Mardi Gras jesters, *Harrah's* is a sedate and rather boring affair, filled with the kind of middle-American visitors whose eyes light up at the prospect of country superstar Toby Keith's restaurant and gaming area. They're gently satirized by the prominent statue of "The Greenbacks," a very lifelike tourist couple dripping dollars from every pore and pocket. The main reasons outsiders might actually bother to pass through are either to catch the comedy shows at the *Improv* (see p.149), or to use the spacious parking garage, handy for other nearby Strip attractions.

The North Strip

xactly where the northern end of the Strip is deemed to start seems to change almost year on year. Now that a solid block of Harrah's-owned casinos cuts the Strip in two, however, it makes sense to think of the **North Strip** as starting with the **Mirage** and the **Venetian**. Since it also includes the showcase **Wynn Las Vegas**, that makes it a very glamorous neighbourhood indeed.

While all those properties are very much worth seeing, it doesn't mean the North Strip is thriving. Less than ten years ago, the North Strip label was taken to refer to a fading cluster of long-standing casinos half a mile or so further north, which it was promised would soon be swept away and replaced with vastly ambitious upscale new developments. Two have indeed been demolished – the *New Frontier*, which dated back to 1942, and 1958's *Stardust* – but extravaganzas such as *Echelon* and *Fontainebleau* never materialized, and things are looking worse than ever. Long empty lots are interspersed with abandoned construction sites, and analysts believe other ailing veterans like the *Riviera*, *Circus Circus* and *Sahara* may not survive either.

The Mirage

3400 Las Vegas Blvd S ⓣ 702/791-7111, ⓦ mirage.com. Hotel accommodation is reviewed on p.122; restaurants include BLT Burger (p.135) and the Cravings buffet (p.129); bars and clubs include BB King's Blues Club (p.142), Japonais (p.142) and the Revolution Lounge (p.143); Terry Fator & His Cast of Thousands is reviewed on p.151, and the Cirque du Soleil show Love on p.150.

Perhaps the best measure of the impact the **Mirage** has had upon Las Vegas is that now, over twenty years since it opened, it's hard to remember quite what was so different about it. Completed in 1989, the *Mirage* was the first new hotel to be built from scratch on the Strip since 1973. Its high-rise Y-plan design was perfect for its prime position, commanding the point where the Strip curves northeast to parallel the rail tracks towards downtown. Original owner **Steve Wynn**, however, eschewed many of Las Vegas' most time-honoured traditions. He spared no expense on fixtures and fittings for the three thousand guest rooms, he neglected neon in favour of plating the entire facade with 24-carat gold stripes, and he even proclaimed that from now on Las Vegas was going to be a family destination.

By common consent, Wynn's $620 million gamble was risky even by Las Vegas standards, and it was no secret that the *Mirage* could only pay its way by making $1 million clear profit from its gaming tables every day of the year. The fact that it succeeded – not in every specific goal, but in the one detail that counts in Las Vegas, financially – transformed the city. However, in due course the opening of *Bellagio* – Wynn's next brainchild – saw the *Mirage* relegated to second-best even

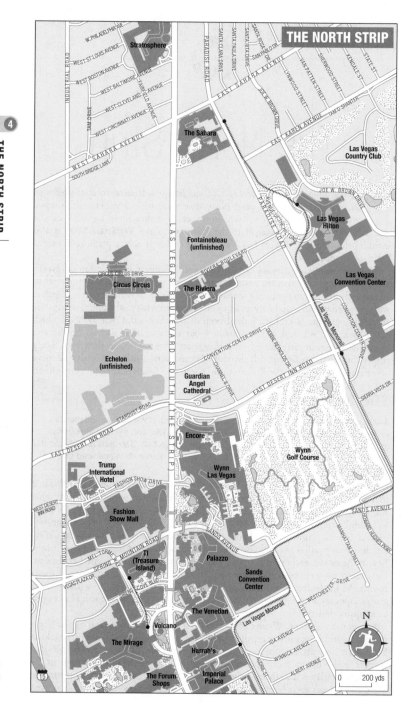

within the Mirage Resorts organization, and since 2000 it has been just another cog in the vast MGM machine.

The volcano

The much-vaunted **volcano** outside the *Mirage* was created to lure passing pedestrians into the property at night – just when they're in the mood to spend money. Within 48 hours of the *Mirage* opening, though, Wynn was kicking himself for failing to create a vantage point inside the casino overlooking the volcano, which meant that the jostling crowds were outside on the Strip instead. Twenty years on, in 2008, the volcano was finally entirely rebuilt, by the company responsible for fountains at *Bellagio* and *Aria*. It remains basically a lumpy fibreglass island, topped by palm trees and poking from a shallow artificial lagoon, which "erupts" in 12ft fireballs and cascades of water every hour on the hour between nightfall and midnight. Choreographed to a percussive soundtrack by Grateful Dead drummer Mickey Hart and tabla player Zakir Hussain, the show is once more drawing large crowds.

Inside the Mirage

Entering the *Mirage*'s opulent central **atrium**, housed beneath a geodesic dome, feels like stepping into a lush garden. Narrow footpaths meander away in various directions, skirting flowerbeds planted with an artful mix of fake and real vegetation. Off to the right, a massive thatched roof shelters the hotel's **registration area**, while the giant fish tank located behind the check-in desks teems with pygmy sharks and stingrays.

There's little scope for leisurely sightseeing within the *Mirage*. It's simply not on the scale of the newer mega-casinos, and the one narrow walkway through the heart of the casino always seems to be busy with visitors eager to get from A to B. It has, however, thoroughly upgraded its restaurants and bars in the last few years, even if shopping opportunities remain minimal. The pool complex out back is also impressive, and now features an "adult" (ie topless) area, imaginatively entitled Bare.

The *Mirage*'s strongest hand has always been **entertainment**. Until 2003,when a wayward white tiger finally declared enough was enough, it was home to high-camp Germanic illusionists **Siegfried and Roy**. The injured Roy Horn recovered sufficiently for the duo to make a final charity appearance in 2009, with the self-same tiger, but they've been superseded at the *Mirage* by an even more prestigious double act, the **Cirque du Soleil** joining forces with the **Beatles** to stage the spectacular and highly recommended show *Love* (see p.150). A separate theatre hosts the extraordinary singing ventriloquist **Terry Fator** (see p.151) and there's also a branch of **B.B. King's Blues Club**.

While there's a bronze statue of Siegfried and Roy out on the Strip, and their **Secret Garden** is still there at the back of the property, the glass-walled cages that formerly housed their tigers in the casino proper have been converted into bars and restaurants.

Secret Garden and Dolphin Habitat

The Mirage ⓦ miragehabitat.com. Mon–Fri 11am–6.30pm, Sat & Sun 10am–6.30pm; adults $15, ages 4–12 $10.

One relic of the Siegfried and Roy era survives – the **Secret Garden and Dolphin Habitat**, reached via a landscaped ramp that leads up from the pool area at the back of the *Mirage*. This surprisingly spacious zoo – a better deal than *Mandalay Bay*'s Shark Reef aquarium (see p.34) – is as the name suggests divided into two

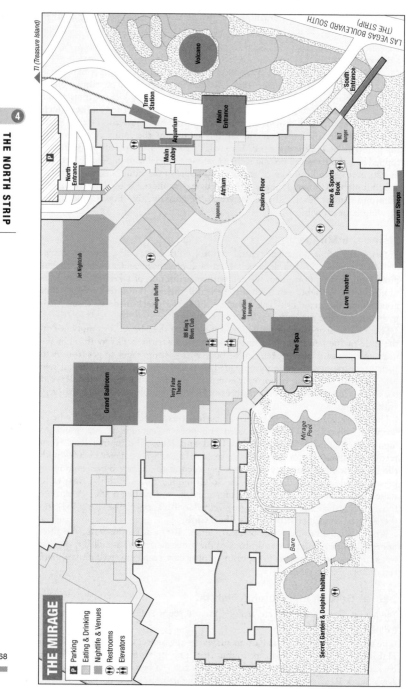

THE MIRAGE

Legend:
- P Parking
- Eating & Drinking
- Nightlife & Venues
- Restrooms
- Elevators

TI (Treasure Island)

LAS VEGAS BOULEVARD SOUTH (THE STRIP)

Volcano

Tram Station

Main Entrance

South Entrance

Aquarium

Main Lobby

North Entrance

P

Atrium

Japonais

Casino Floor

BLT Burger

Race & Sports Book

Forum Shops

Jet Nightclub

Cravings Buffet

BB King's Blues Club

Revolution Lounge

Love Theatre

The Spa

Grand Ballroom

Terry Fator Theatre

Mirage Pool

Bare

Secret Garden & Dolphin Habitat

distinct parts. The first consists of two interconnected pools, in which you can watch dolphins experience "random interactions" both above and below the water (as opposed to performing tricks, because this is supposedly an educational facility, though it comes to much the same thing). Enclosures beyond hold the world's greatest concentration of big white cats, including snow leopards and hetero-zygous white lions, as well as the signature white tigers.

TI (Treasure Island)

3300 Las Vegas Blvd S ⓣ 702/894-7111, ⓦ treasureisland.com. Hotel accommodation is reviewed on p.123; restaurants include Isla (p.135) and Phô (p.135); Gilley's Saloon is described on p.142; and the Cirque du Soleil show Mystère is reviewed on p.150.

The casino known as both **TI** and **Treasure Island** perfectly epitomizes the many recent changes Las Vegas has gone through. When Steve Wynn built it in 1993, using the first profits from *Mirage* next door, the city was in thrall to the notion that it was about to become a child-friendly destination. *Treasure Island* took the Mirage's volcano concept several stages further by having its entire lower facade sculpted into a novelty attraction – an intricate, pastel-pretty seafront village straight out of *Pirates of the Caribbean*. Amid much yo-ho-ho-ing and cannonfire, two "pirate ships" clashed nightly on the moat in front, drawing crowds of kids and their parents to the boardwalks and rigging that still line the Strip.

As the years went by, the whole Vegas-for-kids notion passed away, taking with it most of *Treasure Island*'s lovingly crafted fripperies, like the skull motifs that adorned everything from its main sign to the door handles. Even the very name was replaced by the anodyne acronym *TI*, though it's a sign of ongoing ambiva-lence that the words "*Treasure Island*" still seem to crop up everywhere.

Most ludicrous of all, the pirate battle was revamped as a "sexy" adult show, in which the victorious ship is now crewed by the lingerie-clad **Sirens of TI**, who screech rock songs to lure the few remaining "renegade pirates" into their clutches (nightly: spring and summer 7pm, 8.30pm, 10pm & 11.30pm; autumn and winter 5.30pm, 7pm, 8.30pm, & 10pm).

Then MGM-Mirage ran into stormy waters building CityCenter, and sold *TI* out of the blue to **Phil Ruffin**, the former owner of the veteran, recently-imploded *New Frontier* casino a little further north. When Ruffin took over *TI* in 2009, business was ticking over nicely, and he was in no hurry to make changes. Bit by bit, however, he's showing his hand, targeting "budget-minded tourists with blue-collar tastes" to leave *TI* with more of a split personality than ever. While the sirens are still doing their thing outside, the fancy Italian restaurant and nightclub indoors have been replaced by **Gilley's Saloon**, a country-themed beer-and-barbecue joint previously at the *New Frontier*.

The whole place is an entertaining mix of discordant tastes. A shiny customized motorbike – the Sirens of TI Chopper – jostles for space alongside Ruffin's prized collection of antique Oriental carvings, such as an enormous 35,000-year-old mammoth tusk. You can still buy pirate souvenirs, but further back Ruffin's ex-model wife, a former Miss Ukraine, has been given free rein to create the lavish Oleksandra Spa.

Treasure Island is still home to *Mystère*, Las Vegas' first-ever **Cirque du Soleil** show (see p.150), but on spare nights the showroom hosts country stars like LeAnn Rimes. And while *TI* still holds a handful of high-end restaurants, departing theatregoers can now buy pizza by the slice, or cubic zirconia jewellery from the Bling Co.

TI remains umbilically connected to its estranged parent; they share the same driveway, and a stand-alone monorail runs to the front of the *Mirage*. It's also perfectly sited to take advantage of pedestrian traffic from its high-profile, big-money neighbours. Quite how far downmarket Ruffin manoeuvres its profile will make fascinating watching.

The Venetian

3355 Las Vegas Blvd S ☎ 702/414-1000, ⓦ venetian.com. Hotel accommodation is reviewed on p.124; restaurants include Bouchon (p.136), Delmonico Steakhouse (p.136), Tao Asian Bistro (p.136) and Zefferino's (p.136); bars and clubs include Smokin' Hot Aces (p.143), Tao (p.145), and the V Bar (p.143); the Blue Man Group show is reviewed on p.148 and the Phantom Of The Opera on p.151; and the Grand Canal Shoppes are also described on p.172.

The **Venetian** occupies a legendary Las Vegas location, which as home to the *Sands* casino from 1952 onward played host to the fabled antics of the **Rat Pack**. Although Howard Hughes announced plans for the "new *Sands*" during the late 1960s, the old structure was not demolished until 1996, and the *Venetian* only just managed to make its debut in the twentieth century. It was the brainchild of one man, **Sheldon Adelson**, who made his fortune establishing Las Vegas' annual COMDEX exhibition as the world's premier computer-industry trade show, and then selling it for $800 million in 1995.

The birth of the *Venetian* was plagued with complications, and its eventual emergence in 1999, with only a handful of restaurants in action and no shops, was acclaimed as a textbook example of how *not* to open a casino. Initial prognostications were gloomy, and having cost around $1.4 billion to build it soon racked up heavy losses. But a dozen years on, and now holding a staggering seven thousand rooms if you include the supposedly distinct *Palazzo*, it's a major success. While every bit as lavish as *Wynn Las Vegas* or *Bellagio*, for example, it's much more user-friendly, with architecture and attractions to lure in passing tourists, and the conference centre and luxury accommodation to keep it packed with business travellers.

When he originally sketched out plans for the *Venetian*, Mr Adelson apparently set out to cram all the snapshots of his real-life 1991 honeymoon in Venice into a single frame. The Venetian's Strip facade incorporates facsimiles of six major Venice buildings – from south to north, the **Library**, the **Campanile**, the **Palazzo Contarini-Fasan**, the **Doge's Palace**, the **Ca' d'Oro** and the **Clock Tower** – as well as the **Rialto Bridge**, the **Bridge of Sighs** and a small stretch of "canal".

Inside the Venetian

Although Venice was the first European city to have a public gambling house – it opened in 1638, and guests were obliged to wear masks – the challenge of making the casino itself particularly Venetian has been largely ignored. The coolness of its marble floor comes as a welcome relief after the heat of the Strip, but the slot machines and tables in the gaming area beyond are much like any others. The internal layout of the *Venetian* focuses around extravagant public spaces like the huge hallway that leads to the hotel lobby, paved with Escher-like *trompe-l'oeil* marble tiles, and the magnificent central stairwell, topped by vivid frescoes, that leads to the breathtaking Grand Canal.

The Grand Canal

A preposterous recreation of the waterways of Venice, complete with gondolas and opera-singing gondoliers, the **Grand Canal** is quintessential Las Vegas – for God's sake, it's *upstairs*. Topped by a Forum-esque fake sky, it's lined by the **Grand**

Canal Shoppes (see p.172) and passes by the broad St Mark's Square, where musicians and living statues do their stuff in between the gelato stands and restaurants. A store at the far end sells tickets for gondola rides, both inside and also on the section of canal outside (indoors Sun–Thurs 10am–11pm, Fri & Sat 10am–midnight, outdoors much shorter hours, varying seasonally and dependent on wind and weather conditions; $16 per person, $8 under-13s, or $64 for a 2-person private ride).

Madame Tussaud's

The Venetian, 3355 Las Vegas Blvd S Ⓣ 702/862-7800, Ⓦ mtvegas.com. Daily 10am–10pm, some seasonal variations; $25, over-60s $18, ages 7–12 $15, 25 percent discount online.

The *Venetian*'s one major Strip-level attraction is the first US outpost of **Madame Tussaud's** waxwork museum. Set on the second and third floors of the Library, it's styled as "Interactive Wax," on the grounds that visitors can shoot hoops with Shaq, sink a putt with Tiger, sing karaoke for Simon Cowell, or even put on a wedding dress and marry George Clooney. The actual effigies remain completely static, so the main objective for most visitors is to subject them to such indignities as posing for photographs with them, prodding them gently, or making sarcastic remarks about them. Come in a lively group and you might have a great time; wander through solemnly inspecting wax models of chef Wolfgang Puck or assorted TV hosts, and you may well feel the whole experience is seriously overpriced. There's an extra charge of $15 to have a souvenir photo taken with President Obama in a replica Oval Office.

The Palazzo

3325 Las Vegas Blvd S Ⓣ 702/607-7777, Ⓦ palazzolasvegas.com. Hotel accommodation is reviewed on p.123; restaurants include Dos Caminos Mexican Kitchen (p.136) and Lavo (p.137); and the musical Jersey Boys is reviewed on p.149.

It's far from obvious why the **Palazzo**, which opened in 2008, is officially regarded as being a resort in its own right rather than simply Sheldon Adelson's latest addition to his adjoining *Venetian*. Although it does have its own separate Strip entrance, most visitors stumble across the *Palazzo* by walking the full length of the *Venetian*'s Grand Canal Shoppes and finding to their surprise that another casino lies immediately beyond.

Perhaps it's just that if the *Palazzo* did count as part of the *Venetian*, that would make it the world's largest hotel, and that somehow wouldn't fit comfortably with the image of luxurious exclusivity that each tries to cultivate. Even so, the company president is quite happy to refer to the two combined as "the largest building in the world".

Thanks to its relatively small site, and to Clark County forcing Adelson to provide the obligatory level of parking for the *Venetian* and its Convention Center, the *Palazzo* was the first Las Vegas casino to be constructed atop its own underground parking garage. It was also, at 642ft, briefly the tallest building in Las Vegas, though it was swiftly surpassed when *Wynn Las Vegas* added its *Encore* tower next door.

Inside, the *Palazzo* has its own fair share of high-end stores, arranged on two levels around the atrium that connects to the Grand Canal. In total, though, it seems remarkably devoid of any identity; it just feels like a big, bland mall, with the odd good restaurant, the overblown *Lavo* club-cum-restaurant, and a theatre that's currently hosting the hit show **Jersey Boys**. If you're sightseeing on the Strip, you're better off giving it a miss.

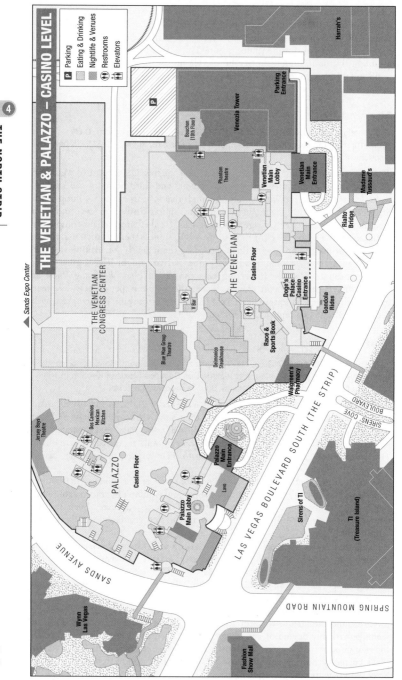

THE VENETIAN & PALAZZO – CASINO LEVEL

P Parking
Eating & Drinking
Nightlife & Venues
Restrooms
Elevators

Sands Expo Center

Harrah's

P

Parking Entrance

Venezia Tower

Bouchon (10th Floor)

Phantom Theatre

Venetian Main Lobby

Venetian Main Entrance

Madame Tussaud's

Rialto Bridge

THE VENETIAN CONGRESS CENTER

V Bar

THE VENETIAN

Casino Floor

Doge's Palace Casino Entrance

Gondola Rides

Blue Man Group Theatre

Delmonico Steakhouse

Race & Sports Book

Walgreen's Pharmacy

SIRENS' COVE BOULEVARD

Jersey Boys Theatre

Dos Caminos Mexican Kitchen

PALAZZO

Casino Floor

Palazzo Main Entrance

Lavo

Palazzo Main Lobby

Sirens of TI

TI (Treasure Island)

LAS VEGAS BOULEVARD SOUTH (THE STRIP)

SANDS AVENUE

SPRING MOUNTAIN ROAD

Wynn Las Vegas

Fashion Show Mall

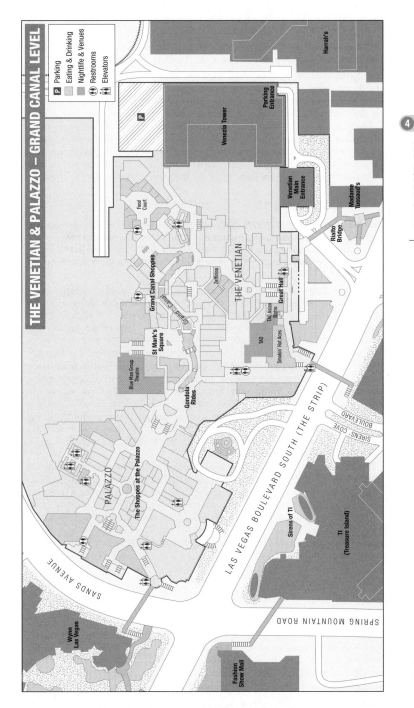

THE VENETIAN & PALAZZO – GRAND CANAL LEVEL

P Parking
Eating & Drinking
Nightlife & Venues
Restrooms
Elevators

Venezia Tower

Parking Entrance

Food Court

Venetian Main Entrance

Madame Tussaud's

Grand Canal Shoppes

Zeffirino

Rialto Bridge

THE VENETIAN

St Mark's Square

Great Hall

TAO Asian Bistro

Blue Man Group Theatre

TAO

Smokin' Hot Aces

Gondola Rides

LAS VEGAS BOULEVARD SOUTH (THE STRIP)

PALAZZO

The Shoppes at the Palazzo

SIRENS COVE BOULEVARD

SANDS AVENUE

Sirens of TI

TI (Treasure Island)

Wynn Las Vegas

SPRING MOUNTAIN ROAD

Fashion Show Mall

Harrah's

Fashion Show Mall

3200 Las Vegas Blvd S ⊤ 702/784-7000, Ⓦ thefashionshow.com. Mon–Sat 11am–9pm, Sun 11am–7pm; shopping reviewed on p.74.

The **Fashion Show Mall** caused a sensation when it opened in 1981 as the first significant shopping mall to appear on the Strip. Thirty years on, it has grown out of all proportion, and it's now ensconced behind a glittering frontage and topped by the bizarre 300ft disc-shaped "Cloud" (which sometimes resembles a high-fashion hat and sometimes a UFO). Strangely enough, it's still the only mall on the Strip that's not attached to a casino, which is both a strength and a weakness. While it's certainly not a must-see attraction like the Forum or Grand Canal Shoppes, it surpasses both by offering full-sized department stores, and if you just want to shop quickly and efficiently without all the frippery, this is the place to come.

Wynn Las Vegas

3131 Las Vegas Blvd S ⊤ 702/770-7000, Ⓦ wynnlasvegas.com. Hotel accommodation is reviewed on p.124; restaurants include Red 8 (p.137) and the Buffet at Wynn (p.129); bars and clubs include Blush (p.142), Parasol Up/Parasol Down (p.143) and Tryst (p.146); Le Rêve show is reviewed on p.151; and the Wynn Esplanade shops are described on p.173.

Wynn Las Vegas, widely seen as Las Vegas' premier upscale property, is yet another brainchild of entrepreneur extraordinaire **Steve Wynn**. After selling his beloved *Bellagio* to MGM in 2000, he used his personal profit of $275 million to buy – and destroy – the 50-year-old *Desert Inn*. Five years to the day later, he opened *Wynn Las Vegas*.

Wynn's initial plan was to build a resort called *Le Rêve* (French for "The Dream"), named for his favourite among those Picassos he owns, but his bankers felt that was too abstract, and the project took on his name instead (with its obvious gambler-friendly connotations). Wynn suffers from an eye disease called retinitis pigmentosa, which severely limits his field of vision; indeed in 2006, he agreed to sell Picasso's *Le Rêve* for $139 million, potentially the most expensive price ever paid for a painting, only to abort the deal by accidentally poking his elbow through the canvas. His affliction, however, clearly enhances his appreciation of colour, for bright colours are the major defining characteristic of his resorts.

In a nutshell, *Wynn Las Vegas* is *Bellagio* reimagined for a younger, hipper crowd, with a marked shift away from European elegance in favour of contemporary Asian design. A pleasant and surprisingly intimate space to stroll around, it features several stores and some excellent restaurants – Wynn has the very rare policy for Las Vegas of insisting his celebrity chefs actually move to the city. Even though the colours are fading somewhat as the years go by, and Wynn's attentions have moved on, both towards *Encore* next door and further afield, *Wynn Las Vegas* remains a breathtaking creation.

Lake of Dreams

The Strip facade of Wynn Las Vegas consists of assorted gardens and waterfalls, tumbling down the outer slope of an artificial "mountain". Once you find your way inside, you discover that the mountain frames the bizarre, enormous Lake of Dreams, an "environmental theatre" in which a massive waterfall serves as the backdrop, and a large expanse of water serves as the stage. Thanks to intricate light projections, everything is in a constant state of flux, with the colour of the waterfall, trees and indeed the entire mountain endlessly changing, and all sorts of strange figures appearing and disappearing. Most of the best views of the lake

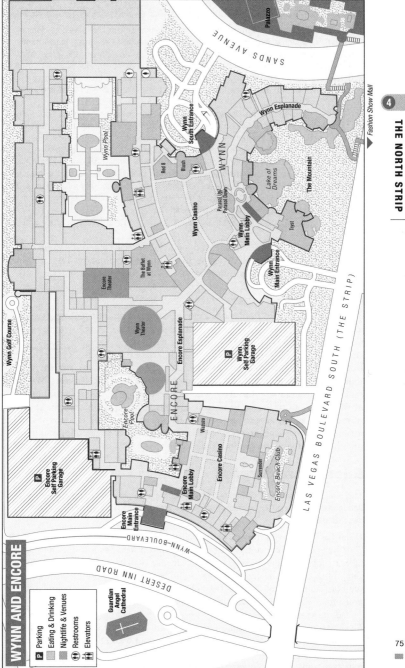

WYNN AND ENCORE

P Parking
◻ Eating & Drinking
◻ Nightlife & Venues
🚻 Restrooms
🛗 Elevators

Guardian Angel Cathedral

DESERT INN ROAD

WYNN BOULEVARD

Encore Main Entrance

Encore Self Parking Garage

Encore Main Lobby

Wazuzu

ENCORE

Encore Pool

Encore Theater

Encore Esplanade

Encore Casino

Surrender

Encore Beach Club

Wynn Golf Course

Wynn Theater

Wynn Self Parking Garage

Wynn Pool

The Buffet at Wynn

Wynn Casino

Red 8

Blush

Parasol Up/ Parasol Down

Wynn Main Lobby

Wynn Main Entrance

WYNN

Wynn South Entrance

Wynn Esplanade

Lake of Dreams

Tryst

The Mountain

LAS VEGAS BOULEVARD SOUTH (THE STRIP)

SANDS AVENUE

Palazzo

▶ Fashion Show Mall

> ## Howard Hughes in Las Vegas
>
> By welcoming **Howard Hughes** as a guest at Thanksgiving in 1966, the now-defunct *Desert Inn*, which was demolished to make way for *Wynn Las Vegas*, inadvertently spearheaded Las Vegas' move toward corporate domination. As New Year approached, the management insisted that the non-gambling Hughes check out before the annual influx of high-roll gamblers arrived. Hughes instead took over the whole hotel, buying its licence to operate until 2002 (although not the casino itself) for $13.2 million.
>
> Hughes remained at the *Desert Inn* for four years, living on the ninth floor with curtains drawn and windows taped over, and keeping the entire eighth floor empty. During that time, he bought enough casinos to become Nevada's largest single operator, despite seldom, if ever, allowing even his closest associates to see him. Tales of his eccentricity abound; quite apart from storing all his urine in jars in his closet, and having total transfusions of Mormon blood, he cancelled the hotel's traditional Easter Egg hunt because he loathed children, and abandoned its pro golf tournaments because he couldn't bear the thought of golfers coming onto his property after putting their hands in those dirt holes.

come from the various restaurants and nightclubs arrayed along the water's edge, but you can get a good overall perspective from the North Show Terrace, which opens off the main hotel registration area.

Inside Wynn Las Vegas

The **interior** of *Wynn Las Vegas* is a riot of colour, with spectacular patterns and motifs sprawling all over carpets, mosaics and tiles, and a central atrium, open to natural light, that's filled with sparkling trees and dazzling hydrangeas and chrysanthemums. Lanterns and parasols add to the Eastern theme. Other than the Lake of Dreams, it holds few specific attractions, though the affluent thirty-somethings who are its prime target audience are drawn to the **Ferrari-Maserati** car dealership alongside the lobby, where typical vehicle prices are in the hundreds of thousands of dollars. Ordinary folk can buy toys and accessories in a souvenir store alongside, but have to pay even to take a peek at the sleek red beauties in the main showroom (ⓦpenskewynnferrari.com; $10, free for under-13s and owners of either brand who can produce their keys).

Encore Las Vegas

3121 Las Vegas Blvd S ⓣ702/770-8000, ⓦencorelasvegas.com. Hotel accommodation is reviewed on p.121; restaurants include Wazuzu (p.137); the club Surrender is described on p.145.

Wynn Las Vegas having proved an immediate success, Steve Wynn followed up in 2008 by opening **Encore Las Vegas** immediately north. *Encore* is not only slightly taller than its predecessor, but by no coincidence at all it's 11ft higher than *Palazzo* and 8ft higher than the nearby *Trump*, Wynn having waited until both those phallic symbols had topped out before completing his own. Just to rub the point home, he posed for TV ads sitting at *Encore*'s very apex, dangling his legs over the side.

Clad in the same glossy colour as its parent, officially known as **Wynn Bronze**, *Encore* stands in much the same relationship to *Wynn* as does the *Palazzo* to the *Venetian*. Interior passageways connect the two, and while *Encore* is certainly seen as being every bit as opulent and exclusive, it doesn't have any particular attractions – or even very much identity – of its own.

When *Encore* first opened, its main Strip entrance opened onto a huge open atrium much like that at *Wynn*. The original idea was that this would offer views of all sorts of new developments, including the *Echelon*. Within a year, however, those projects were scuppered by the recession, so Steve Wynn ripped up that whole side of his new property to make room for the **Encore Beach Club**. This extraordinarily lavish over-21s pool complex also incorporates a nightclub, *Surrender*.

An even more unexpected twist came in 2009 when Steve Wynn signed up the supposedly retired country star **Garth Brooks** – the bestselling solo performer in US musical history – for a five-year engagement to perform sixteen weekends per year in the *Encore Theater*. Tickets for Brooks' one-man acoustic show have been kept to a reasonable price (by Las Vegas standards) of less than $150.

Inside Encore

Encore is linked to *Wynn* via the **Encore Esplanade** of shops (see p.173), which leads directly off *Wynn*'s main casino floor and includes the theatres of both properties. Not that the transition is imperceptible; as soon as you cross the threshold to enter *Encore*, everything grows almost hallucinogenically redder and redder. While the interior holds no specific sights or attractions, chief designer Roger Thomas plays such endless variations on his basic components – besides the predominant red, the fundamental motifs are butterflies and dragonflies – that it's never boring or repetitive. Even if it's all too extravagantly ostentatious to be exactly tasteful, it's certainly not kitsch.

The actual **casino** in *Encore* forms a large rectangle, formally divided into four quadrants by awnings, each of which is then divided in four again. Each segment features a different style of colossal red chandeliers, creating a glorious panoply. The baccarat area – the high-rollers' favourite – is set in a candy-striped marquee in a sort of flower garden at the far end, while yet another splendid selection of restaurants is arrayed around the periphery.

Guardian Angel Cathedral

302 Cathedral Way Ⓣ 702/735-5241, Ⓦ lasvegas-diocese.org. Sunday masses take place at 8am, 9.30am, 11am, 12.30pm & 5pm.

Immediately north of *Encore*, a small spur road to the right leads to one of the Strip's least likely sights. Though dwarfed to the point of invisibility by the

Echelon

In March 2007, the veteran *Stardust* casino – which despite standing only two storeys high when it opened in 1958 was nonetheless the world's largest hotel – was finally demolished. Soon afterwards, the Boyd Gaming Corporation set about constructing the new **Echelon** development on the site the *Stardust* had occupied for almost fifty years. Barely a year later, however, the project stalled. There's currently no scheduled date for its completion, but Boyd continues to talk the talk, and it's just possible that it may finally materialize.

Echelon is designed very much along the lines of CityCenter. Of its five planned towers, one is due to hold three distinct hotels – the 2500-room *Echelon* itself, the 650-room *Enclave* and the 350-room *Shangri-La Las Vegas* – plus an Asian-style spa known as *Chi*. Another will contain two further hotels, the 860-room *Mondrian Las Vegas* and the 550-room *Delano*, an offshoot of the Miami original, which will share use of the Agua spa. The whole project will also have one giant casino, the usual array of restaurants, bars and stores, and a 4000-seat theatre used for permanent production shows. For updates, visit Ⓦ www.echelonlv.com.

surrounding cathedrals to Mammon, the starkly angular **Guardian Angel Cathedral** is a genuine Roman Catholic cathedral. Looking very spruce, and much newer than its actual construction date of 1963, it's a welcome haven from the frenzy outside its doors, but it does feature some true Las Vegas touches. The baptismal font resembles an over-sized marble Jacuzzi, coin-in-the-slot electric "candles" line the aisles, and of course there's a gift store. Best of all is the stained-glass window to the right of the altar, depicting the *Stardust*, the *Sands* and the *Hilton* rising above a maze of concrete freeways.

The Riviera

2901 Las Vegas Blvd S ⓣ 702/734-5110, ⓦ rivierahotel.com. Hotel accommodation is reviewed on p.123.

In 1955, the new **Riviera** held considerable novelty value. Merely by remaining erect, it confounded sceptics who predicted that the sands of Las Vegas could never bear the weight of its unbelievable nine storeys. Furthermore, its style, derived in theory from the French Côte d'Azur, seemed both exotic and romantic – even if in practice the decor owed more to the Florida resorts already run by its Miami backers.

More than fifty years on, the *Riviera* is continuing to defy expectations by its very existence. Despite endless rumours that it may soon go the way of neighbours and contemporaries like the *New Frontier* and the *Stardust*, it's still here, and indeed has undergone a major internal refurbishment. Any pretence of creating a sophisticated Mediterranean ambience is long gone, however. These days the *Riviera* boasts an exuberantly garish facade, with neon stars, stripes and curlicues swirling across a towering curved mirror.

After that, the interior comes as a disappointment; while the *Riviera* claims to devote more floor space to gambling than any of its rivals, the casino area into which you're plunged straight off the Strip is relentlessly mundane. A separate arcade known as Penny Town is devoted exclusively to nickel and penny slots and cheap snacks.

Ever since the *Riviera* began, it has stuck to the old formula of enticing in gamblers with traditional semi-sexy entertainment. When it first opened, it set new records by paying Liberace $50,000 per week – by no coincidence, it went briefly broke within three months – and it still has four showrooms in nightly operation. However, nothing of what's on offer is worth going out of your way to see.

Circus Circus

2880 Las Vegas Blvd S ⓣ 702/734-0410, ⓦ circuscircus.com. Hotel accommodation is reviewed on p.121, and the Horse-a-Round Bar on p.142.

"The aspect of Circus that has me disturbed is the popcorn, peanuts and kids side of it. And also the Carnival Freaks and Animal side of it …The dirt floor, sawdust and elephants…After all, the Strip is supposed to be synonymous with a good-looking female all dressed up in a very expensive diamond-studded evening gown and driving up to a multi-million dollar hotel in a Rolls-Royce. Now you tell me what, in that picture, is compatible with a circus in its normal raiment, exuding its normal atmosphere and its normal smell?"

Howard Hughes

A rare constant in the ever-changing world of Las Vegas, **Circus Circus** has remained true to itself for over forty years. Back in the 1960s, combining children's entertainment with casino gambling under a single roof was a radical concept. Later on, that idea was embraced as a surefire money-spinning formula.

When it subsequently became a discredited cliché, *Circus Circus* carried on regardless. Only now does it finally seem to be running into the rails. Since the recession hit, and it turned out that the stalwarts along this portion of the Strip had been destroyed to make room for replacements that never materialized, pedestrian traffic hereabouts has plummeted, and *Circus Circus* has become very much the weakest link in the MGM portfolio.

Circus Circus began life as Jay Sarno's follow-up to his mega-hit *Caesars Palace*, reinvesting the profits from the sale of *Caesars* to create a new property that would appeal to fun-seeking families and high rollers alike. The basic theme, of a hectic, spit-and-sawdust gaming area at street level overlooked by a carnival-style "midway" on the mezzanine, featuring sideshows and circus performers, was much as it remains today. It took a while to get the details right, however. Not only did the original *Circus Circus* lack any hotel accommodation, but it even charged an admission fee to visitors. On top of that, Hughes' revulsion had some basis in fact. The midway was at first the sleazy preserve of unsavoury independent operators. One sideshow, for example, "Bed Toss", invited patrons to throw softballs in the hope of spilling naked showgirls out of giant satin beds. At least Sarno was forced to abandon his experiments with propelling "flying" elephants along a concealed monorail system, when it became clear that his would-be Dumbos couldn't contain their excitement and would have to wear diapers. Only once Sarno sold his stake in 1974 did *Circus Circus* turn both wholesome and profitable, so much so that Circus Circus Enterprises went on to become the leading casino operator in the country, before eventually being subsumed into the MGM-Mirage empire.

Inside Circus Circus

Though the main building of *Circus Circus* is very low-rise by Las Vegas standards, its presence on the Strip is unmistakable, thanks both to its 123ft Lucky-the-Clown neon sign and its marquee-like Big Top canopy. Clowns, contortionists and trapeze artists still cavort on **The Midway** stage upstairs between 11am and midnight daily, surrounded by a more consistently child-oriented array of fairground stalls and attractions. Behind it, the whole complex stretches so far back that there's an in-house monorail link to help exhausted guests return to their rooms. Aside from the extraordinarily **low rates** it charges for those rooms, *Circus Circus*'s other big attraction for tourists with children is the five-acre **Adventuredome** theme park, described below.

No one could mistake *Circus Circus* for a sophisticated joint. It's the one truly kitsch casino still surviving on the Strip, and its pervasive clown motifs even have a slight down-at-heel creepiness, while the *Horse-a-Round Bar* is downright weird. Hunter S. Thompson made great play with the whole place in *Fear and Loathing in Las Vegas*, writing "*Circus Circus* is what the whole hep world would be doing on Saturday night if the Nazis had won the war," and calling it the "Sixth Reich". Small wonder that its owners refused permission to film here for the 1998 movie version.

Even the most gung-ho apologist for the gaming industry would be hard pressed to find anything glamorous about *Circus Circus*'s three low-stakes, high-volume casinos. What's more, while it may have pioneered the provision of no-smoking areas, its low ceilings actually make it one of the most claustrophobic and smoky places to gamble in town.

The Adventuredome

Circus Circus, 2880 Las Vegas Blvd S ⓣ702/734-0414, ⓦadventuredome.com. Hours vary: typically daily 10am–midnight during school holidays, otherwise Mon–Thurs

The Floundering Fontainebleau

Said to be the most expensive uncompleted building in the US, the half-built blue-glass skyscraper that stands on a 24.5-acre site immediately north of the *Riviera* was originally intended to open in 2009 as the 3812-room **Fontainebleau Las Vegas**. Its financing was thrown into such disastrous disarray by the recession, however, that despite having so far cost $2 billion, it was sold to investor Carl Icahn for a mere £156 million. Quite what he'll do with it remains unclear. Although it was planned as a chic luxury resort, modelled on the *Fontainebleau* in Miami Beach, if it does ever open for business it's more likely to be as a mid-range property more in keeping with the current economic climate, and under a different name. Its rooms were fully furnished by the time work was abandoned, but their upscale fixtures and fittings were sold to the *Plazza* down town in 2010

11am–6pm, Fri & Sat 10am–midnight, Sun 10am–9pm; $4–7 individual attractions, $25 all-day wristband, $15 kids under 4ft.

Sheltered beneath a huge bubble of pink glass at the back of *Circus Circus*, but entered only through the casino proper, the **Adventuredome** encloses a Disney-land-esque melange of rides and sideshows. Its central feature is a big red-rock mountain holding the corkscrewing Canyon Blaster roller coaster (rated by aficionados as among the best in town), the spinning Disk'O ride, and the Rim Runner water chute, which passes such dioramas as an Indian pueblo village and a herd of animatronic dinosaurs.

The Sahara

2535 Las Vegas Blvd S ☎702/737-2654, ⓦsaharavegas.com. Hotel accommodation is reviewed on p.123 and the NASCAR Café on p.137.

The **Sahara** looks set to be the last bastion of a once-ubiquitous Las Vegas tradition. Strip casinos used to relish the city's desert setting, but with the demise of soulmates like the *Dunes*, the *Sands* and the *Aladdin*, only the *Sahara* still caters to those who nurture *Arabian Nights* fantasies of sheiks at play in the shifting sands.

Sixty years have elapsed since 1952, when the combined efforts of LA jeweller Milton Prell and Phoenix developer Del Webb went into replacing the bankrupt *Bingo Club* with the gleaming new *Sahara*, but only recently has the hotel made any significant changes. On the down side, the trademark camels above the main entrance have been put out to pasture, in favour of a glittering golden dome encircled by Moorish arches. Inside, the *Sahara*'s theme was always pretty rudimentary, and it still resembles a Third World airport more than a sultan's palace, though at least the venerable *Casbar Lounge* and the *Caravan Cafe* are still going strong.

The *Sahara*'s long-standing association with **cars** is epitomized by the prominent *NASCAR Café* beside its main entrance. That passion for speed dates back to the 1960s, when Las Vegas was the auto-racing capital of the West. Indeed, **Elvis Presley** and his entourage made the *Sahara* their home during the filiming of the racing-themed movie *Viva Las Vegas*.

The Speed Ride

Sahara. Mon–Thurs noon–8pm, Fri–Sun noon–10pm; $10 per ride or $23 for all-day combo pass with Cyber Speedway.

A constant eye-catching distraction to motorists passing by on the Strip, the *Sahara*'s conspicuous **Speed Ride** might look like a roller coaster to you or me, but

The changing face of the Strip

The Las Vegas Strip has been a byword for architectural excess since the 1940s, when the first Western-themed casinos sprang up along Las Vegas Boulevard. Whether appalled or exhilarated, critics have always reacted with the same wide-eyed amazement. The Strip never rests on its laurels though, and is forever sweeping away the old to replace it with something bigger and better. While the essential spur for every innovation remains the desire to attract gamblers, the seduction strategies have been endlessly refined.

The *Desert Inn*, 1967 ▲

Roman statue at *Caesars Palace* ▼

"Little emphasis is placed on the gambling clubs and divorce facilities – though they are attractions to many visitors – and much is being done to build up the cultural attractions. No cheap and easily parodied slogans have been adopted to publicize the city, no attempt has been made to introduce pseudo-romantic architectural themes or to give artificial glamour or gaiety. Las Vegas is itself – natural and therefore very appealing to people with a wide variety of interests."

WPA Guidebook to Nevada, 1940

The birth of the Strip

During its earliest decades, when most visitors arrived by car, **the Strip** was entirely geared towards motorists. The casinos presented themselves as lush oases at the end of the long, hot drive from California. Huge billboards and glittering neon signs towered beside the highway, while the casinos stood back far enough to be admired in their entirety, behind expansive parking areas. Sporting names like the *Sands* and the *Desert Inn*, they celebrated their desert setting, with cowboy imagery, like the *New Frontier* and *El Rancho*, or Arabian-Nights fantasy, like the *Dunes*, the *Aladdin* and the *Sahara*.

The next generation of travellers came by air, with their rooms already booked. The casinos responded by becoming self-contained **fantasy lands**. When *Caesars Palace* opened in 1966, its high-camp Roman extravagance caught the eye, but it also introduced two crucial features. Its interior was both a **trap**, in that it lacked windows, natural light, or conspicuous exits, and a **maze**, laid out so that wherever you wanted to go you had to cross the casino floor, and potentially be lured into gambling.

The Strip goes wild

The triumphant opening of Steve Wynn's *Mirage* in 1989, the first new Strip casino to appear after sixteen years of gloom, heralded a new era. Wynn had realised that increasing **foot traffic** called for a new kind of architecture. Driving past a casino, you've barely time to read the billboards; walking past, you're free to stop, change your plans and wander inside. Every night, the spectacular sound-and-light show of the "volcano" outside the *Mirage* drew huge crowds of pedestrians, who would then investigate the casino itself.

▲ The volcano outside the *Mirage*

▼ The *Aladdin* meets its fate in 1998

Suddenly it was a problem for a casino to be set too far back from the Strip. *Caesars Palace* came up with a pragmatic solution, by constructing **moving walkways** to haul passers-by into the property, but no corresponding walkways to allow them to leave. Other approaches including building localized **monorail** systems; making the casinos look smaller, and thus closer, by visual tricks like using a single exterior "window frame" to serve four rooms; and filling in the former parking lots with fountains, flower gardens or simply long extensions that snaked all the way to the Strip.

▼ The fairytale spires of the *Excalibur*

The most obvious solution of all was to blow up the old casinos and build new ones. Whereas before the roadside signs had always been taller than the actual buildings, the new breed of casinos served as their own signs, by adopting such attention-grabbing forms as **fairytale castles** (*Excalibur*) and **Egyptian pyramids** (*Luxor*), or simply colossal towers (the *Stratosphere*). The very notion of what constitutes a "building" was up for grabs; the pirate ships in the facade of *Treasure Island* not only moved and fought, they were crewed by live actors.

Paris ▲

Monorail going through CityCenter ▼

Las Vegas today

For a brief moment, Las Vegas seemed about to turn into a giant Disney-esque theme park. Then the casinos realised that travellers with kids don't gamble. The next, more adult-oriented craze was to erect squashed-up **replicas of entire cities**: New York, Paris and Venice appeared in quick succession. Now the casinos are crammed so close together, they've given up trying to keep guests from leaving and connected them with malls and bridges.

Since then, the Strip has lost some of its sense of fun. When Steve Wynn unveiled **Bellagio** in 1998, it seemed po-faced rather than playful. While visitors to *Luxor*, say, were invited to enjoy the illusion, *Bellagio* wanted to be taken more seriously. The process went a stage further with the modernism of **CityCenter** in 2009, which refused to pander to its setting with tropes of luxury or whimsical novelties. Arriving just as the economy nose-dived, however, it may prove a step too far.

Five Strip casinos that never were

▶▶ **Elvis Presley** The King never built his Las Vegas promised land; down at the end of Lonely Street perhaps?

▶▶ **London** MGM almost built this opposite *Luxor*, complete with Big Ben, Harrod's and a London Eye.

▶▶ **San Francisco** Having said he'd replace the *New Frontier* with this, Phil Ruffin bought *Treasure Island* instead.

▶▶ **Titanic** The blueprints looked great; it was the inevitable metaphor that scuppered things.

▶▶ **Xanadu** Proposed in 1975, this "stately pleasure dome" would have been the first mega-resort.

officially it's a "magnetic-induction ride". Its cars crash through the outer wall of the *NASCAR Café*, loop through the open air above the Strip and then climb a 250ft tower. The thrill is real enough, but at $10 for 48 seconds, it's all over a bit too fast.

The Cyber Speedway

Sahara. Daily noon–10pm; $10 per ride or $23 for all-day combo pass with Speed Ride.

In the *Sahara*'s indoor Cyber Speedway, each participant faces a private screen and "drives" a three-quarter-size Indy car that bucks and surges in response to the slightest touch of the controls. At any one time, eight cars race each other around video renditions of either the Indianapolis racetrack or the streets of Las Vegas; printouts at the end reveal which driver beat the rest. The more you do it, the more likely you are to win, so the whole experience is fiendishly addictive. Alternatively, you can pay $5 for the much less heart-thumping experience of watching a 3-D movie of the real thing.

The Stratosphere

2000 Las Vegas Blvd S ⓉⒷ702/380-7777, ⓌⒷstratospherehotel.com. Hotel accommodation is reviewed on p.123, while restaurants include Top of the World (p.137).

The unsavoury stretch of Las Vegas Boulevard north of Sahara Avenue is still seen by locals as not really belonging to the Strip – not least because it lies within the city limits of Las Vegas rather than Clark County. This area was long known as Naked City, at first because the showgirls who lived here in the 1940s were said to sunbathe in the nude, but later to denote its status as one of Las Vegas's poorest and most crime-ridden neighbourhoods. These days, however, it's dominated by the mighty **Stratosphere Tower**, which serves as a symbolic northern border to the great neon way.

In 1979, one of the great Las Vegas hucksters, Bob Stupak, opened the immensely tacky **Vegas World** casino here, half a dozen blocks up from the *Sahara*, and immediately began talking about building the world's tallest tower alongside it. Thanks to the strong desert winds, and the fact that the foundations could only be twelve feet deep, by the time the *Stratosphere* was eventually completed in 1996, it was simply the tallest building west of the Mississippi, while panicking investors forced Stupak to replace *Vegas World* itself with a higher-class hotel.

Initially a financial disaster, in the longer run the *Stratosphere* has done surprisingly well, kept busy particularly by European tour groups, perhaps less sensitive than Americans to its off-Strip location. Passing pedestrian traffic is minimal at this point, and a fit of sour grapes from its owners ensured that it was never connected to the Monorail system, but in the current budget-conscious era its no-nonsense room rates continue to strike a chord.

The Stratosphere Tower

The Stratosphere, 2000 Las Vegas Blvd S. Sun–Thurs 10am–1am, Fri & Sat 10am–2am; $16, discounts for guests.

Riding to the "pod" at the 1149ft summit of the *Stratosphere* is a Las Vegas experience not to miss. Tickets are sold up on the second floor, while the actual elevators start at the far end of a tacky but usually busy shopping-and-souvenir mall. After a 75-second ascent, you emerge outdoors, on the 109th floor, to be confronted by an astounding 360° panorama of the city. The views are even better from the floor below, where the windows of the indoor gallery are angled out over the edge, and detailed captions and photographs explain every discernible detail. The next floor down holds the *Top of the World* restaurant, reviewed on p.137.

Stratosphere thrill rides

The Stratosphere, 2000 Las Vegas Blvd S ⓣ 702/380-7711. Sun–Thurs 11am–1am, Fri & Sat 11am–2am. Insanity $12; X-Scream $12; Big Shot $13; various combination tickets up to $36 all-day unlimited package.

As originally planned, the *Stratosphere* would have held a wonderful-sounding ride called **Belly of the Beast**, in which a King Kong-shaped elevator would carry passengers up the outside of the tower, and then, under airplane attack, let them go. That was never built, but the uppermost level does offer three magnificently demented **thrill rides**. **Insanity**, a sort of giant crane, dangles riders over the edge strapped into individual seats, then spins them round fast enough for them to be facing straight down; **X-Scream** does much the same thing with its passengers crammed into a precarious gondola; and the ludicrous but terrifying **Big Shot** is a four-person open-air couch that shunts to the top of an additional 160-foot spire, then free-falls down again.

SkyJump

The Stratosphere, 2000 Las Vegas Blvd S ⓦ skyjumplasvegas.com. Sun–Thurs 11am–1am, Fri & Sat 11am–2am; $100; minimum age 14.

The principle of the **SkyJump** – the *Stratosphere*'s latest attraction, unveiled in 2010 – is easy to grasp. You simply jump off the top and plummet 855ft. At least it offers the small consolation that you're strapped into a jump suit and harness. It's actually a "controlled free-fall", more like a zip line than a bungee jump, so your speed is limited to 40mph, and you don't bounce back up again, you just walk shakily away at the bottom. There's no refund if you chicken out once you're standing out on the precarious platform.

Downtown Las Vegas

To be clear from the outset, **downtown Las Vegas** is an entirely distinct area from the Strip; in fact the Strip is not strictly speaking in Las Vegas at all, but stretches south from the city limits, two miles south of the original downtown core.

That said, downtown Las Vegas has never been a "downtown" in the conventional sense of the word. True, it does stand on the site where the city was founded, a little over a century ago. Having just laid its tracks across the valley, the San Pedro, Los Angeles & Salt Lake Railroad established Las Vegas in May 1905 by auctioning parcels of land close to the railroad station. A simple grid was mapped out, with the station itself on Main Street at the head of the principal thoroughfare, **Fremont Street**.

However, the city never grew to any size before gambling was legalized in the 1930s; even in 1940, it had a population of just eight thousand. Fremont Street failed to develop a significant infrastructure of stores and other businesses, and those few it did acquire were in any case to be supplanted by the advent of the casinos. As a result, downtown today is much like the Strip, in that the only conceivable reason to come here is to visit the casinos.

Las Vegas has always had the strongest of incentives to promote downtown at the expense of the Strip; as the Strip lies outside the city, in Clark County, only the downtown casinos pay city taxes. In the 1940s, it officially baptized Fremont Street as "**Glitter Gulch**," and for several decades downtown more or less kept pace with the burgeoning Strip. At the time the *Mirage* opened on the Strip in 1989, for example, the veteran *Horseshoe* downtown remained the city's most financially successful casino.

The revitalization of downtown

As the Strip subsequently raced ahead, downtown appeared to be in terminal decline. It was clear that something drastic had to be done. The idea of turning Fremont Street into a *Venetian*-style canal was rejected, but the ultimate solution was almost as absurd; they built a **roof** over it instead. As the **Fremont Street Experience**, it has become the scene of banal but undeniably spectacular nightly light shows. These have done a certain amount to entice the crowds back, although many visitors are disappointed at how little there is to do once the show's over – except gamble, of course, which was the point of the thing.

Despite endless attempts by Las Vegas Mayor **Oscar Goodman** to revitalize downtown, nothing has significantly impacted on tourism. Currently his hopes rest on the forthcoming **Mob Museum** (see p.87). If that fails, maybe another pet Goodman scheme will be revived – legalizing prostitution.

As things stand, Fremont Street today is downtown restyled as a sanitized suburban mall, its block-spanning casinos now seeming like little more than identical department stores. It has to be said that none of them, not even the

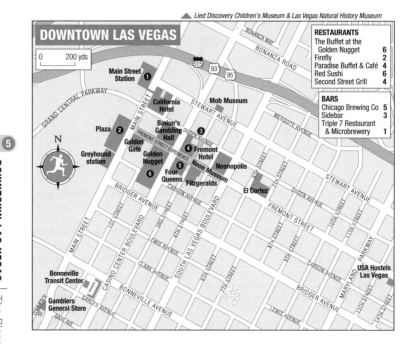

DOWNTOWN LAS VEGAS

0   200 yds

Main Street Station ❶

GRAND CENTRAL PARKWAY

BONANZA WAY

BONANZA ROAD

515 93 95

MAIN STREET

California Hotel

STEWART AVENUE

Mob Museum

MESQUITE AVENUE

Plaza ❷

Binion's Gambling Hall

FREMONT STREET EXPERIENCE

OGDEN AVENUE

❸

N

Golden Gate

Greyhound station

Golden Nugget

Fremont Hotel ❹

Neon Museum

Neonopolis

STEWART AVENUE

❺

Four Queens ❻

Fitzgeralds

El Cortez

7TH STREET

OGDEN AVENUE

10TH STREET

11TH STREET

BRIDGER AVENUE

CARSON AVENUE

FREMONT STREET

1ST STREET

3RD STREET

4TH STREET

SOUTH LAS VEGAS BOULEVARD

LEWIS AVENUE

8TH STREET

CARSON AVENUE

MARYLAND PARKWAY

MAIN STREET

CASINO CENTER BOULEVARD

CLARK AVENUE

6TH STREET

9TH STREET

USA Hostels Las Vegas

Bonneville Transit Center

BONNEVILLE AVENUE

BRIDGER AVENUE

13TH STREET

14TH STREET

Gamblers General Store

COMMERCE ST

GARCES AVENUE

CASS AVE

LEWIS AVENUE

RESTAURANTS
The Buffet at the Golden Nugget	6
Firefly	2
Paradise Buffet & Café	4
Red Sushi	6
Second Street Grill	4

BARS
Chicago Brewing Co	5
Sidebar	3
Triple 7 Restaurant & Microbrewery	1

much-vaunted *Golden Nugget*, would merit a second glance on the Strip. If you come to Las Vegas specifically to **gamble**, there's a strong case for spending time downtown – the odds tend to be better, the room rates cheaper and the atmosphere a bit more casual – but otherwise you miss little by avoiding it altogether.

Downtown used to be seen as an area where you could **walk** around, but nowadays there's little scope for strolling anywhere other than the few central blocks of Fremont Street. The streets to the south hold the occasional interesting shop, like the Attic (see p.173) or the Gamblers General Store (see p.174), or budget restaurant, but although they may seem close enough on the map, they're grim and unsettling places to walk, and unbearably hot in summer.

The Plaza

1 Main St ☎ 702/386-2110 or 800/634-6575, ⓦ plazahotelcasino.com. The Firefly restaurant is reviewed on p.138.

The giant **Plaza** casino faces the west end of Fremont Street from the site of Las Vegas's defunct railroad station. After Amtrak abandoned rail service here in 1997, its facilities were absorbed into the *Plaza*'s capacious bowels, but Greyhound buses continue to use the adjoining depot.

The *Plaza*'s one positive feature is the glass dome above its front entrance, which is currently occupied by the excellent *Firefly* restaurant and offers great views of the Fremont Street light-show. But the rest of the *Plaza* is in a very sorry state. Heavy financial losses resulted in the **closure** of all of its hotel operations and most of its casino space in 2010, and the entire property was put up for sale. In 2010, its new owners bought the high-end room furnishings from the never-completed *Fontainebleau* (see p.80), so it may indeed reopen in better shape. The eternally optimistic Mayor Goodman hopes the revived Plaza will serve as a gateway to the **Symphony Park** area to the west, which will feature a performing arts centre and shopping mall.

Main Street Station

200 N Main St ☎ 702/387-1896 or 800/713-8933, ⓦ mainstreetcasino.com. Hotel accommodation is reviewed on p.124 and the Triple 7 Restaurant & MicroBrewery on p.144.

Despite unpromising beginnings – it went broke within a year of opening in 1991 – **Main Street Station** (not part of the Stations chain of casinos scattered around the city) has turned into a rare downtown success story.

Standing two blocks off Fremont Street, it benefits from a tasteful design intended to evoke New Orleans in the 1890s, with an abundance of authentic antiques ranging from wrought-iron fences to Teddy Roosevelt's private railroad car and even bronze chandeliers from Buenos Aires. Thanks to the very high ceilings and natural lighting, all that period detail is never oppressive, and a well-thought-out array of good-value, down-to-earth restaurants and other facilities have put *Main Street Station* firmly on the tourist map. The *Triple Seven Brewpub* is a particularly good spot for a downtown drink.

California Hotel

12 Ogden Ave ☎ 702/385-1222, ⓦ thecal.com. Hotel accommodation is reviewed on p.124.

The **California Hotel** is a run-of-the-mill downtown casino notable solely for the fact that it's heavily dominated by Hawaiian customers. Sam Boyd (whose company also owns the neighbouring *Main Street Station*) named it thus in 1975 in the understandable expectation that most of the clientele would be Californian. He soon turned his attention to Hawaii, however, where he had run bingo games in his youth, and that scheme proved so successful that the majority of its eight hundred guestrooms still tend to be taken by Hawaiian tour groups.

The *California* is a pleasant enough, if very low-profile place, with Hawaiian menu items prominent in the bars and restaurants. Even the slot machines are labelled in Hawaiian.

The Fremont Street Experience

Fremont Street, between Main and Fourth ⓦ vegasexperience.com. Nightly, hourly on the hour from sunset until midnight. Free.

The gigantic metal mesh of the **Fremont Street Experience** stretches over Fremont for four entire blocks, the area once known as "Glitter Gulch". Ninety feet high, this so-called "Celestial Vault" shades the pedestrianized street during the day, but comes into its own at night, when over twelve million LED modules turn it into a giant movie screen. There's no plot or content to the free hourly shows, just pure eye-catching spectacle and a blast of soft rock; spectators gather below to gasp, stagger and applaud as they're catapulted into space, draped with US flags, or menaced by colossal swarming snakes.

Completed in 1995, the Fremont Street Experience is sponsored by the downtown casinos, which cooperate by turning off their lights during each fifteen-minute show. The original idea was that at the end of the show, the audiences would find themselves milling around on the street with nowhere to go except into the nearest casino. These days, however, Fremont Street keeps partying all evening, and in summer especially a changing roster of **live bands** – often tribute acts performing, say, the songs of Queen or KISS – play on stages set up along the street. Current schedules are listed on the website.

The Golden Gate

1 E Fremont St ⓣ 702/385-1906 or 800/426-1906, ⓦ goldengatecasino.com. Hotel accommodation is reviewed on p.124.

What's now the **Golden Gate** is unique for Las Vegas in being genuinely old, rather than simply themed to look old. The city's most venerable establishment, it has occupied its prime position at the west end of Fremont Street since 1906, when Las Vegas itself was just a year old. As the *Nevada Hotel*, it catered to travellers who arrived at the railroad station opposite, and was styled on the grand hotels of San Francisco, many of which were destroyed in that year's earthquake. As the first hotel in southern Nevada, it boasted a distinguished phone number: 1. It later became first the *Sal Segav* (Las Vegas spelled backwards), and then, in 1955, the *Golden Gate*.

Barely changed since a third storey was added in 1931, its dark, wood-panelled interior still has a frontier feel, though by comparison with almost any other Las Vegas casino the *Golden Gate* is absolutely tiny, and now thinks of itself as a B&B. Many repeat Las Vegas visitors, however, make a special pilgrimage to its *Shrimp Bar and Deli*. Having served over thirty million shrimp cocktails since 1959, it has recently, finally, abandoned its legendary 99¢ price tag, in favour of charging $1.99 (though that's actually the "original", and for more than the merest hint of shrimp you'll need to opt instead for the $3.99 "Big").

The Golden Nugget

129 E Fremont St ⓣ 702/385-7111, ⓦ goldennugget.com. Hotel accommodation is reviewed on p.124; restaurants include Red Sushi (p.138) and the Buffet (see p.129); and the Gordie Brown show is reviewed on p.148.

The **Golden Nugget** is generally described, not least in its own publicity material, as being the one downtown casino that matches the extravagance and splendour of the Strip. It doesn't quite. While indeed a bright, glittery place that attracts a hipper, more upmarket clientele than any other downtown casino, it's nonetheless very far from counting as a must-see destination.

It opened in 1946, the same year that the *Flamingo* was unveiled on the Strip, with a decor modelled on the opulent saloons of nineteenth-century San Francisco. Several decades later, it's best known as the place where Las Vegas's premier gaming entrepreneur, **Steve Wynn**, gained his foothold in the casino business. During the early 1970s, the young Wynn – then a liquor distributor and real-estate speculator – accumulated enough shares in the ailing *Nugget*, together with inside knowledge of corruption among its staff, to engineer a boardroom coup. The *Nugget* swiftly prospered under his control, which enabled Wynn first to develop another *Golden Nugget* in Atlantic City, and subsequently to build the *Mirage*, *Treasure Island*, *Bellagio*, *Wynn* and *Encore* on the Strip.

MGM-Mirage eventually sold the *Golden Nugget* in 2004, showing that the major players were no longer interested in the paltry profits to be made downtown. Since then, under successive owners, the *Nugget* has been considerably remodelled, toning down its formerly golden facade in favour of a more sober, Deco-influenced look. Its centerpiece is **The Tank**, the very fancy open-air pool area around which the building curls – not only does it have a large aquarium, but there's an enclosed three-storey waterslide, naturally reserved for the use of guests only, that shoots right through the middle of it, sharks and all. Poolside sunbathers while away the afternoon within inches of the casino,

The Mob Museum

Housed in a former downtown courthouse at 300 Stewart Ave, the **Mob Museum** – or to give it its full title, the Las Vegas Museum of Organized Crime and Law Enforcement – represents the latest attempt by Las Vegas Mayor **Oscar Goodman** to lure tourists back downtown.

Intended as an interactive bid to "set the record straight" on the role played by organized crime in the city's development, it had yet to open when this book went to press. Displays were expected to focus as much on the FBI's ultimately successful campaign to break the Mafia's stranglehold on the casino business as on the mobsters themselves, though Goodman himself is never averse to glamourizing his own history as a defence lawyer for such notorious figures as Meyer Lansky and Anthony "Tony the Ant" Spilotro.

For the museum's opening hours and admission fees, visit ⓦthemobmuseum.org.

separated only by floor-to-ceiling windows; it's all carefully calculated to make passing visitors wish they were hotel guests.

A surprisingly inconspicuous case near the lobby shows off the hotel's collection of genuine golden nuggets. Pride of place goes to the **Hand of Faith** nugget, found with a metal detector in Australia in 1980. At 61 pounds 11 ounces, it's currently worth just under a million dollars. *Golden Nugget* spokespersons admitted some years ago that the one on display used to be a replica, but claim it's now genuine; don't try putting them to the test. Alongside are several sizeable Alaskan lumps, including one worn smooth from being carried in the pocket of its owner as a good-luck charm for 25 years. In that time, a full two ounces were rubbed off.

Binion's Gambling Hall

128 E Fremont St ⓣ702/382-1600, ⓦbinions.com.

If the *Golden Nugget* represents downtown at its most pretentious, then **Binion's Gambling Hall**, the latest incarnation of the property long known as **Binion's Horseshoe**, has always gone to the other extreme, promoting itself as the definitive downtown gambling den and nothing more. That ethos dates back to its founder, **Benny Binion**, affectionately remembered as one of the great Las Vegas characters despite a record for violence exceptional even by local standards. An itinerant Texan horse trader with at least two killings to his name, he ran the criminal underworld in Dallas during the 1940s, before a bloody gang feud persuaded him to relocate to Las Vegas. Acquiring two faltering Fremont Street casinos, he replaced them with the *Horseshoe*, which opened as downtown's first "carpet joint" (as opposed to the rougher "sawdust joints" that had long characterized the area) in 1951.

Binion himself lost control of the casino when he was jailed for tax evasion in the 1950s – he took advantage of the interlude to learn to read and write – and never regained his gaming licence. However, his family bought it back in 1964, with Benny very much in charge behind the scenes. By the time he died, on Christmas Day 1989, the *Horseshoe* was the most profitable casino in Las Vegas. To Benny, the explanation was simple: "We got a little joint and a big bankroll, and all them others got a big joint and a little bankroll." The *Horseshoe* had in 1988 taken over the legendary *Mint* next door, simply bashing down the party wall, and in the process finally acquired a significant number of hotel rooms.

Following Binion's death, the *Horseshoe* fell spectacularly from grace, thrown into turmoil by both a good old-fashioned family feud and a sensational murder. Benny Binion's son Ted had his gaming licence first suspended due to drug use, and then, in 1998, revoked altogether because of his Mob connections. Later that year, he was suffocated, after being forced to take an involuntary overdose, by his live-in lover and her new man, who were caught a few days later digging up $6 million in silver bullion at his desert ranch.

Meanwhile, Ted's estranged sister Becky took over the *Horseshoe*, only to mismanage its finances so badly that she first raided the casino's famous million-dollar display case, and then in 2004 closed the place altogether. It reopened within months, having been sold to Harrah's, who are widely believed to have bought it simply to get hold of the Horseshoe name and the **World Series of Poker**, which was established there in 1970. They swiftly moved the World Series to the *Rio*, but have yet to fulfil expectations that they'll eventually build a new *Horseshoe* casino on the Strip. Meanwhile the original has changed hands a couple of times, while so far continuing to lose money, and is currently owned by Terry Caudill, who also owns the *Four Queens* nearby.

Although the million-dollar exhibit has now reopened, enabling visitors to pose for photos surrounded by a million dollars in banknotes, *Binion's* today is in a sorry state. Its reputation for offering the best gambling odds and lowest minimums in town is a thing of the past, and its 24-hour coffee shop, legendary for offering the best dining bargains in town, finally closed down in 2009. It no longer even functions as a hotel.

The Four Queens

202 E Fremont St ⓣ 702/385-4011 or 800/634-6045, Ⓦ fourqueens.com. Hotel accommodation is reviewed on p.124 and the Chicago Brewing Company on p.143.

Named not for a poker hand but for the four daughters of its original owner, the **Four Queens** has been a fixture on the downtown scene since 1966. Now occupying an entire block, it has prospered along with the three better-known neighbours with which it shares Fremont Street's busiest intersection, adding two nineteen-storey hotel towers and sprucing up its lobby away from its old New Orleans theme in favour of matching the sparkling lights of the *Golden Nugget*.

The Fremont Hotel

200 E Fremont St ⓣ 702/385-3232, Ⓦ fremontcasino.com. Hotel accommodation is reviewed on p.124; restaurants include Second Street Grill (p.138) and the Paradise Buffet & Café (see p.130).

Hard though it is to imagine, the **Fremont Hotel** was at fifteen storeys the tallest building in Nevada when it was completed in 1956. The still-visible concrete facade of its main hotel tower was seen as shockingly modern and marked a deliberate eschewal of downtown's previously universal Wild West style of architecture. These days the *Fremont*, which was bought by Sam Boyd of *Sam's Town* fame in 1985, and still belongs to the Boyd Corporation, is just another downtown gambling palace. It's not quite as fashionable as the *Golden Nugget*, despite boasting the excellent *Second Street Grill* restaurant, but with its bright lights and purple baize tables it's jazzier than the rest of the pack.

Fitzgeralds

301 E Fremont St ⓣ 800/274-5825 or 702/388-2400, Ⓦ fitzgeraldslasvegas.com. Hotel accommodation is reviewed on p.124.

Until a few years ago, **Fitzgeralds**, which occupies an entire block of Fremont Street, was a tacky Irish-themed casino that sported every Celtic cliché imaginable, from shamrocks to a piece of the Blarney Stone. Owned since 2001 by

Detroit businessman Don Barden – the first black person to own a casino in Nevada – it's now changed its image.

By and large, the tired old Irish decor has gone; poor old Mr O'Lucky, the 34-foot leprechaun effigy who formerly greeted customers, belied his name by catching fire and burning to the ground. New features include lots of free entertainment, a prominent *Krispy Kreme* outlet on the sidewalk (which enables passers-by to get free wifi), and upgraded restaurants including *Don B's Steakhouse*. The small balcony of the second-floor *Vue Bar* makes a good vantage point for watching the light show outside.

Neonopolis

450 E Fremont St Ⓦneonopolislv.com.

What if they built a mall and nobody came? You might imagine the intersection of Fremont Street and Las Vegas Boulevard would be the perfect location to build a big new shopping mall and entertainment centre. The city of Las Vegas certainly did. However, the block-long **Neonopolis** mall has been a disaster ever since it opened in 2002.

Despite the location, just across the street from the Fremont Street Experience, the complex, now entirely in private hands, almost always seems to be empty. Only a few tenants ever leased space, and even fewer lasted: its eleven-screen cinema currently stands vacant, while even its food court seems to have been abandoned.

Rumours suggest that **Star Trek: The Experience**, an interactive theme-park ride previously at the *Las Vegas Hilton*, will at some point reopen at Neonopolis, and that the whole place may be relaunched as **Fremont Square**, but don't count on either.

El Cortez

600 E Fremont St Ⓣ702/385-5200, Ⓦecvegas.com. Hotel accommodation is reviewed on p.124.

Surrounded by pawn shops and T-shirt stores, a couple of somewhat uneasy blocks' walk east of the Fremont Street Experience, the quasi-Moorish **El Cortez** traditionally represented downtown at its most downmarket.

The Neon Museum

Las Vegas is seldom sentimental about erasing the traces of its past, but as casino after casino upgrades its image, eschewing "vulgar" neon in favour of "classy" gilt trimmings, dewy-eyed preservationists have campaigned to save its abandoned neon glories. As a result, the block between the end of the canopied section of Fremont Street at Fourth Street, and Las Vegas Boulevard to the east, has been grandly designated as the **Neon Museum**.

This open-air neon graveyard displays ten restored, fully functional signs gathered from all over the city. Some of these winking, blinking, garish delights are perched on street-level pedestals; larger examples cling to the corners of adjacent offices or car parks. The oldest piece is a classic "Red Indian" motel sign that adorned the *Chief Hotel Court* in 1940; others include the Horse and Rider from the *Hacienda*, demolished to make way for *Mandalay Bay*, and the original magic lamp from the old *Aladdin*.

Long-term plans seem to have pretty much stalled, but the museum hopes in due course to open a two-acre outdoor **Neon Boneyard** of unrestored signs at 770 Las Vegas Blvd N; its centrepiece will be the restored lobby of the space-age **La Concha Motel**, which formerly stood alongside the *Riviera* on the Strip. Check its **website**, Ⓦneonmuseum.org, for the latest progress, and for details of occasional tours of the collection.

In 1941 it was the largest downtown hotel – albeit with a mere 59 rooms – while in 1946 it served as a stepping stone for early investor "Bugsy" Siegel en route to the *Flamingo*. From 1963 until 2008, however it belonged to **Jackie Gaughan**, who also at various times owned all or part of the *Plaza, Flamingo, Golden Nugget* and many others. The consortium that bought it included both his son and his long-term business partner, and as of 2010, Jackie, in his ninetieth year, was still living in a penthouse flat upstairs.

Scurrilous local legend had it that Gaughan barely changed a thing during his tenure, not even emptying the ashtrays, let alone cleaning the carpets. These days, however, following an extensive overhaul, it's looking considerably smarter. Its upgraded rooms and suites are still available at rock-bottom rates, however – the one thing *El Cortez*, which flirts with calling itself the cooler-sounding **EC**, can never change is its location – so it's still the haunt of budget travellers and local low-rollers. As well as some of the lowest-stakes gambling in town, it also offers some of the lousiest, featuring regular drawings of Social Security numbers, with a $50,000 prize for matching all nine digits.

Lied Discovery Children's Museum

833 Las Vegas Blvd N ☎702/382-5437, ⊛ldcm.org. June–Aug Mon–Sat 10am–5pm, Sun noon–5pm; Sept–May Tues–Fri 9am–4pm, Sat 10am–5pm, Sun noon–5pm. $8.50, ages 1 to 17 $7.50.

The **Lied Discovery Children's Museum**, a bit less than a mile north of downtown on a very pedestrian-unfriendly stretch of Las Vegas Boulevard, is a rather poor specimen of the modern breed of hands-on children's museums. Occupying a few rooms of a city library building, it's far less likely to stimulate childish imaginations than the wonders on the Strip.

Local kids on school trips enjoy the chance to paint, draw and sculpt, but even the youngest tourists may resent being dragged away from *Luxor* or *Circus Circus*. There are a few typical Las Vegas touches, like the fact that infant artists are rewarded for each work of art that they create with forty "Discovery Dollars," which they can withdraw from the Discovery ATM. However, a significant proportion of the more sophisticated displays tends to be broken at any one time, so unless a good temporary exhibition is taking place (call ahead) there's not a lot of point coming all the way up here.

Las Vegas Natural History Museum

900 Las Vegas Blvd N ☎702/384-3466, ⊛lvnhm.org. Daily 9am–4pm. $10 adults, $8 students and seniors, $5 ages 3–11; look for discount coupons on website.

A mile or so north of downtown, a block beyond the children's museum, the **Las Vegas Natural History Museum** has at least tried to move beyond its traditional dioramas of stuffed animals. Thus the Marine Life Gallery features a smallish tank of live sharks alongside its mounted specimens, while the Prehistoric Life Gallery offers five large animatronic dinosaurs, including a roaring Tyrannosaurus Rex. Even the old-fashioned exhibits in the Africa section downstairs are less static than you might expect; note the zebra frantically trying to fend off two lions.

A slightly incongruous new pavilion, added in 2010, houses the **Treasures of Egypt** exhibition, which repeat Las Vegas visitors may recognize as having been the core of the King Tut displays that were formerly housed in the *Luxor* casino. You reach replicas of the various golden artefacts found buried with the pharaoh in 1922, by way of a reconstruction of the tomb's entrance passageway.

The rest of the city

L
as Vegas may look enormous on the map, but as far as tourists are concerned the only significant neighbourhoods are the Strip and downtown. Nowhere else even deserves to be called a "neighbourhood," in the sense of having a distinctive identity, a variety of attractions and being explorable on foot. If you think the individual blocks along the Strip are large, wait until you drive into the rest of the city. Soon the streets start to be spaced half a mile or more apart, and often there really is nothing between one and the next. As it has grown, the city has repeatedly vaulted across acres of empty space, and sizeable portions of the grid remain completely undeveloped.

Certain districts of Las Vegas are known for their **shopping**, as detailed in Chapter 15, and there's the occasional concentration of **restaurants**, such as on Paradise Road south of Twain. However, no area of the city ranks as a destination in its own right, nor is likely to tempt you out of your car should you happen to pass through.

Instead, your only ports of call away from downtown and the Strip are likely to be specific individual attractions, such as the various so-called **"locals' casinos"**. Aimed primarily at local gamblers, the latter tend to have bowling and/or skating facilities and cinemas rather than white tigers and sphinxes, but with their good-value restaurants and low-stakes gambling (concentrating on slot machines and video poker), they do at least have something to offer the out-of-state visitor.

Since the venerable Liberace Museum closed its doors in 2010, none merits an excursion on public transport. Note that Las Vegas has fewer public parks than any major city in the US. If you want to get out into the **open air**, your best bet is to head for nearby Red Rock Canyon, as described in Chapter Seven, *Out from the City*.

Boulder Station

4111 Boulder Hwy ⓣ702/423-7777, Ⓦboulderstation.com. The Railhead lounge and music venue is reviewed on p.146.

Boulder Station stands roughly five miles east of the Strip along Desert Inn Road, at the point where Fremont Street passes under US-93/95 and becomes Boulder Highway. The second of the so-called Stations casinos to open, back in 1994, it's also ranked among the chain's top-four best-performing properties, and was thus expected to survive the chain's 2010 bankruptcy relatively unscathed.

Not that *Boulder Station* has all that much to boast about. Customers are lured in by the usual combination of cheap and cheerful restaurants, bingo, an eleven-screen cinema, the *Railhead* lounge and childcare facilities ($7–8/hr), but what truly sets this casino apart from its brethren is how seriously betting is taken here.

The huge Race and Sports Book has a positively Dickensian atmosphere, with rows of pencil-chewing gamblers overlooked by dark Victorian "stained glass" as

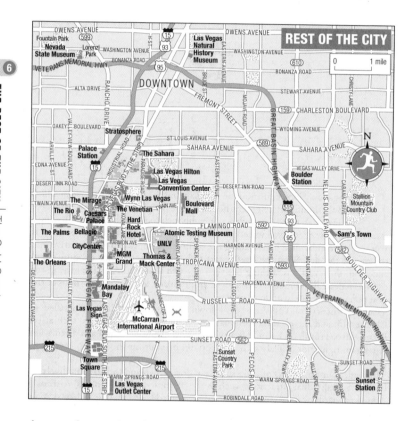

REST OF THE CITY

they scan the news from far-off racetracks. Railroad motifs permeate the whole place, especially in the *Railhead* lounge (see p.146), where the sizeable stage plays host to nationally known country stars plus a smattering of R&B musicians and up-and-coming local bands.

The Gold Coast

4000 W Flamingo Rd ☏ 702/367-7111, ⓦ goldcoastcasino.com. Hotel accommodation is reviewed on p.125; restaurants include Ping Pang Pong (p.140).

Though located just half a mile west of the Strip, across from both the *Rio* (see p.95) and the *Palms* (see p.95), the **Gold Coast** is much more of a locals' casino than its two higher-profile neighbours. Built only four years before the *Rio*, in 1986 – by Michael Gaughan (son of Jackie), who made his money running the slot concessions at the airport – its old-style Western decor always gave it the feel of a much earlier era. Recent upgradings, by current owners Boyd Gaming, have left it looking spruced-up enough to lure in passing trade, without actually adding anything substantial inside.

In truth, it's not a bad little place, offering the city's best **Chinese restaurant**, *Ping Pang Pong* (see p.140), and a *TGI Friday's*, plus a handful of other cheap eateries; a 70-lane **bowling alley**; and a large bingo room. Killers' frontman Brandon Flowers worked briefly as a bellhop at the casino.

Hard Rock Hotel

4455 Paradise Rd ☏ 800/473-7625, ⓦ hardrockhotel.com. Hotel accommodation is reviewed on p.125; restaurants include Mr Lucky's 24/7 (p.139) and Nobu (p.139); the Joint music venue is described on p.146.

If you don't already share the widespread delusion that the *Hard Rock* is by definition the coolest place in any city worldwide, little about the **Hard Rock Hotel**, a mile east of the Strip, is likely to convince you. Its own publicity material drones on about how "hip" the place is, how it's "the first ever rock'n'roll resort," and that "this is not your father's Vegas any more", but it's really not a patch on the current generation of Strip giants. Yes, guitars signed by the likes of Bob Dylan and George Michael hang above the check-in desk; the cashier's cage bears the slogan "In Rock We Trust"; and The Who's John Entwistle even died here. Display cases scattered throughout the property hold such treasures as Billy Idol's sequined suit and a drum that once belonged to Puddle of Mudd, while motorcycles and microphone stands sit atop banks of slot machines.

Killing the whole rockin' fantasy, though, is the hard fact that the *Hard Rock* is just another hotel/casino, and rather a lame one at that, populated by pony-tailed men and designer-label women trying to look twenty years younger than they really are, and hanging out in bars and clubs with names like "Rehab" and "Wasted Space".

In fairness, the *Hard Rock* does boast a better-than-average line-up of musical acts, some great restaurants and a showpiece pool, but it's not really worth going out of your way to see it. Like so many off-Strip properties, it's also said to be struggling in the face of the current recession.

Note that the *Hard Rock Café* is not in the casino; it used to stand just across the parking lot, but is now located on the Strip itself, in the Showcase Mall just north of the *MGM Grand*.

The Las Vegas Hilton

3000 Paradise Rd ☏ 702/732-5111 or 888/732-7117, ⓦ lvhilton.com. Hotel accommodation is reviewed on p.125.

The **Las Vegas Hilton** stands a full half-mile east of the Strip, set back behind the *Riviera* on Paradise Road. Traditionally, its location alongside the Convention Center enabled it to compete on equal terms with the major Strip casinos, but since the advent of places like *Bellagio*, the *Venetian* and *Wynn Las Vegas*, the *Hilton* has become the casino that Las Vegas forgot. Following a few years as part of the Bally's/Caesars Palace empire, who effectively asset-stripped the property by shunting its former high-rolling regulars to their other casinos, it was taken over in 2004 by the Resorts International conglomerate, but has seen no significant subsequent upgrading.

Though it's hard to believe now, for its first eight years this was the city's most prestigious resort. In the late 1960s, **Kirk Kerkorian** (see p.41) hoped that building the largest hotel in the world on this site – the *International Hotel* – would spur the development of Paradise Road as a second, parallel Strip. Existing Strip owners felt threatened enough to attempt to prevent the project ever breaking ground. When it finally went ahead, Howard Hughes tried to spoil things by buying up the *Landmark Hotel* nearby – a miniature *Stratosphere* – and reopening it as a casino on the self-same weekend, in July 1969.

In any event, the *International* was an instant success, thanks in large part to **Elvis Presley**, as described in the *Entertainment* colour insert. Kerkorian himself swiftly tired of his creation, though, and sold his stake to Hilton after just a year. Renamed the *Las Vegas Hilton*, its symmetrical trefoil shape made it easy to double its initial

1500 rooms to more than three thousand in 1973, simply by extending each of its three wings (if you look closely you can see the joins). However, it had to wait 25 years before Paradise Road acquired its second casino, the *Hard Rock*, about two miles south. Pedestrians being the rarest of species on Paradise Road, and the Monorail having proved a resounding failure at luring walk-in visitors, the *Hilton* remains a place you're only expected to reach by car, and it doesn't even bother to present an enticing facade to the visitor.

M Resort

12300 Las Vegas Blvd S, Henderson ☎702/797-1000, ⓦthemresort.com. The Studio B buffet is reviewed on p.130.

Despite its address on Las Vegas Boulevard – and for that matter its swanky appearance – the *M Resort*, which opened in 2009, is very definitely not on the Strip. Perched on a low bluff ten miles' drive due south of *Mandalay Bay*, the southernmost Strip casino, the *M* is instead a particularly upscale "locals' casino". While targeted primarily at the generally prosperous residents of the surrounding suburb of Henderson (technically a town in its own right), it also benefits from being the first casino seen by drivers arriving from California as they enter the Las Vegas Valley.

Although MGM Resorts contributed $160 million of the total $1 billion construction costs, the *M* was built by the Marnell family, the original owners of the *Rio*. Their design and construction firm was also responsible for the *Mirage*, *Bellagio* and *Wynn*, and the *M* incorporates lessons learned from all those properties. The *Rio*'s early years proved how much local customers value good service, attention to detail and, in particular, well-priced eating and drinking, while design elements from the latest Strip casinos permeate the new property. It has nonetheless struggled in the face of the recession Penn National Gaming bought it in late 2010 for a mere $230 million, though so far little has changed.

Inside the M

The *M* is broadly divided between the casino proper, which looks like a somewhat brighter version of *Aria*, with its earth tones and stylish minimalism, and the resort areas, where the hotel lobby with its plush red ceiling and rows of flowers more closely resembles *Wynn*. Outside, the opulent pool complex has an attractive retro feel. For visitors, the main reason to call in at the *M* is its top-class *Studio B* buffet (see p.130), though it also holds a fabulous patisserie, *Baby Cakes*. Locals are also attracted by its good-value gambling, and especially the ultra-modern Race and Sports Book. In an unusual policy, all visitors can help themselves to free soft drinks from dispensers located throughout the casino.

The Orleans

4500 W Tropicana Ave ☎702/365-7111 or 800/675-3267, ⓦorleanscasino.com. Hotel accommodation is reviewed on p.125.

A mile west of the Strip on Tropicana Avenue, a fake facade of pastel-painted townhouses and intricate balconies conceals the warehouse-like **Orleans** casino. When it opened in 1996, this previously untested location seemed destined to drive it into rapid bankruptcy, but things eventually turned around, and its extensive outdoor car parks are now usually full. Don't expect much from its New Orleans theme though, beyond a few half-hearted nods to the Crescent City; there's little New Orleans music on offer in its lounges and showrooms.

As a casino, however, it's quite exciting, with the loud commentaries in its Race and Sports Book matched by the enthusiasm of the clientele. Low stakes are offered on all table games, there's video poker galore and penny slots, and the croupiers are decked out in Mardi Gras beads. Most of the customers are local, though busloads of tourists arrive on the free shuttle buses from its sister property, the *Gold Coast* (see p.92), and also from *Bill's Gamblin' Hall* on the Strip, a hangover from the days when *Bill's* shared the same ownership too.

Other features of the *Orleans* include a reasonable buffet; a games arcade; the 70-lane, 24-hour bowling arcade upstairs; and the eighteen-screen Century Theatres, equipped with sofa seats and rocking chairs.

The Palms

4321 W Flamingo Rd ⓣ 702/942-7777, ⓦ palms.com. Hotel accommodation is reviewed on p.125; restaurants include Bistro Buffet (p.128) and N9ne Steakhouse (p.139); bars, clubs and music venues include Ghostbar (see p.144), the Pearl Theater (see p.146) and Rain (see p.145).

The **Palms** casino, which opened in 2001, has been a wildly successful experiment in appealing to both hip, high-rolling tourists and canny, cost-conscious locals. Thanks to the aggressive marketing campaign of owner George Maloof (whose family also owns the Sacramento Kings basketball team), it also ranks among Las Vegas's top celebrity hangouts. There's a particularly close connection with **hip-hop artists**; Eminem, Dr Dre and 50 Cent, for example, spent three weeks in the in-house recording studio in 2009, while countless music videos have been filmed in the casino.

While the *Palms'* closest equivalents are probably *Mandalay Bay* and the *Hard Rock*, both of which target a similarly cool crowd, its most obvious rival was originally the *Rio*, which stands just a few yards away, across Flamingo Road. It outdoes its neighbour by being just one storey taller – though it should be noted that the *Palms* calls its topmost 42nd floor its "55th", on the basis that for "good luck" it doesn't have a fourth, a thirteenth, or indeed anything from forty to forty-nine (the last being for the benefit of its Chinese guests). Other weapons in the *Palms'* arsenal include the *Moon*, *Rain* and *Ghostbar* **nightclubs**; the *Playboy Club*; the *Pearl Theater*, which seats up to 2500 and is often used for awards ceremonies; a batch of very classy restaurants; and a deluxe spa.

Elements designed to please locals, on the other hand, include ample parking space, a fourteen-screen cinema, and an abundance of (allegedly "loose") video poker machines.

The Rio

3700 W Flamingo Rd ⓣ 866/746-7671, ⓦ riolasvegas.com. Hotel accommodation is reviewed on p.125; restaurants include Búzio's (see p.138), Gaylord (p.138) and the Carnival World buffet (p.129); bars and clubs include the VooDoo Lounge (see p.144); and the Penn & Teller magic show is reviewed on p.150.

Despite being stranded half a mile west of the Strip, on the other side of I-15, the **Rio** quickly established itself as a major Las Vegas player after it opened in 1990. Acclaimed by locals and tourists alike, it was even hailed at the time as the world's best-value hotel. Two decades on, however, it has definitely sunk back into the pack. Now owned by Harrah's, the *Rio* still boasts a fine array of restaurants, plus big-name shows such as Penn & Teller, but it's lost much of the cachet that formerly lured visitors away from the Strip.

The *Rio*'s most impressive feature remains its dramatic red- and blue-glass exterior, together with the stunning purple light show (visible from all over the city) that plays across both its original building and the newer hotel tower. In turn, the top of that tower, occupied by the *VooDoo Lounge*, makes a great vantage point for viewing the Strip.

Harrah's ownership of the *Rio* has long been considered an uncomfortable fit. All the company's other casinos stand cheek-by-jowl along the Strip itself, which makes it easy to market them together. It's widely assumed that only the economic malaise has so far prevented the *Rio* from being sold off to the highest bidder. When such a sale finally goes through, Harrah's will almost certainly move the **World Series of Poker** to one of its Strip giants; the annual event has been staged at the *Rio* ever since they took it away from the *Horseshoe* downtown in 2005.

Inside the Rio

The "Rio" theme can be a bit tricky to pin down, having mutated from being specifically Brazilian to incorporating pretty much anything that's either tropical, carnival-related, or at the very least eye-catching. The **Masquerade Village** section stages its own twelve-minute **Show In The Sky** (Thurs–Sun, hourly 7pm–midnight), in which parade "floats" suspended from overhead rails pass above the casino floor while lingerie-clad dancers cavort on the central stage – over-16s can ride their own float for $13. In addition, the unfortunate cocktail waitresses have been restyled as "bevertainers," and sing as they deliver drinks to gamblers.

Typical of the *Rio*'s recent faltering attempts to roll the clock back was its opening of the topless *Sapphire Pool* in 2008, in a joint venture with a local strip club. The pool was forced to close down again the next year, after undercover police operations revealed prostitution and drug-related activity.

Sam's Town

5111 Boulder Hwy ⓣ 702/456-7777 or 800/897-8696, ⓦ samstownlv.com. Hotel accommodation is reviewed on p.125.

A last hold-out of Las Vegas's once-ubiquitous Wild West theme, **Sam's Town**, six miles east of the Strip, is the quintessential locals' casino. After years of low-profile prosperity from providing bargain-basement grub-and-gambling, it has blossomed into a genuinely appealing place whose biggest downside is being so far out of the way; see it while en route to or from the Hoover Dam.

Though the "Sam" of the name honours the late casino operator Sam Boyd, *Sam's Town* was the brainchild of his son, Bill Boyd. During his daily drive to work in 1979, he was struck by the sheer volume of traffic along this hitherto uncommercialized stretch of highway. *Sam's Town* was soon drawing in crowds of thrill-seeking commuters, giving them hearty old-style Western meals then clawing back their wages via its endless banks of slots.

While its general decor is still bursting with boots'n'spurs'n'cactuses, *Sam's Town* now centres on a bright, spacious glass-roofed atrium, overlooked on all sides by the high-rise brownstone facades of its hotel towers. Officially known as Mystic Falls Park, and kitted out with fibreglass mountains, waterfalls, real trees, recorded birdsong and even animatronic beavers, it's reminiscent – if you're in the right mood – of New York's Central Park. A free water, laser and light show takes place four times daily (2pm, 6pm, 8pm & 10pm); the three after-dark performances have a strong patriotic theme.

Upstairs, **Sheplers** sells a fabulous array of cowboy boots and other paraphernalia. On the south side of the casino, the **Sam's Town Live** complex is an 1100-seat performance and dining space, most commonly hosting country entertainers. There's also an 18-screen cinema and a 56-lane, 24-hour bowling centre, plus two large **RV parks**.

Sunset Station

1301 W Sunset Rd, Henderson ⓣ702/547-7777, ⓦsunsetstation.com. Hotel accommodation is reviewed on p.125; restaurants include the Oyster Bar (p.139) and the Feast buffet (p.130); and the Gaudí Bar is described on p.144.

Eight miles southeast of the southern end of the Strip, in suburban Henderson, **Sunset Station** is a long drive from the centre of Las Vegas. En route to Hoover Dam, however, and opposite the Galleries at Sunset mall (see p.174), it's not exactly off the beaten track, and it's worth seeing in its own right.

Completed in 1997, *Sunset Station* was designed to look something like an old Spanish mission. The attempt is enjoyable enough, even if it's not all that coherent, and some of the interior trimmings are truly spectacular. An extraordinary adobe-styled and mushroom-shaped canopy of stained and coloured glass undulates above the gaming area, reaching a climax in the central *Gaudí Bar* (see p.144). A fantastic mosaic-enhanced tribute to the Catalan architect Gaudí, it's Las Vegas at its most surreal.

Sunset Station also features a thirteen-screen cinema; the 72-lane *Strike Zone* bowling centre; some good restaurants and the great-value *Feast* buffet; childcare facilities; and a games arcade, plus free shuttle buses to the Strip.

Other attractions

The Atomic Testing Museum

755 E Flamingo Rd ⓣ702/794-5151, ⓦatomictestingmuseum.org. Mon–Sat 10am–5pm, Sun noon–5pm. $12, seniors, students and ages 7–17 $9, under-6s free.

This offshoot of the Nevada Test Site Historical Foundation – which preserves the history of the nearby desert location where nuclear weapons were tested from 1951 to 1992 – exhibits a mix of kitschy and serious artefacts, including nuclear-tinged pop-culture items, film clips and a recreation of a bomb shelter. There's also a library with hundreds of thousands of declassified documents. The main attraction, however, is a full-sensory simulation of an above-ground nuclear explosion in the so-called "Ground Zero Theater."

Nevada State Museum

700 Twin Lakes Drive ⓣ702/486-5205, ⓦmuseums.nevadaculture.org. Wed–Sun 9am–5pm. Adults $8, under-18s free.

The **Nevada State Museum** is both hard to find – follow Washington Avenue three miles west of downtown to Valley View Boulevard, then look for signs to Lorenzi Park – and hardly worth finding. Despite ample floor space, and a potentially fascinating subject in the history of the Las Vegas valley ever since it was roamed by mammoths, its displays are perfunctory and lifeless, aimed at school parties with short attention spans. What's more, the chronology peters out altogether in the 1950s, right when things start to get really interesting; the only glimpse you get of contemporary Las Vegas is a door once used by Bugsy Siegel – quite the dullest door you ever saw.

Out from the city

Spend more than a day or two in Las Vegas and you'll soon find yourself gasping for a blast of sunlight and fresh air away from the casinos. A glance at the horizon makes it clear that you'll have to cross an expanse of empty desert before you reach anywhere interesting, but exhilarating day-trip destinations do exist.

Perhaps the most obvious targets lie in the eye-catching **Spring Mountains** to the west. At their base, monumental walls cradle the desert fastness of **Red Rock Canyon**, while further north wooded slopes rise toward the summit of **Mount Charleston**. If Red Rock Canyon whets your appetite for other-worldly desolation, you'll also enjoy the longer excursion to the incandescent moonscape of the **Valley of Fire**, northeast of the city. Finally, neither **Hoover Dam** nor **Lake Mead** counts as a natural wonder, but each is in its own way every bit as breathtaking.

This chapter only includes places that can be reached and explored in a self-guided day-trip from Las Vegas. For details of trips further afield, to the **Grand Canyon** and the awe-inspiring **Zion** and **Bryce Canyon** national parks of southern Utah, see chapter 8. On the basis that Las Vegas holds enough casinos to last any sane human being a lifetime, this guide does not cover the nearby state-line gambling resorts of Primm, Mesquite and Laughlin.

Red Rock Canyon

The closest concentration of classic Southwestern canyon scenery to Las Vegas lies a mere twenty miles west of the city centre. The sheer 3000ft escarpment that towers above **Red Rock Canyon National Conservation Area** is clearly visible from hotel windows along the Strip, with every fiery detail picked out each morning by the rising sun. What you can't see until you enter the park, however, is that there's a cactus-strewn desert basin set deep into those mighty walls, surrounded by stark red cliffs that are pierced repeatedly by narrow canyons accessible only on foot.

Run by the Federal Bureau of Land Management, Red Rock Canyon covers almost 200,000 acres of wilderness. Like other such BLM areas, it's less groomed for tourists than a national park or monument. Thus while it includes over thirty miles of hiking trails, they're not as well signed or maintained as you might expect, and it's all too easy for novice walkers to get lost.

To reach the canyon, just keep going west on Charleston Boulevard, from the extreme north of the Strip. The pink leaves of the trees lining the road perfectly complement the pink strata of rocks on the mountains straight ahead, though this vista has been somewhat marred by the construction of the **Summerlin** residential and resort development at the west end of Charleston. This only opened in 1999, but has swiftly mushroomed to become a fully fledged suburb of the city.

OUT FROM THE CITY

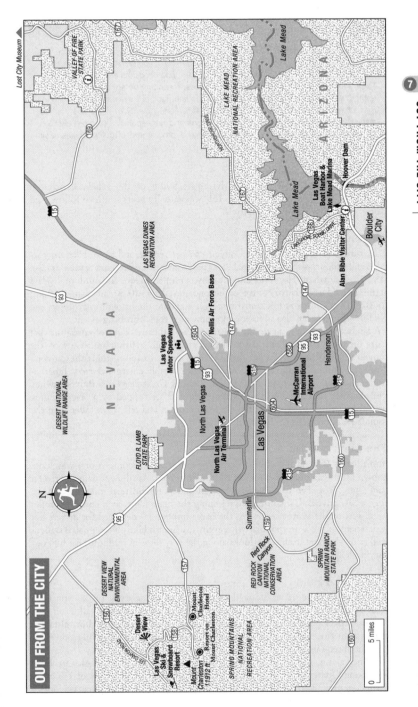

VALLEY OF FIRE
STATE PARK

LAKE MEAD
NATIONAL RECREATION AREA

Lake Mead

A R I Z O N A

Hoover Dam

Las Vegas
Boat Harbor &
Lake Mead Marina

Boulder
City

Alan Bible Visitor Center

LAKESHORE SCENIC DRIVE

LAS VEGAS DUNES
RECREATION AREA

Nellis Air Force Base

Henderson

McCarran
International
Airport

Las Vegas Motor Speedway

North Las Vegas

DESERT NATIONAL
WILDLIFE RANGE AREA

N E V A D A

FLOYD R. LAMB
STATE PARK

North Las Vegas Air Terminal

Las Vegas

DESERT VIEW
NATURAL
ENVIRONMENTAL
AREA

N

Summerlin

Red Rock Canyon

RED ROCK CANYON
NATIONAL CONSERVATION
AREA

SPRING MOUNTAIN RANCH
STATE PARK

Desert View

Las Vegas Ski &
Snowboard Resort

Mount
Charleston 11,912 ft.

Mount Charleston Hotel

Resort on Mount Charleston

LEE CANYON ROAD

SPRING MOUNTAINS
NATIONAL
RECREATION AREA

0   5 miles

99

Red Rock Canyon hiking practicalities

While Red Rock Canyon is great for hiking and camping (call ☎702/515-5050 for permits), there are a number of things to keep in mind. If you plan to **hike**, buy a good map from the visitor centre before you set off; the free handouts aren't up to the job. The canyon is subject to "leave no trace" rules, meaning you should minimize your contact with wildlife, stay on established trails and pack out everything you bring in. Since temperatures can soar above 105°F/41°C, bring plenty of water. Be warned also that the desert is home to mountain lions and rattlesnakes. For more detailed information on Red Rock Canyon hiking, and a programme of guided hikes, visit ⓦredrockcanyonlv.org.

Having continued due west for the entire width of the valley, Charleston Boulevard – by now officially **Hwy-159** – eventually veers south to follow Red Rock Wash as far as the canyon itself.

The visitor centre

The **admission fee** to Red Rock Canyon – $7 per vehicle, and $3 for bikes, motorbikes and pedestrians, with National Parks passes accepted – becomes payable as soon as you turn north off Hwy-159 into the canyon proper. Indoor and outdoor displays at the splendid new **visitor centre** just beyond, unveiled in 2009 (daily 8am–4.30pm; ☎702/515-5350, ⓦredrockcanyonlv.org), explain the canyon's geology and wildlife. Rangers can also advise on recommended **rock climbing** ascents.

A landscaped terrace, facing into a natural amphitheatre of Aztec sandstone that soars on three sides of the central basin, commands a panoramic view of the canyon's main features. An enclosure of rare desert tortoises holds the canyon's "spokes-tortoise," **Mojave Max**, whose unpredictable emergence from hibernation each spring makes him the local equivalent of *Groundhog Day*'s Punxsutawney Phil. Farther back, the **Wilson Cliffs** to the left are topped by a layer of grey limestone, which has preserved them from erosion and left them taller than the rounded **Calico Hills** to the right.

The Scenic Drive

Immediately beyond the visitor centre, the access road becomes a one-way loop, known as the **Scenic Drive** (daily: March 7am–7pm, April–Sept 6am–8pm, Oct 6am–7pm, Nov–Feb 6am–5pm), which meanders for thirteen miles around the edge of Red Rock Canyon before rejoining the main highway a couple of miles southwest of the visitor centre. As the name implies, it's designed for drivers not pedestrians, but it's also popular with cyclists, who can bike on designated trails as well as on the road itself. Overlooks along the way serve as trailheads for hikes of varying lengths.

The Calico Hills

The most dramatic views along the Scenic Drive come early on, as you head straight toward the **Calico Hills** that form the basin's northeastern wall. From two successive overlooks, Calico Vistas 1 and 2, it's possible to scramble short distances down from the road to find yourself dwarfed amid these crumbling domes of cream and red sandstone.

Further along, the **Calico Tanks Trail**, a 2.5-mile round trip, heads up from Sandstone Quarry and beyond the visible rim to reach the largest of the area's natural "tanks." The rainwater collected and stored in such depressions was once a valuable resource for nomadic desert peoples. On a clear day, you can see the Strip from up here.

Willow Spring

The easiest trail in the canyon starts at **Willow Spring**, a short way up a well-signed spur road seven miles from the visitor centre. Following the tree-filled minor canyon formed by Lost Creek, it passes rock shelters once used by Native Americans. Adults can enjoy a comfortable 1.5-mile stroll, while kids who complete a shorter half-mile section designated as the **Children's Discovery Trail** can claim a certificate and badge at the visitor centre, which provides full details on request.

Pine Creek Canyon Trail

Energetic hikers who lack the urge to do out-and-out rock climbing should enjoy the **Pine Creek Canyon Trail**, which sets off a little less than eleven miles from the visitor centre. From the trailhead, look down and to the left to see the row of ponderosa pines that reveals the presence of Pine Creek. Reaching the ruined homesite beside it takes around twenty minutes, along a sandy red footpath fringed with cactuses.

To reach and potentially follow the clear stream itself, rippling over red-rock boulders and lined with lush flowers, take your pick from various imprecise trails. The main trail, on the other hand, continues up to the right. If you keep going all the way to the foot of a red-capped monolith that divides two forked canyons, it will add up to a round-trip hike of roughly five miles.

Mount Charleston

Las Vegas residents desperate to escape the desert heat flock in summer to the **Spring Mountains National Recreation Area**. Thirty miles northwest of the city and forming part of the Toiyabe National Forest, it's more widely known as **Mount Charleston**, on account of its highest point, the 11,918ft Charleston Peak. Ten thousand years ago, this isolated range formed a natural refuge for wildlife from the lakes that filled the Las Vegas Valley, and it retained its own unique ecosystem as the rest of the region dried out. In fact, many of its plants and animals, including one unique species of chipmunk, are found nowhere else on earth.

The cool wooded slopes of Mount Charleston are much less of a novelty for most tourists, of course, but they do offer some great **hiking**, and in winter you can even drive out for a day of **skiing** or **snowboarding**. Higher elevations usually remain covered by snow between mid-October and mid-May each year, while the streams and waterfalls only carry substantial flows during the thaw in spring and early summer.

To reach Mount Charleston, follow either **US-95** itself, or **Rancho Drive** which feeds into it, northwest out of the city for a total of fifteen miles from the Strip. Six miles beyond the point where they intersect, head west along Hwy-157, **Kyle Canyon Road**, which for its first ten miles continues to cross flat, barren desert. Shortly after dipping through a jagged rocky "reef" that pokes from the valley floor, the highway enters Kyle Canyon.

Kyle Canyon

As it penetrates the Spring Mountains, Hwy-157 itself remains relatively level; the hills rise on either side. When it begins to climb, the ascent is gradual and not all that dramatic. Only as you feel your ears popping do you realize you've left the valley behind. As the closest part of the mountains to Las Vegas, **Kyle Canyon** is the main day-trip destination. With each passing year, a few more buildings appear on its slopes, and it's becoming a residential community. Although there are a couple of hotels with year-round restaurants, there's nowhere up here to buy gas or basic groceries, so stock up accordingly beforehand.

The Resort on Mount Charleston

Set below the highway on the left, seventeen miles up from US-95 and facing a towering rocky outcrop, the recently renovated **Resort on Mount Charleston**, at 2 Kyle Canyon Rd (☎702/872-5500 or 1-888/559-1888, ⓦmtcharlestonresort .com), is the finest **accommodation** option in the mountains, with rates for its 62 rooms and suites that start as low as $29 per night in summer, and rise to around $100 in winter. Despite its somewhat forbidding facade, on the inside it resembles an old-fashioned national park lodge, with lots of wooden furnishings, a high vaulted ceiling, and a 360-degree open fireplace. It even has a few discreet slot machines, if you're pining for the city. Downstairs, the *Cut Above* serves $13–16 wraps, sandwiches and burgers at lunchtime, and pricier steak, chicken and seafood dinners – though be warned it closes at 8pm on weekdays.

Mary Jane Falls and around

Beyond the hotel, you pass from the lower "life zone" of yuccas and cacti into forests of pine, fir and mahogany. Hwy-158, branches right in less than a mile, while a little under two miles beyond that turnoff, Hwy-157 doubles back sharply on itself and starts back along the other side of Kyle Canyon. A short spur road, **Echo Road**, keeps going straight on for a few hundred yards up to the trailhead for the **Mary Jane Falls Trail**. This 2.5-mile round-trip hike follows a disused road for a little under a mile, before requiring hikers to ascend a series of exhausting switchbacks to reach the twin Mary Jane Falls at the head of the canyon. Fed by separate springs, the falls are at their strongest in early summer, but that's not a good time to enter the caves immediately behind them, which remain icy until later in the year.

Cathedral Rock Trail

Half a mile further along Hwy-157, the **Cathedral Rock Trail** sets off from a roadside car park. Starting at 7600ft and climbing a further thousand feet along a rough but not very steep footpath, the three-mile round-trip can be pretty gruelling for anyone unused to such elevations. En route to the top of the promontory known as **Cathedral Rock**, you have to circle around Mazie Canyon, by way of denuded hillsides cleared by countless winter avalanches. You're eventually rewarded with views all the way back down Kyle Canyon – though not as far as Las Vegas – as well as onward to **Charleston Peak**. Its smooth bald dome is the only point in the mountains that pokes out above the treeline.

Mount Charleston Lodge

Hwy-157 comes to a dead end shortly after Cathedral Rock, looping around the parking lot of **Mount Charleston Lodge** (☎702/872-5408 or 800/955-1314, ⓦmtcharlestonlodge.com; Mon–Thurs $135, Fri–Sun $200). This large and unexciting Southwestern restaurant is usually packed with day-trippers, with lunchtime pizzas, Mexican dishes and chillis at $13–15, and more substantial dinners for $20–30. If you can get a table on the terrace – which tends to be closed off due to ice in winter – you'll be treated to fine views over the canyon and up to Charleston Peak. The 23 comfortably appointed **log cabins** alongside the parking lot are rented out by the night, and are popular with honeymooners escaping Las Vegas.

Hwy-158

The most scenic stretch of road in the Spring Mountains is **Hwy-158**, which runs for nine miles across the face of the mountains to connect Kyle Canyon with **Lee Canyon** to the north. Parking at the roadside at various unmarked spots along the way will provide opportunities to survey the desert far below, and you may even spot caves apparently used by bandits preying on travellers using the old Mormon Trail across the valley.

Desert View Trail

A mile before you reach Lee Canyon, the clearly signed **Desert View Trail** is a short paved footpath with an unlikely history. During the A-bomb tests of the 1950s (see p.188) the Mount Charleston area was designated by the Atomic Energy Commission as being the best vantage point for spectators. On eight separate days in 1957, announced far enough in advance for tourists to plan their vacations to coincide, vast crowds assembled up here to watch the explosions. Metal poles erected to hold official cameras recording the events still stand just below the viewing platform. These days, you have to settle simply for a vast desert panorama, which doesn't extend as far as Las Vegas itself.

Lee Canyon

From the north end of Hwy-159, Hwy-156, also known as Lee Canyon Road, runs eighteen miles northeast to rejoin US-95 thirteen miles up from the Kyle Canyon turn-off. Heading three miles southwest instead brings you into the heart of **Lee Canyon**. Like Kyle Canyon, this was once the scene of commercial logging; more recently, the trees have been cut back to create southern Nevada's only **ski** area.

Las Vegas Ski and Snowboard Resort

Just under fifty miles from the Strip is the rather tiny **Las Vegas Ski and Snowboard Resort** (see p.181), at the head of Lee Canyon. For more details, or to arrange a $20 round-trip **shuttle ride** from town, visit Ⓦ skilasvegas.com.

Lake Mead

The single most popular day-trip from Las Vegas is the thirty-mile drive southeast to the vast artificial reservoir of **Lake Mead**, and to the mighty **Hoover Dam** that created it. In many ways, the dam is also responsible for modern Las Vegas's very existence. Not so much as a source of energy – contrary to popular belief, only four percent of Las Vegas's electricity comes from hydroelectric power – but because the workers who built it triggered the city's first gambling-fuelled boom (see p.186). As for the lake, it makes a bizarre spectacle, utterly unnatural yet undeniably impressive, with its blue waters a vivid counterpoint to the surrounding desert. Both the lake and its 550-mile shoreline, however, can be excruciatingly crowded all year round.

As the crow flies, the western edge of Lake Mead is barely fourteen miles east of the Strip, but no road follows that route. Although two minor highways provide the most direct access, most visitors choose instead to take **Boulder Highway**, climbing out of the valley at Railroad Pass and reaching **Boulder City** – still the only city in Nevada that doesn't allow gambling – thirty miles out from the Strip. The first surreal vista of the lake arrives as you drop out of Boulder City on Business-93.

Lakeshore Scenic Drive

On a stark sandstone slope beside US-93, four miles northeast of Boulder City, the **Alan Bible Visitor Center** (daily 8.30am–4.30pm; ☎702/293-8990, ⓦnps.gov /lame) is the main source of information on the Lake Mead National Recreation Area. Even if you don't need details of how to sail, scuba-dive, water-ski or fish from its various marinas, it's worth calling in to get your bearings. Pick up some safety advice, too – notorious for drunken shenanigans, the lake averages three fatal water accidents per month.

Though the lake straddles the border between Nevada and Arizona, the best views come from the Nevada side. From the visitor centre, Hwy-166, better known as **Lakeshore Scenic Drive**, parallels its western shore as far as Las Vegas Bay. Despite the name, water levels have dropped so low in recent years that the lake is not always visible, and several marinas, accessible via spur roads, have had to be relocated.

Both **Lake Mead Marina** (☎702/293-3484, ⓦriverlakes.com) and the adjoining **Las Vegas Boat Harbor** (☎702/293-1191, ⓦboatinglakemead.com) offer restaurants and stores, as well as boat and jet-ski rental, although they're functional rather than pleasant places to stop. The harbour's **Lake Mead Cruises Landing** is the base of operations for the *Desert Princess*, an imitation paddlewheeler that makes up to four excursions daily, with evening dinner cruises in summer ($24–49; ☎702/293-6180, ⓦlakemeadcruises.com).

Hoover Dam

Staying on US-83 beyond Boulder City takes you through the rocky ridges of the Black Mountains to reach **Hoover Dam**. Designed to block the Colorado River and supply low-cost water and electricity to the cities of the Southwest, the 726ft-high structure ranks among the tallest dams ever built. And at 660ft across at the base, it's nearly as wide as it is tall – amazingly, during its construction enough concrete was used to build a two-lane highway from San Francisco to New York. It was completed in 1935, as the first step in the Bureau of Reclamation programme that culminated in the Glen Canyon Dam at the far end of the Grand Canyon, and the creation of Lake Powell. **Bus tours** to the dam from Las Vegas, with Gray Line (☎800/966-8125, ⓦgrayline.com) for example, cost around $60 for a five-hour trip.

Seeing the dam

A new **bypass** bridge, long suggested but finally constructed after the 9/11 attacks prompted fears that the dam might be a potential terrorist target, now carries all traffic across the Colorado River a few hundred yards south of the dam.

Although you can't drive across the actual dam into Arizona, if you're happy just to get a general view of the thing, you should be able to squeeze into one of the car parks on its far side accessed from the Arizona side of the new bridge. To see the dam close up, you'll have to pay $7 to park in the huge multi-storey facility on the Nevada side of the river (daily 8am–5.45pm). From here, you can walk down to the dam itself and walk along the top, looking towards Lake Mead from one side of the road and then peering down the awesome drop to the Colorado River from the other.

Across from the splendid Art Deco monument, on the Nevada side of the river, which commemorates the dam's opening by Franklin Roosevelt in 1935, stands the **Hoover Dam Visitor Center** (daily April–Sept 8.30am–5.45pm, Oct–March 9.15am–4.15pm; ☎702/293-1824, ⓦwww.usbr.gov/lc/hooverdam). Paying a further $8 (no reductions) entitles you to inspect its displays on the dam's history and construction. A total fee of $11 ($9 seniors & ages 4–16) entitles you to join a

Powerplant Tour (first tour always 9.15am, last ticket sold April–Sept 5.15pm, Oct–March 4.15pm), by taking an elevator ride down to the foot of the dam, where you can see the giant turbine room and even step out into the open air. Finally, the extended, hour-long Dam Tour (daily 9.30am–3.30pm, every half hour; total fee $30, no reductions) includes more than a mile of walking along the damp, eerie tunnels and passageways that riddle the dam.

Valley of Fire

While Red Rock Canyon certainly makes a tasty appetizer, to experience the true scale and splendour of the Southwestern deserts you need to make the hundred-mile round-trip drive to the **Valley of Fire**, northeast of Las Vegas. Its multicoloured, strangely eroded rocks are the solidified remains of sand dunes laid down at the time of the dinosaurs, 150 million years ago. If they seem familiar, you may have seen them in any number of movies, from *One Million Years BC* to *Star Trek – The Next Generation*.

The road into the valley, state Hwy-169, cuts away east from I-15 thirty long, empty miles up its course toward Salt Lake City. Passing briefly through a corner of the desolate Moapa River Indian Reservation, it then starts to undulate and climb the aptly named Muddy Mountains, whose grey-ochre wall forms the eastern boundary of the Dry Lake Valley.

Seeking to cut costs, Nevada's state government has recently threatened both the Valley of Fire State Park, and the Lost City Museum just beyond it, with temporary or even permanent **closure**; check the relevant websites, given below, before you set off.

Valley of Fire State Park

Twelve miles from the interstate, Hwy-169 crests the Muddy Mountains and enters **Valley of Fire State Park**. A huge panorama opens up ahead, stretching down toward Lake Mead, but the road has to pick its way gingerly down, threading between abrupt, jagged outcrops. Having paid the $10-per-vehicle fee at the entrance station, you soon come to the first of the big red rocks, the ridged, bulbous **Beehives**.

A little further on stands the park's **visitor centre**, located at the start of the spur road that holds the park's most spectacular formations (daily 8.30am–4.30pm; ☎702/397-2088, ⊛parks.nv.gov/vf.htm). Besides displays on the geology and history of the region, the centre provides an introduction to local wildlife, with reptilariums holding live rattlesnakes.

The broad, paved road beyond the visitor centre leads through a wonderland of misshapen stone monstrosities, worn smooth by millennia of wind and rain and striped in a broad palette of colours. Cream, yellow, gold, pink and purple strata are interspersed among the lurid omnipresent red. Many hikers set off walking when the road ends 5.5 miles along at the White Domes, but that entails ploughing through thick sand drifts, and there are better trails earlier on.

Mouse's Tank

Less than a mile north of the Valley of Fire visitor centre, an easy and interesting half-mile hike follows a sandy wash through **Petroglyph Canyon**. The rock walls at the base of certain sandstone monoliths here are thought to have been decorated by prehistoric Ancestral Puebloan farmers (see p.185). Some symbols have been recognized as being similar to those used by the modern Hopi people of Arizona, but not all is necessarily what it seems. The depictions of bighorn sheep, for example, probably represent shamans rather than actual sheep.

The trail is forced to stop when the ground suddenly drops away at the far end of the canyon, where run-off after occasional desert storms has cut deep channels into the rock. Scrambling up the slopes adjacent to the edge enables you to peer down into a natural "tank" that can hold collected rainwater for months at a time. Known as **Mouse's Tank**, this remote reservoir was the hideout of Mouse, a fugitive Paiute Indian, during the 1890s.

Elephant Rock

One of the most photographed features of the Valley of Fire is located alongside Hwy-169 three miles east of the visitor centre. Reached via a short but steep trail from the car park at the park's east entrance, **Elephant Rock** does indeed bear an amazing resemblance to a petrified pachyderm, dipping its trunk into the hillside.

The Lost City Museum

A mile outside the park, Hwy-169 meets Hwy-167, Northshore Drive, which circles back south toward Las Vegas. Staying on Hwy-169 as it heads north from this intersection is a much less attractive option – maps that depict this as a scenic route are pretty wide of the mark – but it brings you in nine miles to Overton's intriguing **Lost City Museum** (Thurs–Sun 8.30am–4.30pm; ☎702/397-2193, ⒲museums.nevadaculture.org; $10).

Between around 300 BC and 1150 AD, people known as the **Ancestral Puebloans** are thought to have farmed in the Moapa Valley, immediately north of the Valley of Fire. This was the western extremity of their domain, which extended across the entire Colorado Plateau, from modern Utah and Arizona into New Mexico and Colorado. The first to build the characteristic adobe villages that the Spaniards later called "pueblos," they were the ancestors of today's Pueblo Indians – hence their modern name, now used by archeologists in preference to the former term of "Anasazi."

The "**Lost City**," by far the largest Ancestral Puebloan settlement in Nevada, was really more of an elongated village. Stretching for around thirty miles along the Moapa Valley, and originally known to archeologists as the Pueblo Grande de Nevada, its ruins were partly submerged by the creation of Lake Mead. At that time, in the 1930s, the finest artefacts from the site were gathered into this museum, which was given a catchy name in the hope of making it easier to raise funds.

Displays at the museum are still very much rooted in the 1930s – techniques like painting over a slab of genuine petroglyphs would appal modern archeologists – but there's still plenty to fascinate casual visitors. The whole structure is designed in a mock-Pueblo style, with a replica of a dig on a genuine site inside, and reconstructions of Pueblo buildings, also on their original sites, in the garden outside.

Northshore Drive

The fifty-mile drive back to Las Vegas from the Valley of Fire along Hwy-167, **Northshore Drive**, takes you through some utterly stunning wilderness. Desolate and forbidding sandstone mountains soar in your path, the road dwindling to a thin grey streak dwarfed beneath stark serrated cliffs. Its name, however, referring to its position by Lake M. ad, is misleading – you almost never see the lake itself, which remains on the far side of a high ridge. Here and there, side roads lead down to marinas on the lake, but unless you're going boating they're dismal spots.

The national parks

A trip to Las Vegas provides the perfect opportunity to explore a little further afield in the magnificent deserts of the Southwest. Although many visitors think of the **Grand Canyon** as being the most obvious potential destination, as explained below that's neither as near nor as convenient as you might imagine. This chapter therefore suggests a couple of additional possibilities to consider, in nearby southern Utah – breathtaking **Zion National Park**, and bizarre, unforgettable **Bryce Canyon National Park**.

If you're prepared to pay premium prices for an **air tour**, then it's possible to take a day-trip to the Grand Canyon. Otherwise, it's worth setting aside at least one night for a short **road trip**. Ideally, you'd get away from Las Vegas over the **weekend**, when the city's room rates rise enormously, and the whole place becomes hugely crowded.

The Grand Canyon

Las Vegas tour companies perpetuate two great **myths** about the Grand Canyon: first, that the Grand Canyon is close to Las Vegas, and secondly, that seeing the so-called Grand Canyon West – also known as the West Rim, and home to the **Skywalk** – amounts to the same thing as seeing the Grand Canyon.

Neither is true. To see the full majestic sweep of the canyon, you have to go to **Grand Canyon National Park**, which holds two main concentrations of viewpoints. Both those along the **South Rim**, and those along the higher and less-visited **North Rim**, lie over 270 miles by road from the Strip, making them far beyond the scope of a driving day-trip from Las Vegas.

As for **Grand Canyon West**, it's a scenic spot, with impressive canyon views, and makes an adventurous destination, but it entirely lacks the scale, let alone the panoply of rock formations, that characterizes the canyon proper. A shorter but still long and bleak drive from Las Vegas, it's just possible to make the round-trip in a day by car, or take a day-long bus tour, but it's not recommended.

The only practical way to see the Grand Canyon as a **day-trip** from Las Vegas, therefore, is to take an **air tour**, in which case it's just as easy to see the real thing, at the South Rim of the national park, as it is to go to Grand Canyon West.

If you want to take a **road trip** from the city, on the other hand, and make at least one overnight stop, **lodging** is available at both rims of the national park, but not at Grand Canyon West. For a truly memorable getaway, there's also a further possibility – hiking down to stay near the extraordinary waterfalls of the remote **Havasupai Reservation**.

Grand Canyon West

As a rule, any "Grand Canyon tour" you see advertised in Las Vegas is almost certainly going not to the national park, but to the area known as either **Grand**

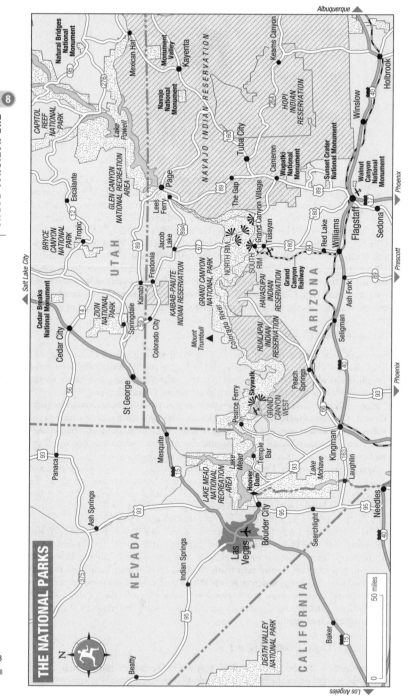

THE NATIONAL PARKS

N

0   50 miles

Albuquerque

Los Angeles

NEVADA

UTAH

ARIZONA

CALIFORNIA

NAVAJO INDIAN RESERVATION

HOPI INDIAN RESERVATION

KAIBAB-PAIUTE INDIAN RESERVATION

HAVASUPAI INDIAN RESERVATION

HUALAPAI INDIAN RESERVATION

GRAND CANYON NATIONAL PARK

LAKE MEAD NATIONAL RECREATION AREA

GLEN CANYON NATIONAL RECREATION AREA

CAPITOL REEF NATIONAL PARK

BRYCE CANYON NATIONAL PARK

ZION NATIONAL PARK

DEATH VALLEY NATIONAL PARK

Cedar Breaks National Monument

Natural Bridges National Monument

Navajo National Monument

Wupatki National Monument

Sunset Crater National Monument

Walnut Canyon National Monument

Mexican Hat

Monument Valley

Kayenta

Kearns Canyon

Holbrook

Winslow

Flagstaff

Sedona

Prescott

Phoenix

Phoenix

Tuba City

Cameron

Red Lake

Williams

Ash Fork

Seligman

Page

Lees Ferry

The Gap

Grand Canyon Village

Tusayan

NORTH RIM

SOUTH RIM

Grand Canyon Railway

Jacob Lake

Fredonia

Kanab

Springdale

Colorado City

Escalante

Tropic

Cedar City

St George

Mesquite

Panaca

Ash Springs

Indian Springs

Las Vegas

Boulder City

Searchlight

Laughlin

Kingman

Needles

Peach Springs

GRAND CANYON WEST

Skywalk

Pearce Ferry

Temple Bar

Hoover Dam

Lake Mead

Lake Mohave

Baker

Beatty

Mount Trumbull

Colorado River

Lake Powell

Lake Mead

Red Lake

Salt Lake City

Grand Canyon West Air Tours

Several companies fly day-trip **air tours** from Las Vegas to the rudimentary airstrip alongside the West Rim headquarters.

Helicopter trips are offered by Papillon (☏702/736-7243 or 1-888/635-7272, ⒲www .papillon.com), Maverick (☏702/261-0007 or 1-888/261-4414, ⒲www.maverick helicopter.com) and Sundance (☏702/736-0606 or 1-800/653-1881, ⒲www.sundance helicopters.com), among others. Prices tend to start at almost $300 per person for a trip that includes perhaps just a brief landing beside the Colorado; approach $400 for a flight that doesn't land at all but provides a longer air tour of the canyon; and approach $500 for a package featuring a visit to the Skywalk.

Airplane tours, with operators like Scenic Airlines (☏702/638-3200 or 1-800/634-6801, ⒲www.scenic.com), are much cheaper. A simple overflight with no landing costs from around $100; a basic package including a ground tour of Grand Canyon West starts at around $170; and add-ons like a walk on the Skywalk or a helicopter descent to the river can bring the cost up to $300 or more.

Be sure you know exactly what your package does and does not include; surprisingly little help or guidance is available once you arrive.

Canyon West, or the **West Rim** of the Grand Canyon, 125 miles by road from the city. This canny marketing name has recently been attached to a cluster of overlooks along a small portion of the 108 miles of Colorado River frontage that belongs to the **Hualapai Indian Reservation**.

It can't be emphasized enough that Grand Canyon West bears no relation to the canyon at its best. This far west, the canyon is starting to peter out; it lacks the colossal depth and width of its central section, and holds none of the towering mesas, buttes and temples so conspicuous from the viewpoints in the national park.

Thus, while it's been tremendously hyped in the last few years, thanks to the construction of the glass-floored **Skywalk**, Grand Canyon West is very far from being a must-see attraction. If you're an outdoors type, eager to immerse yourself in the desert wildernesses of the Southwest, it's probably not for you.

That said, the West Rim is undeniably a stunning spectacle, and offers several unique experiences, including helicopter flights down to the Colorado River, and short river trips, as well as the Skywalk. If you're happy to pay premium prices for a once-in-a-lifetime thrill, you may absolutely love it.

Driving to Grand Canyon West

To **drive** to Grand Canyon West, head east from US-93 in Arizona, forty miles south of the Hoover Dam, onto Pierce Ferry Road. Continue for 28 miles, then turn right (east) onto Diamond Bar Road. From there, a rocky 14-mile climb – unpaved but graded, and normally suitable for all vehicles other than RVs – leads through foothills scattered with Joshua trees and up the Grand Wash Cliffs, and up to the Hualapai reservation.

You reach Grand Canyon West five miles later, where you have to pay $20 to **park** at the airport.

Seeing Grand Canyon West

The only entrance to Grand Canyon West is at the **airport**, a few hundred yards short of the rim. To reach the Skywalk and other viewpoints, further down the road, you have to join a **bus tour** from here. If you've flown in, some package will already be included in the overall price you've paid; otherwise, all visitors have to

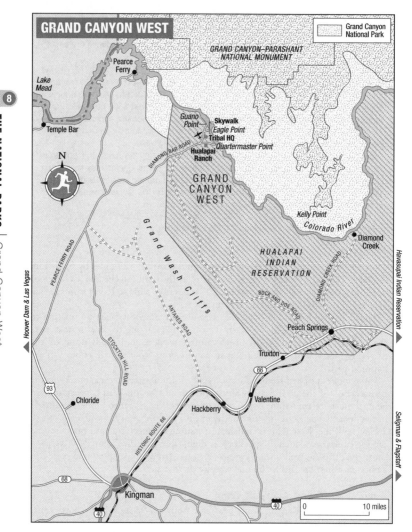

pay an $8 "impact fee", and buy the $30 Hualapai Legacy package, which includes a bus tour to Eagle Point and Guano Point, but not the Skywalk or any food. The Skywalk costs an additional $30; a half-hour horseback ride costs $35 (90min $75); and a helicopter flight down to the river, for a pontoon boat ride, costs $159. A tribal tax adds ten percent to all charges.

The **Skywalk** itself is a short distance from the terminal, at **Eagle Point**. Unveiled in 2007 by astronaut Buzz Aldrin, it's a horseshoe-shaped glass-bottomed walkway that juts out a short way from the rim. Whatever impression the publicity may give, though, it's not on the main canyon rim – and thus not directly above the Colorado River, which is four thousand feet below the rim near this point – but on one rim of a narrow, unnamed side canyon, above a drop of "only" 1200 feet. Supposedly to protect its glass floor, cameras are forbidden on the walkway, so you have to pay an official photographer if you want to capture the big moment.

Across from the Skywalk, the cliff face on the other side of this subsidiary canyon bears an uncanny resemblance to a massive eagle with its wings outstretched. Hualapai **dancers** perform at regular intervals on a stage near the Skywalk, and replica dwellings of the kinds used by various Southwestern tribes stand along a short paved trail.

At the dead end of the road, two miles from the terminal, the unfortunately named **Guano Point** surveys long stretches of the Colorado in both directions. Though the Grand Canyon looks as if it could go on forever, in fact it comes to an end not far beyond the next bend in the river to the west, where it bisects the Grand Wash Cliffs. A small café here serves simple meals.

The Colorado River

No hiking trail connects Grand Canyon West with the Colorado River below, but many visitors take the four-minute helicopter ride down from the terminal. The flight in itself is a major adventure, and it's also a real thrill to find yourself walking down by the river in the depths of the inner gorge.

A short footpath leads down from the landing site to the river's edge, where wooden jetties act as the base for the pontoons and jet boats that sweep visitors out for a quick swirl on the river. The adjoining beach is the terminus for the Hualapai's one-day rafting trips, participants fly out from here.

The Havusupai Reservation

Much less visited than the neighbouring Hualapai reservation, but blessed with magical turquoise waterfalls and deep canyon scenery, the **Havasupai Reservation** offers a total change of pace to Las Vegas. Simply to get there requires a 230-mile drive and an eight-mile hike, so you can only see it on an overnight trip. Even if things have changed a little since a 1930s anthropologist called this "the only spot in the United States where native culture has remained in anything like its pristine condition," it remains a very special place.

Havasu Canyon is a side canyon of the Grand Canyon, 35 miles as the crow flies west of the national park's South Rim. To get here from Las Vegas, follow US-93 southeast from the Hoover Dam to Kingman, Arizona – a total of a hundred miles. Stock up with food, water and petrol, then head northeast for another 57 miles on AZ-66, one of the few surviving stretches of the original cross-country Route 66, before turning left onto Arrowhead Hwy-18. After crossing a further sixty miles of bare sagebrush desert, this reaches a dead end at **Hualapai Hilltop**.

An eight-mile trail zigzags down a bluff from here, leading through the ravishing redrocks of waterless Hualapai Canyon to the village of **SUPAI**. Riding down on horseback with a Havasupai guide costs $70 one way, $120 round-trip, and there's often a helicopter service as well ($85 one way; ☎623/516-2790). Hiking is free, but all visitors pay a $35 entry fee on arrival at Supai. Beyond Supai the trail leads to a succession of spectacular waterfalls, starting with a dramatic and as yet unnamed cascade created by a flash flood in 2008. Beyond that lie **Havasu Falls**, which is great for swimming, and **Mooney Falls**, where a precarious chain-ladder descent leads to another glorious pool.

For all practical details, see the tribe's helpful **website**, ⓦ www.havasupaitribe .com. Supai itself holds the **motel**-like *Havasupai Lodge* (☎928/448-2111; $145 per night), along with a **café**, a **general store** and the only **post office** in the US still to receive its mail by pack train. Further down, and looking rather dilapidated since the latest flood, a **campground** ($17; ☎928/448-2141) stretches between Havasu and Mooney Falls.

Grand Canyon National Park

The **Grand Canyon** remains beyond the grasp of the human imagination. No photograph, no statistics, can prepare you for such vastness. At more than one mile deep, it's an inconceivable abyss; varying between four and eighteen miles wide, it's an endless expanse of bewildering shapes and colours, glaring desert brightness and impenetrable shadow, stark promontories and soaring sandstone pinnacles.

By far the grandest portions of the canyon lie protected within **GRAND CANYON NATIONAL PARK**. The vast majority of visitors come to its **South Rim** – it's much easier to get to, it holds far more facilities (mainly at **Grand Canyon Village**) and it's open year-round. There is another lodge and campground at the **North Rim**, which by virtue of its isolation can be a lot more evocative, but at one thousand feet higher it is usually closed by snow from mid-October until May. Few people visit both rims on a one-way trip; to get from one to the other demands either a tough two-day hike down one side of the canyon and up the other, or a 215-mile drive by road.

Admission to the park, valid for seven days on either rim, is $25 per vehicle or $12 for pedestrians and cyclists.

The South Rim

To reach the **South Rim** from Las Vegas, drive a hundred miles southeast to meet the **I-40** interstate; follow that for 116 miles east, as far as **Williams**; then head north for 56 miles on US-180.

The South Rim area centres on the thirty-mile stretch of the canyon edge that's served by a paved road, and focuses especially on **Grand Canyon Village**, the small community that holds the park's **lodges**, **restaurants** and **visitor centre**. Tourist facilities have been concentrated here ever since the railroad arrived a century ago, while the canyon can be admired from countless vantage points, not only within the village but also along the eight-mile **Hermit Road** to the west and the 23-mile **Desert View Drive** to the east.

The park's main **visitor centre** (daily: May to mid-Oct 7.30am–6pm; mid-Oct to April 8am–5pm; ☎928/638-7888, ⓦwww.nps.gov/grca/), is located close to Mather Point, a good place to get your first glimpse of the canyon itself. Although the village, not far west, is accessible to private vehicles, for most of the year you'll be dependent on the park's free **shuttle buses** to reach the other viewpoints.

South Rim tours from Las Vegas

Airplane tours to the South Rim arrive at the small airport at **Tusayan**, six miles south of the canyon. Both Scenic Airlines (☎702/638-3200 or 1-800/634-6801, ⓦwww.scenic.com) and Grand Canyon Airlines (☎928/638-2359 or 1-866/235-9422, ⓦwww.grandcanyonairlines.com) offer day-trips that include a round-trip flight from Las Vegas plus a bus tour of the South Rim, with prices starting at $190.

It's also possible to do a day-trip from Las Vegas to the South Rim by **bus**, with operators including Papillon (☎702/736-7243 or 1-888/635-7272, ⓦwww.papillon .com). Prices start at $79, but as trips involve a fifteen-hour day and 550 miles of driving, with little more than an hour at the canyon itself, they're not recommended.

Much the best **accommodation** in the village is the magnificent 1905 *El Tovar Hotel* (doubles from $174) and the *Bright Angel Lodge*, which has some great rustic cabins (from $90, rim-side cabins from $110), but even in these and the other "rim-edge" places – the more mundane *Thunderbird* and *Kachina* lodges (both from $170) – very few rooms have actual canyon views. Be sure to make **reservations** (same-day ☏928/638-2631, advance ☏303/297-2757 or 1-888/297-2757, Ⓦwww.grandcanyonlodges.com). All offer plenty of places to **eat**.

The North Rim

Higher, more exposed, and far less accessible than the South Rim, the **NORTH RIM** of the Grand Canyon receives less than a tenth as many visitors. To drive here from Las Vegas, take the **I-15** interstate northeast into Utah; turn east after 131 miles towards Zion National Park (see below); follow Utah Hwy-59 and Arizona Hwy-389 71 miles to Fredonia; and take US-89A for thirty miles to Jacob Lake. As the only road down to the North Rim – the 44-mile Arizona Hwy-67 – is closed by snow in winter, all North Rim tourist facilities, concentrated at **Bright Angel Point**, are only open between mid-May and mid-October.

A cluster of venerable Park Service buildings stand where the main highway reaches the canyon, while a handful of rim-edge roads allow drivers to take their pick from additional lookouts.

Accommodation at *Grand Canyon Lodge* is in cabins and motel-like structures that spread back along the ridge from the lodge entrance, the loveliest of which have canyon views; advance reservations are essential (☏480/337-1320 or 1-877/386-4383, Ⓦwww.grandcanyonlodgenorth.com; rates from $113). The *Lodge* also holds a good **restaurant**.

Zion National Park

With its soaring cliffs, riverine forests and cascading waterfalls, **ZION NATIONAL PARK** is the most conventionally beautiful of Utah's parks. Its centrepiece, the lush oasis of **Zion Canyon**, is a spectacular narrow gorge, echoing with the sound of running water.

Located just 158 miles northeast of Las Vegas, and accessible in under three hours along the I-15 interstate, Zion Canyon makes a superb weekend break from the city. Even the shortest hiking trail within the canyon can escape the crowds, while a day-hike will take you away from the deceptive verdure of the valley and up onto the high-desert tablelands beyond.

Summer is by far the busiest season. That's despite temperatures in excess of 100°F, and violent thunderstorms concentrated especially in August. Ideally, come in spring, to see the flowers bloom, or in autumn, to enjoy the colours along the river. The **admission charge** for Zion, valid in all sections of the park for seven days, is $25 per vehicle, or $12 for motorcyclists, cyclists and pedestrians.

Visiting Zion Canyon

In **Zion Canyon**, mighty walls of Navajo sandstone soar half a mile above the box elders and cottonwoods that line the loping North Fork of the **Virgin River**. The awe of the Mormon settlers who called this "Zion" is reflected in the names of the stupendous slabs of rock along the way – the **Court of the Patriarchs**, the **Great White Throne** and **Angel's Landing**.

Although Hwy-9 remains open to traffic all year, the paved six-mile **Scenic Drive**, which branches north off it, is accessible to private vehicles in winter only.

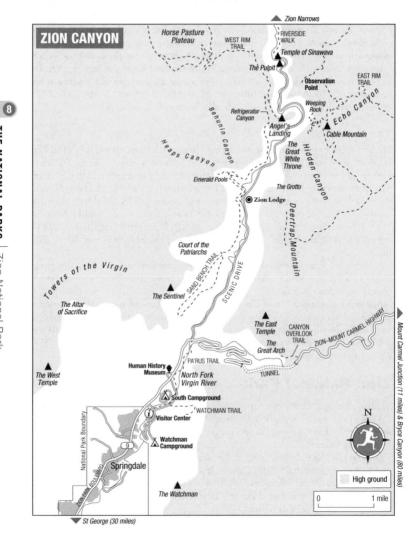

ZION CANYON

Zion Narrows

Horse Pasture Plateau

WEST RIM TRAIL

RIVERSIDE WALK

Temple of Sinawava

The Pulpit

Observation Point

EAST RIM TRAIL

Weeping Rock

Refrigerator Canyon

Behunin Canyon

Echo Canyon

Angel's Landing

Cable Mountain

Heaps Canyon

The Great White Throne

Hidden Canyon

Emerald Pools

The Grotto

Zion Lodge

Deertrap Mountain

Court of the Patriarchs

Towers of the Virgin

SAND BENCH TRAIL

SCENIC DRIVE

The Sentinel

The Altar of Sacrifice

The East Temple

CANYON OVERLOOK TRAIL

ZION–MOUNT CARMEL HIGHWAY

The Great Arch

Mount Carmel Junction (11 miles) & Bryce Canyon (80 miles)

PA'RUS TRAIL

TUNNEL

Human History Museum

North Fork Virgin River

The West Temple

South Campground

WATCHMAN TRAIL

Visitor Center

National Park Boundary

ZION PARK BOULEVARD

9

Watchman Campground

Springdale

N

The Watchman

High ground

0   1 mile

St George (30 miles)

Between late March and October, all visitors, other than guests at *Zion Lodge* (see opposite), have to leave their vehicles either in Springdale (see opposite) or at the large **visitor centre** just inside the park (daily: late May to early Sept 8am–8pm, late April to late May & early Sept to mid-Oct 8am–6pm; mid-Oct to late May 8am–5pm; ☏435/772-3256, ⓦwww.nps.gov/zion/). Free **shuttle buses** run on two separate loops in summer – one between Springdale and the visitor centre, with nine stops en route, and the other between the visitor centre and the end of the Scenic Drive, also with nine stops including *Zion Lodge*.

The Scenic Drive ends at the foot of the **Temple of Sinawava**, beyond which the easy but delightful **Riverside Walk** trail continues another half-mile up the canyon and ends at a sandy little beach. Another undemanding hike leads up to **Weeping Rock**, a straightforward half-hour round-trip from the road to a gorgeous spring-fed garden dangling from a rocky alcove.

From the same trailhead, a mile beyond *Zion Lodge*, a more strenuous and exciting route cuts through narrow **Hidden Canyon**, whose mouth turns into a waterfall after a good rain. Directly across from the lodge a short and fairly flat trail (two-mile round-trip) winds up at the **Emerald Pools**, a series of three clearwater pools, the best (and furthest) of which has a small sandy beach at the foot of a gigantic cliff.

The single best half-day **hike** climbs up to **Angel's Landing**, a narrow ledge of whitish sandstone protruding 1750ft above the canyon floor. Starting on the Emerald Pools route, the trail switchbacks sharply up through cool **Refrigerator Canyon** before emerging on the canyon's west rim; near the end you have to cross a heart-stopping five-foot neck of rock with only a steel cable to protect you from the sheer drops to either side. That round-trip takes a good four hours, but backpackers can continue another twenty miles to the gorgeous Kolob Canyons district.

The high dry plateau above and to the **east** of Zion Canyon, reached by continuing on Hwy-9 at the Scenic Drive turnoff, stands in complete contrast to the lush Virgin River gorge. Its most dramatic sight is the **Great Arch**, best seen from the mile-long **tunnel** via which the highway leaves the park, en route to Bryce.

Zion practicalities

The only **food and lodging** within Zion itself is at *Zion Lodge* (open all year; same-day ☎435/772-7700, reserve through ☎303/297-2757 or 1-888/297-2757, ⓦwww.zionlodge.com; from $159), set amid rolling and well-shaded lawns near the Great White Throne. The terrace of its fine old wooden dining room makes a great lunch stop. Two good **campgrounds**, both charging from $16 per night, are located alongside the visitor centre; the *Watchman* accepts reservations in summer (☎1-877/444-6777, ⓦwww.recreation.gov), while the summer-only *South* is first-come, first-served.

The best alternatives to the in-park lodge are in the appealing small town of **SPRINGDALE**, set among the riverbank cottonwoods half a mile south of the park entrance. **Motels** along Hwy-9, known here as Zion Park Boulevard, include the extremely stylish 🏚 *Desert Pearl Inn*, at no. 707 (☎435/772-8888 or 1-888/828-0898, ⓦwww.desertpearl.com; from $148), which has a great pool, and the somewhat cheaper *Best Western Zion Park Inn*, at no. 1215 (☎435/772-3200 or 1-800/934-7275; ⓦzionparkinn.com; $115), where the spacious rooms have panoramic windows. The 🏚 *Spotted Dog Café*, at no. 428 (☎435/772-3244), is the finest local **restaurant**, while apart from being the liveliest **bar** for miles, the dinner-only *Bit and Spur Saloon*, opposite the *Best Western* at no. 1212 (☎435/772-3498), serves very good Mexican food.

Bryce Canyon National Park

The surface of the earth can hold few weirder-looking spots than **BRYCE CANYON**, an 86-mile drive northeast of Zion. Named for Mormon settler Ebenezer Bryce, who declared that it was "a helluva place to lose a cow," it is not in fact a canyon at all. Along a twenty-mile shelf on the eastern edge of the thickly forested **Paunsaugunt Plateau**, 8000ft above sea level, successive strata of dazzlingly coloured rock have slipped and slid and washed away to leave a menagerie of multihued and contorted stone pinnacles.

In hues of yellow, red and flaming orange, the formations here have been eroded out of the muddy sandstone by a combination of icy winters and summer rains. The top-heavy pinnacles known as **"hoodoos"** form when the harder upper layers of rock stay firm as the lower levels wear away beneath them. **Thor's Hammer**, visible from Sunset Point, is the most alarmingly precarious. These hoodoos look down into technicolour ravines, all far more vivid than the Grand Canyon and much more human in scale. The whole place is at its most inspiring in winter, when the figures stand out from a blanket of snow.

The park approach road runs south from Hwy-12 about twenty miles southeast of the small town of Panguitch; the **entrance fee** is $25 per vehicle, per week. There's a free (summer-only) **shuttle bus** system, but visitors can drive to all the scenic overlooks year round.

Seeing Bryce Canyon

The two most popular viewpoints into **Bryce Amphitheater**, at the heart of the park, are on either side of *Bryce Canyon Lodge*: the more northerly, **Sunrise Point**, is slightly less crowded than **Sunset Point**, where most of the bus tours stop. **Hiking trails** drop abruptly from the rim down into the amphitheatre. One good three-mile trek switchbacks steeply from Sunset Point through the cool 200ft canyons of **Wall Street**, where a pair of 800-year-old fir trees stretch to reach daylight. It then cuts across the surreal landscape into the **Queen's Garden** basin, where the stout likeness of Queen Victoria sits in majestic conde-scension, before climbing back up to Sunrise Point. A dozen trails crisscross the amphitheatre, but it's surprisingly easy to get lost, so don't stray from the marked routes.

Sunrise and Sunset points notwithstanding, the best view at both sunset and dawn (the best time for taking pictures) is from **Bryce Point**, at the southern end of the amphitheatre. From here, you can look down not only at the Bryce Canyon formations but also take in the grand sweep of the whole region, east to the **Henry Mountains** and north to the Escalante range. The park road then climbs another twenty miles south, by way of the intensely coloured **Natural Bridge**, an 85ft rock arch spanning a steep gully, en route to its dead end at **Rainbow Point**.

Practicalities

The **visitor centre**, just past the entrance, carries information on current weather and hiking conditions (daily: May–Sept 8am–8pm; April & Oct 8am–6pm; Nov–March 8am–4.30pm; ☏435/834-5322, ⓦwww.nps.gov/brca). Much the best place to **stay** is the venerable *Bryce Canyon Lodge*, 100 yards from the rim between Sunrise and Sunset points (April–Oct only; ☏435/834-8700 or 1-877/386-4383, ⓦwww.brycecanyonforever.com; from $165), where rustic cabins cost a few dollars more than basic doubles. It also has a **dining room**, a grocery store, a laundry and public showers.

A number of ugly year-round **motels** guard the approach to the park, on and just off Hwy-12, including the large *Ruby's Inn* (☏435/834-5341 or 1-866/866-6616, ⓦwww.rubysinn.com; from $107), and the cheaper *Foster's Motel* (☏435/834-5227, ⓦwww.fostersmotel.com; from $75), both of which have pretty dreadful restaurants. *Ruby's Inn* has its own **campground** ($24), and there are also two first-come, first-served campgrounds within the park ($15): *Sunset Campground*, close to Sunset Point, and *North Campground*, near the visitor centre. To camp below the rim, backpackers require permits from the visitor centre.

Listings

Listings

Accommodation

L as Vegas is the hotel capital of the planet, home to fifteen of the world's twenty largest hotels. The city holds around 165,000 rooms, almost all of them in hotels that also house enormous casinos. The *MGM Grand* alone has five thousand rooms, and the *Venetian/Palazzo* complex over seven thousand, while another twelve casinos boast more than three thousand rooms apiece. All these giants line up along **the Strip**, Las Vegas Boulevard South, though there's a separate concentration of smaller properties **downtown**.

Where to stay

The fundamental choice facing visitors to Las Vegas is whether to stay on the Strip or downtown. The **Strip** is much more glamorous, and home to all the major attractions, restaurants and entertainment. **Downtown** is generally cheaper and more "manageable", on a smaller scale with properties a short walk apart, and has an old-fashioned, less in-your-face atmosphere. Either way, that you'll be staying in a casino is a given; no conventional motels are left either along the Strip or downtown. Some first-time visitors like the idea of basing themselves in a motel elsewhere in the city; such places do exist, but with rates at their current low levels there's absolutely no point in staying in them.

If you opt for the Strip, be warned that not only are the casinos colossal, but they're designed to make it as hard as possible to leave the hotel without having to walk through the whole gaming area. As it can take half an hour to reach the Strip itself from a room in the *MGM Grand* or *Caesars Palace*, it's worth choosing a hotel where you'll be happy to spend most of your time. Obvious factors to consider include the on-site restaurants and entertainment,

the themed attractions, the provisions for children, the pool, and proximity to other places of interest.

For the most part, other than in a handful of top-end properties such as *Wynn*, *Bellagio* and the *Venetian*, the **rooms** themselves are neither more nor less than you'd expect in any standard American hotel chain. Most casinos make only token efforts to match their rooms to their overall "themes"; if you want to know you're in Las Vegas from the moment you open your eyes, *Luxor*, *New York-New York* and *Caesars Palace* offer the most enjoyably themed accommodation.

Room rates

With so much capacity and an uncertain economy, Las Vegas **room rates** are currently lower than they've been for years. Average rates dropped by eighteen percent in 2009 alone, and there are some truly amazing bargains to be had.

The price for every room is in a constant state of flux; each charges a specific rate for each separate night, and when making advance reservations you'll find that the price will repeatedly change. Thus if you stay in the same room for several consecutive nights, you may well pay a different rate for each night; be sure you know exactly what you're letting yourself in for before you book.

Major **factors affecting room rates** include the day of the week; the season; which conventions may be in town; any special events taking place, especially in the hotel or nearby; and the hotel's general level of business. The one surefire way to get a cut-price room is to **visit during the week** rather than the weekend. Rates everywhere rise enormously on Friday or Saturday, so it's not unusual for a room to cost $29 on Tuesday and $149 on Saturday. In general, weekend visitors can expect to pay perhaps $50 extra per night in a lower-end property, and more like $100 extra in the big-name casinos. On top of that, many hotels will only take reservations covering both Friday and Saturday, and won't accept Saturday arrivals. If you're planning a long visit, it's worth considering leaving town over the weekend.

Broadly speaking, you should be able to find a room in a lesser **Strip** casino for under $50 during the week and around $100 on the weekend, while you probably won't get to experience the luxury of *Wynn* or the *Venetian* for less than $175. **Downtown**, it would be unusual to have to pay over $50 for a decent room in midweek – although places like the *Golden Nugget* charge significantly more on weekends – and budget hotels like *El Cortez* come much cheaper than that. The only **hostel** for budget travellers worth recommending, *USA Hostels Las Vegas*, is reviewed on p.124.

Reservations

The easiest way to make a reservation is through each casino's own **website**. Almost all include a rate calendar detailing the available rates for every night in the coming months, and if you're trying to book in a property owned by either of the two main groupings, MGM Resorts International and Harrah's, they'll normally show you rates for all their other properties as well. Look out for **special offers**, such as discounts on longer stays or deals open to users of particular credit cards or motoring organizations. Remarkable recent offers range from a deal that guests who stay two nights at *Aria* or *Vdara* get a free round-trip flight to Las Vegas from anywhere in the US for a repeat stay, to the more banal bonus at the *Hilton* of a $10 per day discount for guests who decline to have their rooms cleaned. You can also get an overview of room rates from the official city website, Ⓦ visitlasvegas.com, or sites like Travelocity and Expedia.

Unless you already have a proven track record, you're unlikely to be offered deals geared towards to serious gamblers, though if you're prepared to commit to betting several thousand dollars – and they *do* check – most casinos will be prepared to offer you a "free" room. Repeat visitors who have joined the various players clubs (see p.153) and wagered significant amounts can expect all sorts of enticements to return.

Resort fees and taxes

The last few years have seen a growing trend for hotels to charge additional **resort fees**, of anything from $1 to $20 per day per room, for services and amenities that were formerly included in the room rates. The usual pretext is that the fees cover **internet access** – which has the spin-off effect of making free wi-fi hard to find (see p.27) – but they're charged whether you use the internet or not. What else is included can vary from day to day, but they may also cover unlimited local or even long-distance calls; a newspaper; bottled water in your room; and use of a fitness centre. None of the **Harrah's** casinos currently charges a resort fee – that's *Bally's, Caesars Palace, Bill's*, the *Flamingo, Harrah's*, the *Imperial Palace, Paris, Planet Hollywood* and the *Rio* – and neither do any of the casinos **downtown**.

In addition, all hotel bills are subject to a **room tax** of twelve percent on the Strip, and thirteen percent downtown.

The Strip

Aria 3730 Las Vegas Blvd S ☎866/359-7757 or 702/590-7111, Ⓦarialasvegas.com. While in keeping with the sophisticated style of the casino downstairs, *Aria*'s chocolate-brown and gold-toned guest rooms feel subdued and somewhat anonymous by Las Vegas standards. High-end amenities include a lavish bath with walk-in shower, huge comfortable beds and wall-mounted flat-screen TVs, though having to use complex electronic controls even to open the curtains of the floor-to-ceiling windows seems counter-productive. Check-in can be chaotic, with individual lines for each desk in the busy public lobby. Weekday rates can make this a real bargain though, especially if you have the time – and the weather – to enjoy the superb pool complex. Sun–Thurs $129, Fri & Sat $259.

Bally's 3645 Las Vegas Blvd S ☎877/603-4390, Ⓦballyslasvegas.com. *Bally's* may once have been the world's largest hotel (as the first *MGM Grand*), but these days it's overshadowed and outclassed by its sister property *Paris* next door, and its many other mighty neighbours. Its central location is a real plus, and the 2816 larger-than-average guest rooms are reasonably well equipped, but it's only worth choosing if you can't find a better rate nearby. Sun–Thurs $59, Fri & Sat $129.

Bellagio 3600 Las Vegas Blvd S ☎888/987-6667 or 702/693-7111, Ⓦbellagio.com. While no longer state-of-the-art, *Bellagio* remains at the top end of the Vegas spectrum. The plush European furnishings and marble bathrooms of its luxurious rooms now give it a slightly retro feel; some face the fountains at the front, others the superb pool complex around the back. The restaurants are among the best in town, and the central location is a plus. Sun–Thurs $129, Fri & Sat $239.

Bill's Gamblin' Hall & Saloon 3595 Las Vegas Blvd S ☎866/245-5745 or 737-2100, Ⓦbillslasvegas .com. The smallest of the Strip casinos is a real throwback, offering a mere 200 large, chintzy guestrooms decked out to recall the San Francisco of a century ago. The rates are not unusually cheap, but it's the only place of this size left, amazing for such a central location. Once you get away from the gloomy public areas, it's all quite cozy, and liable to be heavily oversubscribed at weekends. Guests can use the *Flamingo*'s pool next door. Sun–Thurs $55, Fri & Sat $120.

Caesars Palace 3570 Las Vegas Blvd S ☎866/227-5938, Ⓦcaesarspalace.com. The epitome of Las Vegas luxury ever since the 1960s, *Caesars Palace* matches its newer rivals for both size and amenities. The older rooms still burst with pseudo-Roman splendour – ornate columns, and classical sculptures displayed in wall niches – while those in the newer towers are more conventionally elegant. Although its colossal size can make it a baffling labyrinth to negotiate, the top-class spa, entertainment, pools, restaurants and fantastic shopping at the Forum ranks *Caesars* among the best bets in town. Sun–Thurs $159, Fri & Sat $229.

Circus Circus 2880 Las Vegas Blvd S ☎800/634-3450 or 702/734-0410, Ⓦcircuscircus.com. Only *Excalibur* matches *Circus Circus* for its family appeal and ambience, and both are similarly popular with budget tour groups. With Las Vegas rates generally so low these days, however, *Circus Circus* feels inconveniently far from the main Strip action, and is only really worth it if you're bringing kids to its theme park. Rooms in the motel-like Manor section at the back are pretty grim; pay a little more to stay in one of the Towers instead. Resort fee $5. Sun–Thurs $25, Fri & Sat $60.

Encore Las Vegas 3121 Las Vegas Blvd S ☎888/320-7125 or 702/770-8000, Ⓦencorelasvegas.com. Setting Las Vegas's current standard for high-end luxury, *Encore* ever-so-slightly raised the bar above its adjoining older sister *Wynn* by fractionally increasing the size of its "suites" (in which the wall between the sleeping and living areas does not quite reach the ceiling) and installing even more high-tech controls and flat-screen TVs. Rooms are plush and colourful, though not quite as red as the public areas downstairs, and the pool (sorry, "Beach Club") is the best in town. While *Encore*'s rates broadly match those of its rivals, guests – even big gamblers – can expect fewer freebies and extras than elsewhere. Resort fee $20. Sun–Thurs $186, Fri & Sat $259.

Excalibur 3850 Las Vegas Blvd S ☎877/750-5464 or 702/597-7777, Ⓦexcalibur.com. While the four thousand rooms in this garish fake castle can be very ordinary indeed, the much nicer modernized "wide-screen rooms", typically priced at around $10 extra, are excellent value. Thanks to an endless stream of tour groups and families, the whole place is often uncomfortably crowded; expect long lines at the restaurants. Resort fee $10. Sun–Thurs $24, Fri & Sat $70.

The Flamingo 3555 Las Vegas Blvd S ⊤800/732-2111 or 702/733-3111, ⓦflamingolasvegas.com. Bugsy Siegel's oft-renovated *Flamingo* has dropped well below the top rank of Vegas casinos. The location is great, and so is the tropical-themed pool complex, but the actual accommodation varies enormously; the newer, ultra-pink Go! rooms have real flair, but the standard rooms can be very shabby indeed. Sun–Thurs $50, Fri & Sat $135.

Harrah's 3475 Las Vegas Blvd S ⊤800/214-9110 or 702/369-5000, ⓦharrahsvegas.com. Despite being the flagship location for one of Las Vegas's very major players, *Harrah's* remains resolutely run-of-the-mill. The rooms are generally adequate but strangely dark, and filled with older, old-style visitors lured back by special deals targeted at regular low-rollers. Sun–Thurs $55, Fri & Sat $125.

Imperial Palace 3535 Las Vegas Blvd S ⊤800/351-7400 or 702/731-3311, ⓦimperialpalace.com. Behind its ageing mock-pagoda facade, the *Imperial Palace* is, for travellers happy to forgo Las Vegas luxury, one of the best-value options in the heart of the Strip. Its standard rooms are adequate if not exciting – all have balconies, though, which is quite rare – while the irresistibly bizarre "luv tub" suites, at around $40 extra, offer huge beds, even bigger sunken baths, and mirrors everywhere you can imagine. Sun–Thurs $33, Fri & Sat $90.

Luxor 3900 Las Vegas Blvd S ⊤877/386-4658 or 262-4444, ⓦluxor.com. Spending a night or two in this vast smoked-glass pyramid, even now its Egyptian motifs are vanishing, still counts among the great Las Vegas experiences. All two thousand rooms in the pyramid itself face outwards, with tremendous views, and they're much larger than usual – partly to minimize the effect of the slanting windows, partly because there's space for them to stretch into the hollow interior. Unlike the additional two thousand rooms in the newer tower next door, however – some of which have Jacuzzis next to the windows – most pyramid rooms have showers rather than baths. Resort fee $13. Sun–Thurs $50, Fri & Sat $120.

Mandalay Bay 3950 Las Vegas Blvd S ⊤877/632-7800 or 702/632-7777, ⓦmandalaybay.com. This young-adult playground can feel a little far removed from the bustle of the central Strip, but it has plenty to offer in terms of entertainment and dining as well as its pool. Each of its luxurious rooms has a superb bath and walk-in shower; the vaguely Asiatic theme varies, and the floor plans can be a bit odd, but some have great Strip views. A second 43-storey tower houses the nominally distinct *THEhotel*, which has its own lobby to enable guests to avoid the casino area altogether, and holds around 1100 extremely stylish suites, at broadly similar prices. Resort fee $15. Sun–Thurs $120, Fri & Sat $220.

MGM Grand 3799 Las Vegas Blvd S ⊤877/880-0880 or 891-7777, ⓦmgmgrand.com. Waiting for any kind of service, especially check-in, in this behemoth – 5044 rooms and counting – can be horrendous, but you get a great standard of accommodation for the price. The spacious rooms in the main tower have a fun 1930s Hollywood feel, and come adorned with marble bathrooms and stills from classic MGM movies. In the funkier West Wing, the style is more contemporary, though the rooms are smaller and only have showers. Other bonuses include a fine array of entertain-ment and dining possibilities. Resort fee $10. Sun–Thurs $80, Fri & Sat $180.

The Mirage 3400 Las Vegas Blvd S ⊤800/374-9000 or 702/791-7111, ⓦmirage.com. The glitzy *Mirage* is not the market leader it used to be, and its smallish rooms, now tastefully modernized, are complemented by even smaller bathrooms. The public areas downstairs remain impressive, the pool complex is nicely laid out, and you get to watch the volcano from your bedroom window. Resort fee $15. Sun–Thurs $89, Fri & Sat $175.

Monte Carlo 3770 Las Vegas Blvd S ⊤888/529-4828 or 730-7777, ⓦmontecarlo.com. Despite having over 3000 rooms, the *Monte Carlo* makes little attempt these days at maintaining an identity of its own, positioning itself instead as a quiet, low-key adjunct to neighbouring CityCenter, geared towards comfortably-off older visitors. Its large pool area, complete with wave pool and rafting river, is a boon in summer. Resort fee $6. Sun–Thurs $56, Fri & Sat $130.

New York-New York 3790 Las Vegas Blvd S ☎888/696-9887 or 740/6969, ⓦnynyhotelcasino.com. While not the feast of Manhattan theming it used to be, *New York–New York* remains among the most enjoyable accommodation options on the Strip – and it's small enough that you don't have to spend half your visit shuffling down endless corridors. Although the elevators leave from lobbies designed to resemble specific skyscrapers, the design upstairs varies little. However, the rooms are all very nice, if a bit small (like actual New York hotel rooms). Resort fee $13. Sun–Thurs $60, Fri & Sat $120.

The Palazzo 3325 Las Vegas Blvd S ☎866/263-3001 or 702/607-7777, ⓦpalazzolasvegas.com. At heart, the *Palazzo* is basically an overspill property for its adjoining older sister, the *Venetian*, charging fractionally lower rates for rooms that are all but identical, with split-level "suites" and deep baths. Everything is of an impeccably high standard, but the building itself is much less interesting. Resort fee $17. Sun–Thurs $159, Fri & Sat $229.

Paris 3655 Las Vegas Blvd S ☎877/796-2096 or 877/603-4386, ⓦparislasvegas .com. If not the absolute pinnacle of luxury, standard rooms at the flamboyant French-themed *Paris* are still pretty good, and for location, views and ambience it more than holds its own. The plush new Red Rooms, typically at $40 extra, have an irresistible and exceptionally comfortable Gallic flair. Sun–Thurs $90, Fri & Sat $190.

Planet Hollywood 3667 Las Vegas Blvd S ☎866/919-7472 or 785-5555, ⓦplanet hollywoodresort.com. Some of the nicest mid-rate rooms in town – spacious, with separate bath and shower, and quirkily remodelled with original movie memorabilia. While all lie within easy reach of an elevator, and you don't have to drag your bags through the casino when you check in, they're still an awful long way from the self-park garage though. Sun–Thurs $109, Fri & Sat $219.

The Riviera 2901 Las Vegas Blvd S ☎800/634-3420 or 702/734-5110, ⓦrivierahotel.com. Nothing about the longstanding *Riviera* casino makes it worth staying in one of its two thousand-plus very ordinary rooms. If you do, the newer Monte Carlo and Monaco towers are pricier but preferable to the older main building. Sun–Thurs $30, Fri & Sat $65.

The Sahara 2535 Las Vegas Blvd S ☎866/362-8884 or 702/737-2654, ⓦsaharavegas.com. Despite its consistently low rates, the *Sahara* lacks the location or amenities to appeal to anyone other than diehard NASCAR or roller-coaster enthusiasts. Standard guest rooms look like dull motel rooms, though the superior grade are better value at around $20 more. Resort fee $6. Sun–Thurs $25, Fri & Sat $50.

The Stratosphere 2000 Las Vegas Blvd S ☎800/998-6937 or 702/380-7777, ⓦstratospherehotel.com. Despite its very unfashionable location at the far north end of the Strip, the *Stratosphere* has survived thanks to rock-bottom rates and a steady flow of budget tour groups. No accommodation is in the hundred-storey tower, so don't expect amazing views, just large, plain but good-value rooms, more likely than most to offer last-minute availability or extra discounts on dining or the thrill rides. Resort fee $12. Sun–Thurs $24, Fri & Sat $57.

TI (Treasure Island) 3300 Las Vegas Blvd S ☎800/288-7206 or 702/894-7111, ⓦtreasureisland.com. As yet little altered since its 2009 change of ownership – and thus mingling vestiges of its pirate heyday even as it lures in a new blue-collar clientele – *TI* remains a fun and wonderfully convenient place to stay, even if the rooms are smallish and rather subdued. Resort fee $20. Sun–Thurs $66, Fri & Sat $125.

The Tropicana 3801 Las Vegas Blvd S ☎888/826-8767 or 702/739-2222, ⓦtroplv.com. Redesigned in 2010 with a South Beach/Latin feel, the veteran *Trop* now offers bright, welcoming sunset-toned rooms, huge beds and a fine array of pools. How popular they prove to be, however – and whether the prices remain such good value – will depend on the success of the property's overall makeover. Resort fee $8. Sun–Thurs $69, Fri & Sat $119.

Vdara 2600 W Harmon Ave ☎866/745-7767 or 590-2111, ⓦvdara.com. Aimed especially at business travellers, this hip modern condo-hotel offers a peaceful retreat at the heart of CityCenter, though its much-vaunted lack of a casino hardly seems significant with *Aria* and *Bellagio* just a few steps away to either side. The rooms resemble ultra-modern workspaces, with lots of chrome, glass and black. Other amenities are minimal, with just a small rooftop pool. Resort fee $15. Sun–Thurs $129, Fri & Sat $199.

The Venetian 3355 Las Vegas Blvd S ☎866/659-9643 or 702/414-1000, ⊛venetian.com. The colossal *Venetian* ranks behind only the Wynn properties as the Strip's most luxurious resort. Even its standard rooms are split-level suites, holding decadently comfortable canopied beds on a raised platform, plus marble bath and walk-in shower, and roomy living rooms. As well as a grand rooftop pool complex, a mind-blowing array of shops and restaurants lie within easy walking distance downstairs. The newer Venezia Tower offers even more opulence, plus (with its own check-in desk) a sense of being aloof from the casino bustle; it typically costs from $40 per night extra. Resort fee $17. Sun–Thurs $169, Fri & Sat $239.

Wynn Las Vegas 3131 Las Vegas Blvd S ☎877/321-9966 or 702/770-7000, ⊛wynnlasvegas.com. Ever since the late 1980s, Steve Wynn has defined Las Vegas's highest standard of luxury. *Wynn* (with *Encore*) raises the bar yet higher; its exceptionally large guest rooms (while still rooms rather than suites) boast wonderful beds with fabulous linens (and that extends to the robes and slippers). All have flat-screen TVs in both living areas and bathrooms, which also feature super-sized tubs. Resort fee $20. Sun–Thurs $206, Fri & Sat $259.

Downtown

California Hotel 12 Ogden Ave ☎800/634-6505 or 702/385-1222, ⊛www.thecal.com. Thanks to a long-standing connection with Hawaii, most of the guests in this downtown casino are Hawaiian, and Hawaiian food and drink (not as interesting or flavourful as you might imagine) dominates the bars and restaurants. The actual rooms are plain but adequate. Sun–Thurs $36, Fri & Sat $45.

El Cortez 600 E Fremont St ☎800/634-6703 or 702/385-5200, ⊛ecvegas.com. Veteran downtown casino, transformed by a recent facelift, with cut-price "vintage" rooms in the main building, great-value mini-suites in a newer tower, and the very stylish new Cabana Suites for around $20 extra in a separate building across the street. Sun–Thurs $27, Fri & Sat $60.

Fitzgeralds 301 E Fremont St ☎800/274-5825 or 702/388-2400, ⊛fitzgeraldslasvegas.com. Generic and very central but downtown hotel, where the guestrooms feature standard-issue Holiday Inn decor rather than any locally flavoured glitz, and most offer good views of either the Fremont Street Experience or the desert. There's also a decent pool. Sun–Thurs $29, Fri & Sat $49.

Four Queens 202 E Fremont St ☎800/634-6045 or 702/385-4011, ⊛fourqueens.com. Glittery old-style casino, popular with Vegas veterans, which offers two towers of reasonably tasteful rooms – some of which look right into the Fremont Street Experience – but little by way of diversions. Sun–Thurs $39, Fri & Sat $69.

The Fremont Hotel 200 E Fremont St ☎800/634-6460 or 702/385-3232, ⊛fremontcasino.com. Mid-range, medium-sized casino in the heart of the Fremont Street Experience, with smallish but comfortable rooms and a couple of reasonable restaurants. Sun–Thurs $40, Fri & Sat $80.

The Golden Gate 1 E Fremont St ☎800/426-1906 or 702/385-1906, ⊛goldengatecasino.com. Downtown's oldest joint dates from 1906, when Las Vegas was just a year old. With a hundred retro-furnished rooms – some with flowery windowboxes – it's tiny by Vegas standards, and slightly lower-key than its Fremont Street neighbours. Sun–Thurs $28, Fri & Sat $40.

The Golden Nugget 129 E Fremont St ☎800/846-5336 or 702/385-7111, ⊛goldennugget.com. Still the only downtown casino to make a serious bid for the luxury end of the market, the *Golden Nugget* is undeniably glittery, and has one of the finest pool complexes in town (assuming you feel up to the scrutiny in its goldfish-bowl atmosphere). The rooms are certainly opulent, especially in the newer Rush Tower, but if it's glamour you want it makes more sense to stay on the Strip. Sun–Thurs $49, Fri & Sat $119.

Main Street Station 200 N Main St ☎702/387-1896 or 800/713-8933, ⊛mainstreetcasino.com. This good-value option, two short blocks north of Fremont Street, holds 400 large guestrooms plus a brewpub and an assortment of decent restaurants. Just be sure to request a room on the south side, rather than right next to the freeway. Sun–Thurs $36, Fri & Sat $60.

USA Hostels Las Vegas 1322 E Fremont St ☎702/385-1150 or 1-800/550-8958, ⊛www.usahostels.com. Price-wise, there's no point staying in a hostel in Las Vegas these days, and this former motel is in an inconvenient, somewhat forbidding neighbourhood ten blocks east of downtown. That said, it's much the better of the city's two independent hostels, with dorm beds from $22 and private double rooms from $44.

Rates include free breakfast; cheap dinners are also available. There's also a heated swimming pool. The friendly staff arrange city and national-park tours, as well as a weekly clubbing night.

The rest of the city

Gold Coast 4000 W Flamingo Rd ☎800/331-5334 or 702/367-7111, ⓦ goldcoastcasino.com. The generally Western theme at this old-fashioned locals' casino – at just half a mile west, it's the closest to the Strip – appeals most to older American travellers. While it has nice rooms and good restaurants, the main selling point – unstated, of course – is that the *Rio* and *Palms* casinos, and their fancier facilities (not to mention pricier rooms), are both in easy walking distance, though the Strip itself is too far. Resort fee $3. Sun–Thurs $27, Fri & Sat $59.

Hard Rock Hotel 4455 Paradise Rd ☎800/473-7625, ⓦ hardrockhotel.com. The Hard Rock name has such a high profile worldwide that if you didn't know Las Vegas you might assume that "the world's only rock'n'roll casino" is the best in town; it isn't. Over a mile east of the Strip, it can't match Las Vegas's showcase giants for size or splendour. What it offers is a relatively intimate and even chic alternative, with guest rooms that are well above average, high-class restaurants, a fabulous pool, and of course the odd big-name rock gig. Resort fee $15. Sun–Thurs $79, Fri & Sat $199.

Las Vegas Hilton 3000 Paradise Rd ☎888/732-7117 or 702/732-5111, ⓦ lvhilton.com. The *Hilton* is only a short way off the Strip – and connected to it by Monorail – and its 3000-plus rooms and suites have all the fancy linens and marble trimmings you could ask for. Still, it's a rather sedate property monopolized by conference-goers, and despite the big pool, fun-seeking visitors may feel that they're missing out. At least they don't charge resort fees. Sun–Thurs $79, Fri & Sat $109.

The Orleans 4500 W Tropicana Ave ☎800/675-3267 or 702/365-7111, ⓦ orleanscasino.com. Not a particularly exciting property to begin with, the *Orleans* is at a further disadvantage by being located almost a mile off the Strip. However, the rates are not bad for such well-equipped rooms – many are L-shaped, with inglenook seating by the windows – and it has an on-site bowling alley and cinema. Resort fee $5. Sun–Thurs $29, Fri & Sat $90.

The Palms 4321 W Flamingo Rd ☎866/942-7777 or 702/942-7777, ⓦ palms.com. Although it's still considered among the hippest casinos in town, thanks to some very fancy nightclubs and restaurants and a consistently strong celebrity presence, *The Palms* is in many respects just a presentable but rather dull locals' casino. Thus, while the rooms are very comfortable, you may not feel it's worth paying premium rates for the inconvenient location a mile west of the Strip. Resort fee $1. Sun–Thurs $99, Fri & Sat $199.

The Rio 3700 W Flamingo Rd ☎866/746-7671, ⓦ riolasvegas.com. While not nearly as fashionable as it used to be, *The Rio* still makes a reasonable attempt to rival the Strip giants. The restaurants, bars and buffets are all good, the pool is great, and the rooms are large and luxurious, with floor-to-ceiling windows and great views. But, despite the property's claims to be all-suite, most are not suites – they just have sofas in one corner. And whatever *The Rio* likes to pretend, the Strip stands a good half-mile away, along a highway no one would ever dream of walking. Sun–Thurs $90, Fri & Sat $150.

Sam's Town 5111 Boulder Hwy ☎800/897-8696 or 702/456-7777, ⓦ samstownlv.com. This casino, over six miles east of the Strip, has successfully upgraded its cowboy image, but remains primarily popular with older visitors. The registration desk is in its large central atrium, overlooked on all sides by 650 "Western-themed" guest rooms that aren't nearly as garish as that might sound. There's also a huge caravan park. Resort fee $4.50. Sun–Thurs $27, Fri & Sat $55.

Sunset Station 1301 W Sunset Rd, Henderson ☎800/782-8466 or 702/547-7777, ⓦ sunset station.com. From its Spanish-mission facade to the spacious, well-designed interior, *Sunset Station*, opposite Henderson's huge Galleria Mall, is the quintessential locals' casino. The rooms and pool are good, and you're well poised for an early-morning getaway to Arizona, but it's too far southeast of the Strip to recommend wholeheartedly. Resort fee $15. Sun–Thurs $25, Fri & Sat $60.

Restaurants

T he **restaurant** scene in Las Vegas ranks among the most varied and vibrant in the US. Twenty years ago, the major casinos operated under the assumption that visitors were not prepared to pay for gourmet food, and felt that the longer tourists lingered over their meals, the less time they had left to play the tables. As a result, the only quality restaurants in town were upscale Italian places located well away from the Strip.

These days, however, it's taken for granted that each new casino that opens will hold as many as ten world-class restaurants. The competition to attract culinary superstars has become so fierce that one leading chef, asked what had persuaded him to move to Las Vegas, replied "three million dollars" – though it's worth pointing out that not every celebrity chef whose name stands above the door actually lives in Las Vegas, and Steve Wynn is unique in insisting that his chefs relocate. As a rule, Las Vegas's new breed of gourmet restaurants are a little less expensive than their equivalents in other US cities, and less snootily exclusive.

The downside of all that is that the city's reputation as a haven for cheap eating is no longer deserved. Almost every casino still lays on both a pile-'em-high **buffet**, and a 24-hour **coffee shop/diner**, but prices are not what they were. Buffets tend to charge around $12 for breakfast, $20 for dinner – and the quality in the cheapest can be truly dreadful – while the breakfast special in the coffee shop is much more likely to cost $7.50 than the old-style $1.99.

The latest **recession** has so far changed little. Though a few high-end restaurants have disappeared, and several have made their menus a bit more affordable, as many new ones seem to be opening as ever. There has however been a trend away from expecting visitors to make dining reservations way in advance, in favour of simply hoping to catch their eye once they arrive. Concepts like "designer burgers", novelty diners, and taco or tapas restaurants, more susceptible to spur-of-the-moment impulses, are spreading rapidly. They're still charging premium prices, however, at perhaps $20 per meal for what's often basically fast food.

For anyone staying on the Strip, the choice of restaurants is overwhelming; if you simply feel like eating a particular cuisine, you'll almost certainly find an appropriate and perfectly acceptable option in your own hotel. As it's only possible to review a small proportion of the city's very high number of restaurants in this chapter, the selection inevitably tends towards the higher end of the spectrum.

In terms of price or quality, let alone convenience, there are few reasons to venture off the **Strip**; the best restaurants are right where the tourists are. The one exception to that rule is that certain cuisines have as yet been unable to get a foothold on the Strip; if you want Indian, Thai, or healthy Greek food, for example, you'll have to drive out and find it.

It's usually possible to get a same-day **reservation** for any Las Vegas restaurant; to secure a table for Friday or Saturday night, however, call as far in advance as you can. Guests in the same hotel as a particular restaurant do not get any special priority.

Buffets

In time-honoured Las Vegas fashion, almost every casino offers an all-you-can-eat **buffet**, open to guests and non-guests alike for every meal of the week.

Put simply, the best you can hope for from a buffet, in terms of both flavour and decor, is an experience equivalent to being granted unrestricted access to the food court in an upmarket mall; you'll get high-quality fast food, but not a gourmet feast. The typical buffet offers a broad selection of world cuisines, each available at

Las Vegas Buffets – from the best to the worst

For this book, we sampled every buffet in Las Vegas. Though there's only space here to review the very best, we've ranked them all below in order of preference, with *Wynn Las Vegas* as the best and *More* at *Luxor* as the worst.

Note that a handful of casinos don't have buffets, including *New York-New York*, *Bally's*, the *Venetian*, the *Palazzo* and *Encore*.

Name	Location	Breakfast	Weekend brunch	Lunch	Dinner
Gourmet					
The Buffet	Wynn Las Vegas	$20	$32	$23	$35–39
The Buffet	Aria	$15	$29	$20	$28–36
Le Village	Paris	$16	$25	$18	$25
Studio B	M Resort	$10	$30	$15	$23–30
Carnival World	Rio	$15	$25	$17	$25
The Buffet	Bellagio	$16	$25	$20	$30–37
Worth recommending					
The Buffet	Golden Nugget	$10	$18	$11	$18–21
Cravings	The Mirage	$15	$26	$19	$26
Paradise Buffet	Fremont	$7	$11	$7.50	$13–16
Emperor's Buffet	Imperial Palace	$13	$13	$13	$19
Feast	Sunset Station	$8	$16	$10	$14–19
Adequate					
The Buffet	Monte Carlo	$15	$20	$16	$20–24
Flavors	Harrahs	$15	$21	$16	$22
Spice Market	Planet Hollywood	$15	$23	$19	$28
French Market	Orleans	$7	$14	$9	$14–18
Firelight Buffet	Sam's Town	$6.50	$10.50	$8.50	$11–18
Poor					
Lago Buffet	Caesars Palace	$18	$25	$20	$27
The Buffet	MGM Grand	$14.50	$24–26	$17.50	$26–27
The Buffet	Treasure Island	$14	$22	$16	$22–26
Bayside Buffet	Mandalay Bay	$16	$24	$20	$27
Garden Court	Main St Station	$7	$11	$8	$11–16
Paradise Garden	Flamingo	$14	$21	$17	$22
Bistro Buffet	The Palms	$8	$19	$11	$19
Ports O' Call	Gold Coast	$7	$13	$8.50	$13–18
Circus Buffet	Circus Circus	$10.50	$10.50	$12.50	$13.50
Avoid					
World's Fare	Riviera	$11	$15	$13	–
Round Table	Excalibur	$15	$16	$16	$20
Plates	Stratosphere	$10	$16	$12	$18–22
More	Luxor	$15	$20	$16	$20

the relevant named "station"; a carvery, handing out slices of roast and baked meats; and a certain amount of "action cooking", where a chef prepares a stir-fry, omelette, taco or whatever from your choice of ingredients. Be warned however, that not a single dish in any buffet is likely to meet the standard you'd expect of a reasonably good restaurant, say one that charges $20 or more for an entrée.

In strictly financial terms, the better-value buffets tend to be in **off-Strip** casinos, either downtown or beyond, where they depend on locals as well as tourists, and need to entice diners to drive from elsewhere. By contrast, the buffets at the largest Strip casinos only have to be good enough to ensure that the crowds already in the building don't leave, while also coping with a daily deluge of customers. Hence the poor quality of the buffets at *Excalibur*, *Luxor* and the *MGM Grand*, for example.

If possible, try to avoid eating between 6pm and 9pm, when the queues at the larger casinos can be endless. Arriving early for breakfast (before 8am) and late for lunch (around 2pm or so) can also save time otherwise spent in line. No buffets offer advance reservations, but there's usually some sort of fast-track line, most often for the benefit of favoured gamblers.

As a rule, buffet **prices** include unlimited refills on juices and sodas, but you pay extra for any alcoholic drinks; all are usually delivered by servers rather than being help-yourself. You'll also have to pay tax, and a dollar or two **tip** per person. As most buffets segue seamlessly from breakfast to lunch, and lunch to dinner, you can eat more expensive food at a lower price by arriving just before the change-over. Recent years have seen a growing trend to offer **all-day passes** either to one particular buffet, or to all those within a group of casinos.

Bistro Buffet The Palms, 4321 W Flamingo Rd ☏702/953-7679. Breakfast Mon–Sat 8–10am, $8; lunch Mon–Sat 11am–3pm, $11; brunch Sun 8am–3pm, $19; dinner daily 4–9pm, $19. Belying its bright, stylish setting, the *Palms'* buffet offers a generally poor array of food – the salad choices are particularly bad – and the queues can often be long. It's included here, however, on the sole basis that it features the single tastiest dish of any buffet in the city – the whole barbecued ham hocks are utterly delicious, and the creamed spinach to go with them isn't bad either. If all-you-can-eat ham hocks is your idea of the perfect lunch, you'll be in heaven; if not, don't bother.

The Buffet at Aria Aria, 3730 Las Vegas Blvd S ☏702/590-7111. Breakfast Mon–Fri 7–11am, $15; lunch Mon–Fri 11am–4pm, $20; champagne brunch Sat & Sun 7am–4pm, $29; dinner daily 4–10pm, Sun–Thurs $28, Fri & Sat $36. Although the serving counters feel small compared to the huge dining area – kitted out like a contemporary restaurant, but so bright and large it can't help resembling a canteen – CityCenter's only buffet, upstairs at *Aria*, is a contender for the best in town. Each cuisine is represented by just a couple of dishes, but they're invariably good, and the Indian station, with its fresh-baked naan

bread and tasty curries, is exceptional. The King Crab legs are cut in half, the shrimp are peeled, and assorted sushi includes shrimp nigiri. Salads and desserts alike are exquisite, many prepared in individual shot glasses; in fact courtesy of World Pastry Champion Jean-Philippe Maury, these are the best desserts of any buffet, with a superb Bananas Foster. Weekend dinners include table service of a whole lobster per couple.

The Buffet at Bellagio Bellagio, 3600 Las Vegas Blvd S ☏702/791-7111. Breakfast Mon–Fri 7–11am, $16; brunch Sat & Sun 7am–4pm, $25, or $30 with champagne; lunch Mon–Fri 11am–4pm, $20; dinner daily 4–10pm, Sun–Thurs $30, Fri & Sat $37. Las Vegas's first gourmet buffet, which opened in 1998 charging what were then breathtaking prices, set a standard that subsequent competitors have now surpassed. While it has certainly cut a few corners, there's still a lot to like. Around eight hundred items are prepared fresh in small quantities, and the sheer range of food is impressive. Both lunch and dinner can include sushi, cold cuts, dim sum, green curry duck, coq au vin, roasted salmon and roast lamb with mint sauce, plus fresh-baked focaccia, tasty fruit tarts, and fancy desserts. The large dining area is not especially attractive, but offers spacious seating, and there are even restrooms inside, an astounding innovation.

The Buffet at the Golden Nugget Golden Nugget, 129 E Fremont St ☎702/385-7111. Breakfast Mon–Fri 7–10.30am, $10; champagne brunch Sat & Sun 8am–3.30pm, $18; lunch Mon–Fri 10.30am–3.30pm, $11; dinner daily 3.30–10pm, Mon–Thurs $18, Fri–Sun $21. Downtown's best buffet occupies a plain but bright and spacious room on the *Golden Nugget's* second floor, overlooking the pool complex. The food is wider-ranging than you'll find elsewhere on Fremont Street, especially on the weekend "seafood and more" dinners. Meat entrees like roast beef or Chinese orange chicken are relatively ordinary, but there are unusual dishes like entire roasted heads of garlic or tasty baked catfish. Gentlemen are requested not to wear T-shirts.

The Buffet at Wynn Wynn Las Vegas, 3131 Las Vegas Blvd S ☎702/770-7000. Breakfast Mon–Fri 8am–11pm, $20; brunch Sat & Sun 8am–3.30pm, $32, or $39 with champagne; lunch Mon–Fri 11am–3.30pm, $23; dinner Sun–Thurs 3.30–10pm, $35, Fri & Sat 3.30–10.30pm, $39. Delivering a state-of-the-art buffet being a point of pride for Steve Wynn, it's no surprise that *The Buffet at Wynn* has established itself at the top of the tree. The only snag is that despite prices to match a pretty good restaurant, and although each dish at the serving counter is labelled as though on a gourmet menu – marinated snapper with edamame, five distinct kinds of *ceviche*, and so on – the actual quality is not quite so high. It's the sheer variety that makes it exceptional, with traditional buffet staples like Alaskan crab legs and peeled shrimp prepared to perfection – diners grab phenomenal amounts from the bottomless trays – and some unusual daily specials like baba ganoush or clams in black bean sauce.

Carnival World Buffet Rio, 3700 W Flamingo Rd ☎702/777-7777. Breakfast Mon–Fri 8–11am, $15; champagne brunch Sat & Sun 8am–3.30pm $25; lunch Mon–Fri 11am–3.30pm $17; dinner daily 3.30–10pm $25. Despite prices that match all but the very top tier, this huge buffet enjoys a well-deserved reputation for value that lures bargain-hunting tourists away from the Strip. Little of the food is all that unusual or exceptional – apart from the

juiciest fried chicken in town, and the delicious Bananas Foster dessert – and in fact a lot of it is pretty poor, like the pizzas and corndogs, but it's largely well prepared and presented, and there really is something for everyone, along counters that stretch on forever without any repetition, and range from Thai and Japanese stations (good sushi) to barbecue and fish'n'chips. The only real drawback is that the queues are invariably long.

Cravings The Mirage, 3400 Las Vegas Blvd S ☎702/792-7777. Breakfast daily 7–11am, $15; lunch Mon–Fri 11am–3pm, $19; champagne brunch Sat & Sun 11am–3pm, $26; dinner daily 3–10pm, $26. It may not quite live up to its billing as "the ultimate buffet dining experience," but design-wise the *Mirage* buffet is a stylish reminder that buffets don't have to be boring. The room itself is fabulous, all glitter and sparkle and shiny metal, and the small-scale serving areas do a great job of providing personalized service. Much of the food is cooked to your own order; the rest stands for a few minutes at most. The wide spectrum of offerings includes sushi, stir-fries, dim sum, barbecue, rotisserie chicken and a carvery, plus ice cream and individually prepared salads; dinner sees extra seafood and meat dishes.

Emperor's Buffet Imperial Palace, 3535 Las Vegas Blvd S ☎702/731-3311. Brunch daily 7am–2pm, $13; dinner daily 4–9pm, $19. It would be all too easy to dismiss the *Emperor's Buffet*, tucked away in a dingy passageway on the *Imperial Palace's* third floor, as among Las Vegas's very worst. You couldn't claim the food is good, and it's not even particularly cheap. But the place is nevertheless a real throwback; it's the one unreconstructed, genuinely retro buffet left in the city. With a tiki-hut decor and Hawaiian images that can't have changed in fifty years, it has an irresistible old Vegas charm. It's also the only buffet where you really are expected to help your goddamn self – you get your own coffee, water, condiments, everything, and you might as well do the washing up too, because no one else is going to. There certainly aren't lots of fancy ethnic alternatives, but if you're happy with old-fashioned diner fare it's a much richer experience than the usual bland buffet. And one day soon, no doubt, it'll be gone, and then we'll all be sorry.

Feast Sunset Station, 1301 W Sunset Rd ☎702/547-7777. Breakfast Mon–Fri 8–11.30am, $8; brunch Sat & Sun 8am–4pm, $16; lunch Mon–Thurs 11.30am–4pm, Fri 11.30am–3pm, $10; dinner daily 4–9pm, Sun–Thurs $14, Fri & Sat $19. Locals flock to *Feast*, in the very centre of *Sunset Station*, a ten-mile drive southeast of the Strip, because it epitomizes what the old-style buffet ought to be but never quite is any more on the Strip; a huge, inexpensive array of good-value dishes to suit any taste. Yes, there's some low-quality fast food, like the overcooked burgers stacked in rows, and the dreadful fish'n'chips, but you can easily put together a good meal, with crab salad and raw baby spinach from the salad bar, and, say, sesame chicken from the Asian section, fried chicken from the American, or masala chicken from the Indian. The zestful modern decor is attractive too, with its Southwestern palette of turquoise and orange. Very similar *Feast* buffets can be found in all the casinos of the off-Strip Stations chain.

Paradise Buffet and Café Fremont Hotel, 200 Fremont St ☎702/385-3232. Breakfast Mon–Fri 7–10.30am $7; champagne brunch Sat & Sun 7am–3pm $11; lunch Mon–Fri 11am–3pm $7.50; dinner Sun–Thurs 4–10pm, Fri & Sat 4–11pm, Mon, Wed, Thurs, Sat & Sun $13, Tues & Fri $16. This tropical-themed buffet is a classic slice of old-style downtown Vegas "glamour," compensating for its lack of natural light with glitter, sparkle, splashing water and artificial plants. Unusually, the carvery turkey and beef is actually good, there's some tasty Southern fried chicken, and the shrimp and crab aren't bad either; only the weak salads and run-of-the-mill desserts let the side down. For the pricier "Seafood Fantasy" on Tuesday and Friday evenings, plates are piled high with crabs, lobsters and raw oysters, plus scampi and steamed mussels. Those with smaller appetites can also order à la carte, with dishes aimed at downtown's large Hawaiian contingent such as spam and eggs or "loco moco", a fried egg on a hamburger.

Studio B Buffet M Resort, 12300 Las Vegas Blvd S ☎702/797-1000. Breakfast Mon–Fri 7–10.30am, $10; Lunch Mon–Thurs 11am–4pm, Fri 11am–2.30pm, $15; dinner Mon–Thurs 4–9pm, $23; seafood brunch Sat & Sun 9am–2.30pm; seafood dinner Fri 4–10pm, Sat & Sun 2.30pm–10pm, $30. Ten miles south of *Mandalay Bay* along Las Vegas Blvd, this buffet created a sensation when it opened in 2009. Even though it's now charging much higher prices and you can expect to wait in line for an hour or more, there's still a lot to like. Selections along the all but endless serving counter range from Thai curries and Asian barbecued pork to paella, stuffed vine leaves and all-American mac cheese, and it's all fresh and flavourful. Highlights include the rotisserie chicken, cooked over an open fire, and the huge array of seafood at weekends. Desserts are the real standout, however, with oven-fresh pastries and Italian gelatos. Rates also include unlimited wine and beer, though each drinker has to fetch it in person in a stunningly small glass. The shiny contemporary space has the feel of a TV studio, enhanced by live cooking demonstrations at regular intervals on weekdays, which you can watch close-up or on giant screens.

Le Village Buffet Paris, 3655 Las Vegas Blvd S ☎702/946-7000. Breakfast daily 7–11am, $16; lunch Mon–Fri 11am–3.30pm, $18; champagne brunch Sat & Sun 11am–3.30pm, $25; dinner daily 3.30–10pm, $25. Eschewing the vogue for incorporating every conceivable cuisine, *Paris's* buffet opts instead for exclusively French dishes, and does so extremely well. Although the meat dishes tend to be the best, with roast chicken served fricasseed, as *coq au vin*, or with mustard, along with *duck à l'orange* and a creamy cassoulet of pork and beef, there's also plenty of seafood, from the scallops, shrimp and crab in Sunday's brunch, to the Dover sole and rich *bouillabaisse* midweek. A whole section is devoted to cheesy *raclette* dishes; vegetables such as baby squash and creamed spinach are super-fresh; and there's even a full French cheese board. At busy times, the seating is a little cramped, with the tables squeezed almost like an afterthought into the central square – a very Disney-esque French village – but the food is undeniably *magnifique*.

Restaurants

Mandalay Bay

Aureole ☎702/632-7401, ⓦcharliepalmer.com. **Daily 5.30–10.30pm.** Welcome to wine-lover's heaven, a vision of dazzling white where harnessed "wine angels" swoop around a three-storey "wine tower" that holds ten thousand bottles. Diners use tablet PCs to peruse the online wine list, with prices ranging from $35,000 (for a 1900 Château Mouton Rothschild) down to $38 for an unassuming Oregon pinot gris. New York chef Charlie Palmer's "Progressive American Cuisine" is every bit as impressive. A three-course prix-fixe menu costs $85 or $95 according to whether you dine in the main room or the more private and romantic Swan Court, or you can order à la carte. The specific dishes on offer, all beautifully presented, change frequently, but standouts include the $28 truffled poached chicken supreme, and the $36 seaweed roasted black cod.

Border Grill ☎702/632-7403, ⓦbordergrill.com. **Mon–Fri 11.30am–10pm, Sat & Sun 10am–10pm.** This classy Mexican restaurant at the back of *Mandalay Bay*, run by TV chefs Mary Sue Milliken and Susan Feniger, comes into its own during summer, when tables spread out across an open-air patio towards the spectacular wave pool, but even in winter its high ceilings and light decor give it a spacious feel. Steer clear of the very ordinary *ceviche* for lunch, and focus instead on the tacos ($16–19) and entrees ($16–24). Dinner is more expensive, with pan-seared chicken in pumpkin *mole* sauce at $28 and a 16oz Oaxacan steak for $36, though you can put together a three-course menu for $42.

Hussong's Cantina ☎702/553-0123, ⓦhussongslasvegas.com. **Daily 11am–2am.** The original *Hussong's*, founded over a century ago in Ensenada, Baja California, is the bar that claims to have invented the margarita in 1941. While this first offshoot, in the Mandalay Place shopping mall, serves its own irresistible margaritas, poured by eye and without crushed ice, it's also a restaurant. All the Mexican standards, like a wide array of tacos or the "extreme nachos", are well prepared, but given the chance they'll cook you a fine dinner; whatever white fish they have comes in a blue cornmeal crust with pineapple salsa for $17, and the $5

elote plazero, a grilled white corn cob brushed with cheese, is great value. A trio of *mariachi* musicians perform such south-of-border classics as *Another Brick In The Wall*, and a good time is had by all.

Luxor

Company Kitchen & Pub House ☎702/262-4852. **Mon & Wed–Sat 8pm until late.** A far cry from *Luxor*'s former Egyptian theme, this bistro-turned-pub has a strong contemporary style, its warm earth tones intended to echo a modern Aspen ski chalet. There's little gimmickry about the menu, which ranges from burgers or fish'n'chips at around $15 up to sweet and spicy chipotle salmon for $24 and steaks for $30 or more. Usually, though not invariably, diners can jump the queue for free entry at the neighbouring *LAX* nightclub.

New York–New York

America ☎702/740-6451. **Daily 24hr.** This cavernous diner, tucked in behind the registration desk, derives a retro-chic feel from a large 3-D "map" of the US (measuring 90x20ft) that curls down from the ceiling. Appetizers on the determinedly all-American menu include Wild West potato skins or nachos for around $10, while entrees range from Texan barbecue ribs ($19), via New York pizzas ($12–15), down to a straightforward club sandwich ($13). At any hour of the day or night, you're bound to find something you fancy, and it's all surprisingly good.

Il Fornaio ☎702/650-6500, ⓦilfornaio. com. **Sun–Thurs 7.30am–midnight, Fri & Sat 7.30am–1am.** The nicest place to enjoy the atmosphere of *New York–New York*, offering both a high-ceilinged "indoor" dining room (complete with open kitchen) and terrace seating alongside the casino, this rural-Italian restaurant, staffed by very flirtatious waiters who speak Italian among themselves, is a real joy. Grab a pizza for $13–16, or linger over a full meal, perhaps starting with a $9 tomato and mozzarella or baby spinach salad, followed by seafood linguini ($24), rotisserie chicken ($20) or beef tenderloin ($34). *Il Fornaio* is open for full breakfasts, but its delicious olive breads, pastries and espresso are also sold in the separate deli nearby, close to the hotel's front desk and offering plenty of its own seating.

MGM Grand

Diego ☎702/891-3200. **Sun–Fri 5.30–10pm, Sat 5–10pm.** Both menu and decor at this excellent Mexican restaurant, near the back of the *MGM Grand*, blend Mexican tradition with contemporary design (check out the restrooms for an especially striking combination). The painstakingly prepared food is modelled on home cooking from southern Mexico. Appetizers like guacamole, chicken *empanadas*, and the shrimp and lobster *ceviche* cost $9–13, while entrees include chicken in a delicate red *mole* sauce ($25); and slow-cooked marinated pork ($24). Desserts range from ice-cream sandwiches to Mexican crêpes, and you can even get a margarita popsicle, while they also offer a $34 dinner menu that includes one drink.

Emeril's New Orleans Fish House ☎702/891-7374, ⓦemerils.com. **Daily 11.30am–2.30pm & 5–10pm.** TV chef Emeril Lagasse has given his original Las Vegas outpost a stylish contemporary revamp, but the actual food remains drenched in New Orleans flavour. While Cajun seafood with a modern (but never low-cal) twist is the speciality – there's barbecue shrimp as a $15 appetizer and pecan-crusted redfish as a $35 entree – the menu also includes meat options like pepper-crusted strip steak ($45). If you find the entrees gut-bustingly rich, wait until you see the desserts; but it's all so fabulous you can't help throwing dietary caution to the winds. Reservations are essential in the early evening, but walk-ins can usually be seated immediately at the bar after 9pm.

Grand Wok & Sushi Bar ☎702/891-7433. **Sun–Thurs 11am–10pm, Fri & Sat 11am–1am.** While this makes a great place for a quick pre-show meal, handily located near the Strip with no need to reserve and very reasonable prices, the food is well worth lingering over. Menus range over both Chinese and Japanese dishes, with no attempts at "fusion", and generally the decor is more Japanese, with tasteful features like the "waterfall" that fills one entire wall, flowing over black pebbles. The sushi is excellent – a deep-fried Las Vegas roll, containing crab, salmon, and tuna, costs $15, but most items are under $10 – and so too are Chinese specialities like the $16 Yan Chow fried rice with pork and shrimp.

Nobhill Tavern ☎702/891-7337, ⓦmichaelmina .net. **Sun–Thurs 5.30–10pm, Fri & Sat**

5.30–10.30pm. Formerly refined in the extreme, this earth-toned dining room, occupying a prime location not far off the Strip, has repositioned itself as a more affordable "tavern". San Francisco's Michael Mina, whose namesake seafood restaurant is at *Bellagio*, offers dishes from across his wide repertoire. His signature lobster pot pie, baked in a gleaming copper pan and containing an entire lobster, costs anything up to $95, and there's a $49 tasting menu, but they're complemented by a rota of daily specials that includes fish'n'chips (Wed; $25) and "bangers and mash" (Thurs; $19), and a sublimely incongruous haute-cuisine truffle macaroni cheese for $12.

Rainforest Café ☎702/891-8580, ⓦrainforest cafe.com. Despite belonging to an international chain, this exuberant theme restaurant at the *MGM Grand*'s Strip entrance deserves inclusion here as one of Las Vegas's best options for kids, with decent prices and some of the most fabulously over-the-top decor in town, consisting of a dense jungle filled with huts and waterfalls, giant butterflies and a huge animatronic alligator. How all that running water helps preserve scarce resources is anyone's guess, but at least the food is OK. At breakfast, you can have a fruit plate or eggs Benedict for around $12; later on, there's little for newly converted vegetarian eco-warriors, but you can get a burger for $13, pot roast for $18, or a "primal steak" for $29.

Crystals

Mastro's Ocean Club ☎702/798-7115, ⓦmastrosrestaurants.com. **Sun–Thurs 11am–11pm, Fri & Sat 11am–midnight.** The heavily traditional menu at this steak-and-seafood restaurant, with its clam chowders, shrimp cocktails, lobster tails and bone-in rib-eyes, is in stark contrast to its spectacularly bizarre setting, with the main dining room perched in the "Tree House" high above the Crystals shopping mall (see p.48). Be sure to reserve a table there in advance; otherwise, the food isn't quite thrilling enough to make it worth paying $60 or more per head for dinner in the restaurant's terra-firma piano bar.

Aria

Julian Serrano ☎877/230-2742. **Daily 11am–11pm.** Superb and very stylish tapas restaurant, adjoining *Aria*'s main lobby.

Almost everything comes from different regions of Spain, including the glassware from Segovia and the stylish padded armchairs from Barcelona, as well as ingredients like *pata negra* ham from Extremadura and olive oil from Jaén. As so often with tapas, it sounds inexpensive, at $8–14 per plate, but you can quickly eat $100 worth. In general, the more elaborate the dish, the better; they're unusual without being merely gimmicky. The little balls of cocoa butter filled with chilled *gazpacho* are out of this world, while the avocado *cannelloni* with Scottish salmon and seaweed is exquisite. There are also a few larger entrees, including lamb chops at $28 and paellas, designed to share, at $40 and up. Only the sports TV blaring above the bar strikes a false note, though some people do just drop in for a snack. Good wines start at around $30 by the bottle, or $8 by the glass. A pre-theatre menu, only available if bought with tickets for *Viva Elvis* (see p.151), costs $45.

Silk Road ☎702/590-2800. **Daily 7am–2pm.** This beautiful, futuristic space off the *Vdara* lobby – it looks like an elegant version of a pod from a 1960s sci-fi movie – is only open in daylight hours, so it's always seen at its best, with floor-to-ceiling windows offering outdoor views of the sculptures outside *Aria*. Small portion sizes make it an expensive option, but it's an exquisite experience, all the better for being well removed from any casino action. A full, "Classic American" breakfast costs $22, while à la carte items include three "Morning Sliders", miniature burger-style sandwiches of grilled steak, egg and tomato, and bacon and cheddar, for $15. A $21 set lunch menu changes daily; all the beautifully presented courses are placed on

the table simultaneously. Alternatively, the playful $12 *ahi* bites are irresistible, each of the four stacks or raw minced tuna topped with a tiny fried quail's egg. On Sunday mornings there's a $39 buffet brunch.

Bellagio

Michael Mina ☎702/693-7223, ⊛michaelmina .net. **Mon, Tues, Thurs & Sun 5–9.45pm, Fri & Sat 5–10pm.** This offshoot of the celebrated San Francisco seafood restaurant, in *Bellagio's Conservatory*, is firmly established in Las Vegas's very highest dining echelon, with tasteful, understated decor that matches the exquisite delicacy of the cuisine. The standout appetizer is the $15 black mussel soufflé, while the zestful, $59, phyllo-dusted Dover sole is typical of the entrees. Carnivores can enjoy stuffed Colorado lamb for $49, or a whole roasted foie gras for around $100. A $55 pre-theatre menu is served 5–6pm, and there's also a wholly vegetarian tasting menu at $85.

Noodles ☎702/693-8131. **Daily 11am–2am.** Despite being hidden away behind the *Baccarat* bar and having a lower profile than *Bellagio's* big-name restaurants, this all-purpose Asian eatery is a stylish, high-class affair, kitted out like a postmodern apothecary with display shelves of slender glass jars. The surprisingly inexpensive menu spans Thai, Japanese, Vietnamese and Chinese cuisine, with soup noodles at $13–17, wok-fried noodles $16–21, and similarly priced alternatives such as barbecued pork or duck, and steamed rice or congee. Of the dim sum, served Fri–Sun only (11am–3pm), the $8 *shiu mai* dumplings, packed with minced pork and large pieces of shrimp, and served with a

Casino Coffee Bars

Every Las Vegas casino holds at least one **espresso café**. Most are open long hours, though a few simply take over some other space for a few hours each morning. As you're unlikely to feel like venturing beyond your own hotel for a wake-up java jolt, there's no point reviewing them in detail here.

However, for something a bit different from the Strip's thirty-plus *Starbucks* outlets, it's worth going out of your way to visit the **Jean-Philippe Patisserie** cafés in *Aria* and/or *Bellagio*, which besides coffee offer magnificent European pastries and desserts; the one in *Bellagio* holds a fountain filled with flowing hot chocolate.

Free wi-fi being a very rare commodity along the Strip – see p.27 – the only coffee bars that currently offer it are the *Coffee Bean and Tea Leaf* outlet in the Miracle Mile shops in *Planet Hollywood*, and in the *Venetian*.

searing mustard sauce, are absolutely succulent.

Olives ℡702/693-7223. Daily 11am–2.45pm & 5–10.30pm. Modelled by Todd English and Victor LaPlaca on their Boston original, *Bellagio*'s best-value gourmet restaurant enjoys a lovely terrace setting, facing the Eiffel Tower across the lake. Only a few lucky diners get to sit out there; the rest have to make do with the more formal, elegant dining room indoors. Even if *Olives* is the kind of place that calls a $16 pizza an "individual oven-baked flatbread," and your food is more likely to be arranged vertically than horizontally, the largely Mediterranean menu is uniformly fresh and superb. It's a great spot for lunch, with $12–17 appetizers like tuna or beef carpaccio and slow-braised lamb ribs, pasta dishes like butternut squash tortelli ($17), and specials such as a jumbo lump crab-cake sandwich ($25). Dinner entrees are generally pricier, at up to $50, but at least you get their trademark platter of huge, delicious olives as soon as you sit down.

Planet Hollywood

Koi ℡702/454-4555. Sun–Thurs 5.30–10.30pm, Fri & Sat 5.30–11.30pm. The most successful of *Planet Hollywood*'s determined attempts to lure in A-listers, this Japanese-inspired fusion restaurant, an established celebrity hangout in Hollywood and New York, occupies pride of place on the mezzanine floor, looking across to *Bellagio*'s fountains. With its glamorous Hollywood take on Asian design, not to mention its $14 "saketini" cocktails, it makes a very classy date option. The menu abounds in glossy, faultless modern standards, with lots of sushi and sashimi (costing anything from $7 to $40), plus appetizers like soft shell crab with *ponzu* sauce ($15), and entrees such as miso-bronzed black cod ($25).

Lombardi's Romagna Mia ℡702/731-1755. Sun–Thurs 11am–10pm, Fri & Sat 4–11pm. Dependable, good-value Italian restaurant, with seating both indoors and "outdoors" (under the artificial sky) in the appealing Oasis Square section of the Miracle Mile Shops. *Lombardi's* offers pretty much all things to all comers, whether you fancy a soup or salad for $7–12, a cheap pasta or pizza meal for $12–20, or a gourmet special such as veal *piccata* or sea bass in lemon butter for $20–27. Similarly, tables come with paper tablecloths and crayons, so the

kids can doodle, but a stylish flourish to the service (and bottomless $5 mimosas) ensure that the adults feel catered to as well.

Todai Seafood Buffet ℡702/892-0021, ⦿todai.com. Sun–Thurs 11.30am–2.30pm & 5.30–9.30pm, Sat & Sun 11.30am–2.30pm & 5.30–10pm. Located close to the Merchants Harbor section of the Miracle Mile Shops, *Todai* is one of the very few buffets in Las Vegas that counts as a stand-alone restaurant rather than a casino offshoot. Part of a Californian chain specializing in magnificent all-you-can-eat Japanese spreads, it's seafood heaven, with unlimited sushi and sashimi plus salads, hot entrees, *ramen* and *udon* noodles, and both barbecued and teriyaki meats. Lunch costs $20 Mon–Fri, $22 Sat & Sun, while dinner is $30 Mon–Thurs, $32 Fri–Sun.

Paris

Les Artistes Steakhouse ℡702/967-7999. Daily 5.30–10.30pm. Elegant European-style Art Nouveau grand cafe, set on two levels in the heart of *Paris*, and serving high-quality French steakhouse cuisine. From the mosaics and Monet-inspired upholstery to the graceful double staircase that swirls up toward the Belle Epoque ceiling, the atmosphere is just right. The best of the appetizers is the traditional onion soup ($9); in addition to a full array of steaks and sauces ($35–55), entrees range from halibut ratatouille ($30) to Kurobuta pork shank ($35); and the dessert pastries are out of this world.

Mon Ami Gabi ℡702/944-4224, ⦿monamigabi.com. Mon–Thurs 7–11am, 11.30am–3.45pm, & 4–11pm; Fri 7–11am, 11.30am–3.45pm, & 4pm–midnight; Sat 7am–midnight; Sun 7am–11pm. Las Vegas life doesn't get much better than lunch at *Mon Ami Gabi*, with its open-air seating right on the Strip, facing the *Bellagio* fountains and rendered comfortable by parasols in summer and outdoor heaters in winter. They call it a steakhouse, but the feel is more like a proper French pavement bistro, both outside and in the conservatory-like indoor dining room. As for the menu, it boasts a gloriously authentic onion soup ($9) that's buried so deep in cheese it's almost impossible to find; juicy *moules marinière* (mussels; $11); and thin-cut *steak frites* ($24). The choice expands for dinner, with other steak cuts such as *onglet* ("hanger steak"; $20); oysters or whatever shellfish is in season; and fresh fish entrees. End the meal with a fine, rich French dessert, such as *crêpe suzette* ($6–10).

Caesars Palace

Beijing Noodle No. 9 ☎877/346-4642. **Sun–Thurs 11am–11pm, Fri & Sat 11am–midnight.** Although it pitches itself as a casual noodle shop, *Beijing Noodle No. 9* has perhaps the most delightful and unusual decor of any Las Vegas restaurant. Entered via an avenue comprising six large fish tanks, each holding two hundred Japanese goldfish (for luck), it's a really lovely space, dazzling white and almost dizzying, with white tracery screens that create the feeling of being in an aquarium. The food itself is very good – try the Imperial Seafood Dumplings, each of which contains seafood in a hot chicken broth; the salt and pepper shrimp; or the delicious, very tender beef *chow fun* with flat noodles. With entrees approaching $20 it's more expensive than you'd pay for noodles elsewhere, but "single" portions are very substantial; one each and you've got a good meal. All prices end in nine cents, including a "bird's nest" dessert at $99.09.

Mesa Grill ☎877/346-4642, ⊛mesagrill.com. **Mon–Fri 11am–2.30pm & 5–11pm, Sat & Sun 10.30am–3pm & 5–11pm.** Serving contemporary Southwestern cuisine in a prime location facing the Colosseum doors, Bobby Flay's stylish *Mesa Grill* is a heavyweight addition to *Caesars'* roster of gourmet restaurants. You're in for a flavourful treat; think crunchy cornmeal coatings and sharp chili accents. Appetizers, at $10–16, range from goat cheese *queso fundido* to wild mushroom grits. Entrees are generally $32–48, and include assorted steaks, crusted snappers, and a sumptuous fire-roasted veal chop.

The Palm ☎702/732-7256, ⊛thepalm.com. **Daily 11.30am–11pm.** Classy, upmarket steakhouse, a few steps from the casino floor inside the Forum Shops. Closely modelled on the New York power-dining original, it's festooned with caricatures of local celebrities. The food may not be all that exciting, cooked with a better-safe-than-sorry approach that can make it all pretty heavy, but it's somehow deeply reassuring, and the service is impeccable. At lunchtime, you can get a burger for $13 or a "Business Lunch" of soup or salad and steak for $24; for dinner, choose from various Italian entrees at $24–30, or from 14 different steak options at $42-plus.

Serendipity 3 ☎877/346-4642, **Mon–Thurs 11am–11pm, Fri 11am–midnight, Sat 10am–midnight, Sun 10am–11pm.** Enjoying perhaps the Strip's most prominent location, spreading across a large open-air terrace perched just above the sidewalk outside *Caesars*, this cheerful, colourful diner is an exercise in conspicuous consumption. Its theme – "gigantic portions" – might not seem exceptional in Las Vegas, but the servings truly are gargantuan. The signature frozen hot chocolate soars above a huge sundae dish, while each crouton in the Caesar salad is if not a loaf then at least a roll, the size of your fist. Assuming you can square this level of greed with your conscience – and your relatives – you can treat yourself to a great big meal for under $20, in perfect people-watching territory.

The Mirage

BLT Burger ☎702/792-7888, ⊛bltburger.com. **Sun–Thurs 11am–2am, Fri & Sat 11am–4am.** Celebrity chef Laurent Tourondel's burger restaurant, housed in the *Mirage's* former white tiger enclosure, stays busy late into the night, and makes a convenient stop to grab a high-quality snack. It's not exactly cheap, however, with a "classic" burger priced at $12, or $23 with fries and a beer, and the Kobe beef burger at $17. Be sure to try a shake; the $11 versions are spiked with alcohol.

TI (Treasure Island)

Isla ☎866/286-3809. **Daily 4–10pm.** A lot of people pass quickly through this high-class, good-value Mexican restaurant, pausing for a hasty snack or swift shot, but there's much to savour if you choose to linger. Besides the expected enchiladas and burritos (from $13), chef Richard Sandoval's open kitchen – set through the window of a wall inlaid with blue *azulejo* tiles – serves up imaginative, tasty specialities that range from chicken breast *mole* for $19 up to beef tenderloin for $28. Be sure to sample an appetizer like the trio of crunchy corn masa cakes with different toppings for $8, or the $15 tuna salad. The large tequila bar at the front, open from lunchtime onwards, offers around a hundred varieties by the glass, from $7 up to $40.

Phô at the Coffee Shop ⊤702/894-7111. Sun–Thurs 11am–11.30pm, Fri & Sat 11am–2.30am. If you're looking for a simple, cheap and tasty meal that's a little out of the ordinary, there's no faulting the Strip's only Vietnamese restaurant, which takes over half the space of the *Coffee Shop* at *TI*. The speciality here is hearty bowls of *phô* soup, available in chicken, beef or vegetable flavours for around $15, while rice or vermicelli noodle dishes start at $12.50.

The Venetian

Bouchon ⊤702/414-6200. Mon–Fri 7–10.30am & 5–10pm, Sat & Sun 8am–2pm & 5–10pm. Despite its sky-high reputation and exclusive setting – just off the ornate tenth-floor lobby of the *Venetian*'s Venezia Tower – Thomas Keller's spacious recreation of a classic French bistro (the much smaller original is in Napa Valley) is both friendly and affordable. The interior design is meticulously authentic, but the real joy here is to sit outside on the huge open piazza that spreads beneath the hotel towers. Bouchon's every dish is prepared with perfect precision, and the prices are reasonable by Las Vegas standards, with a delicious French onion soup for $9.75 and a flavourful roast chicken with figs and mushrooms at $29.50. There's also plenty of seafood, like oysters and mussels. Breakfast is a Francophile's dream of croissants, pastries, yogurt and coffee.

Delmonico Steakhouse ⊤702/414-3737, Ⓦemerils.com. Sun–Thurs 11.30am–2pm & 5–10pm, Fri & Sat 11.30am–2pm & 5–10.30pm. Although *Delmonico* is TV chef Emeril Lagasse's Las Vegas version of a classic New Orleans steakhouse, the decor is "modern Tuscan," in deference to the *Venetian*'s Italian roots. Only one of its many dining rooms, equipped with arched ceilings and a fireplace, is at all intimate or appealing; the rest are austere and minimal, and overall it's more refined than Emeril's raucous *Fish House* at the *MGM Grand*. The whole place reeks of money: a humble baked potato costs $9, while several wines hit the $3000 mark. Even the least likely items come swimming in butter – Emeril's not one to stint – but the meat at the core of the experience is excellent, with each large and very tender steak priced at around $50. While there may be just one fish entree, such as a $40 barbecued salmon,

appetizers include pepper-seared ahi tuna at $21 and barbecue shrimp at $18. Lunch consists of smaller, cheaper servings of substantially the same menu.

Tao Asian Bistro ⊤702/388-8338, Ⓦtaolasvegas .com. Sun–Wed 5pm–midnight, Thurs–Sat 5pm–4am. Centred on a 16ft-tall Buddha, this plush, opulent pan-Asian restaurant is a phenomenon. Serving 600,000 dinners a year with an average per-person cost of $70, it has been ranked ever since it opened in 2005 as the highest grossing independent restaurant in the US, with figures double those of its nearest rival. The perennial crowds are attracted by the sheer glitz, buzz and general vibe more than the food, but assuming you have a taste for Chinese, Japanese or Thai cuisine, and don't mind spending $12–18 for an appetizer of dumplings or roast pork, or a plate of noodles, and well over $30 for a meat or fish entrée, you're bound to find something to enjoy. The adjoining *Tao* nightclub is reviewed on p.145.

Zeffirino ⊤702/414-3500. Mon–Sat 11.30am–midnight, Sun 10am–2.30pm & 4pm–midnight. Though purists might not approve of the intrinsic fakery of the *Venetian* branch of this venerable Genoa restaurant, any Las Vegas aficionado just has to love it. It manages to be both very formal, even romantic, with its rich tapestries and curtains and meticulous silver service, but playful, with ornate balconies overlooking the Grand Canal and the songs of the gondoliers wafting up. Typical dinner entrees, such as chickpea-flour shrimp ravioli or grilled swordfish, can be pricey; but there are always some $18 meat or fish specials, while the $20 three-course set lunch (daily except Sun) is exceptional value. Sunday sees a $65 champagne "gourmet brunch," featuring lobsters, oysters and Chateaubriand.

The Palazzo

Dos Caminos Mexican Kitchen ⊤702/577-9600. Mon–Fri 11am–11pm, Sat & Sun 11am–midnight. For flair as well as food, this huge Mexican restaurant – part of a hip New York group – is the pick of the *Palazzo*'s dining options. Beautifully designed in warm bronzes and turquoises with no lack of modern edge – Aztec skulls line one wall, Mexican poster-images are illuminated by neon, and the restrooms lie at the end of a long, mysteriously dark tunnel – it offers a stylish Vegas experience at affordable, New

York prices. The food is authentic and tasty, with inventive twists: at weekends, lunch is replaced by a well-priced, relaxed brunch, designed for lingering, with classy eggs Benedict and tacos from around $13, and frozen prickly pear margaritas to wash them down; dinner, a slightly more elaborate affair, might start with roasted plantain *empanada* ($10) followed by avocado-leaf-crusted big-eye tuna ($25). Whatever you choose, be sure to start with the deliciously creamy, made-to-order guacamole.

Lavo ☎702/791-1800, ⓦlavolv.com. Sun–Thurs 5pm–midnight, Fri & Sat 5pm–1am. Run by the same team as the *Venetian*'s *Tao*, with similar financial success, *Lavo* is a surprising throwback to the days when Italian restaurants were Las Vegas's hippest hangouts, luring (or to be honest, paying) celebrities like Jay-Z to "party" in its dark, soberly decorated dining room and adjoining nightclub. Located alongside the *Palazzo*'s main entrance, with Strip views from some tables, it serves traditional, expensive Italian cuisine. Appetizers like eggplant *parmagiano* or a big bowl of mussels range upwards from $15, pizzas and pastas are largely $20–30, and seafood entrees such as a huge chunk of roasted sea bass cost $30–40. It's all impeccably prepared, though much like *Tao* this is very much a place to come for the glamour rather than just another meal.

Wynn Las Vegas

Red 8 ☎702/770-9966. Sun–Thurs 11.30am–11pm, Fri & Sat 11.30am–1am. Largely open to the casino walkways, but with curtains acting as screens, this airy, relaxed Asian bistro exudes *Wynn Las Vegas*'s trademark fresh take on design. Here it's traditional Chinese restaurant styling that's given a twist, with overstuffed banquettes, slick black tables and naturally, a preponderance of lush, lucky scarlet. The food is traditional Southeast Asian, predominantly Chinese, but with Malaysian and Mongolian thrown in. Subtle, aromatic flavours abound – dim sum ($6–10; daily 11.30am–3pm) includes tasty pan-fried turnip cakes and steamed buns – and you'll also find perfectly executed classics like spicy shredded jellyfish with chicken ($9), barbecued duck or pork ($16), Kung Pao shrimp ($24), potstickers ($9) and all manner of Cantonese noodle dishes.

Encore Las Vegas

Wazuzu ☎702/248-3463. Sun–Thurs 11.30am–10.30pm, Fri & Sat 11.30am–1am. Riffing exuberantly on *Encore*'s trademark red, the decor at this pan-Asian restaurant ranges from a huge dragon composed of ninety thousand gleaming crystals to a brace of giant golden pears. Once past its plush entranceway, however, you'll find it's open to the casino, leaving diners exposed to the comments – and smoke – of passing sightseers. The food itself is consistently good however, whether you go for the dumplings (such as *shu mai*, pork and shrimp, or *har gow*, plump steamed shrimp); the smoky drunken noodles, with onions and Thai basil (chicken or beef $18, shrimp $22), the *Wazuzu* rice bowls (with freshwater eel for example for $18), or $25 entrees like the miso marinated black cod or steamed bass. Sake by the glass starts at $7, wine at $10.

The Sahara

NASCAR Café ☎702/734-7223. Daily 7am–10pm. If you find yourself in the car-mad *Sahara* at all, you're probably here for the NASCAR connection, so this garish sports-themed eatery will be right up your street. Always packed with enthusiastic race fans admiring the memorabilia (especially the centrepiece 34ft "Carzilla," the world's largest stock car), it serves a predictable menu of burgers and barbecue sandwiches for $8–13.

The Stratosphere

Top of the World ☎702/380-7711, ⓦtopofthe worldlv.com. Sun–Thurs 11am–10.30pm, Fri & Sat 11am–11pm. So long as you're happy to settle for good rather than gourmet food, dining at this 106th-floor revolving restaurant is an utterly memorable experience; the view is simply phenomenal. The best time to come is after dark, when the menu – a catch-all mixture of Californian, quasi-Asian and routine American dishes – is more interesting than at lunch, and the lights of the Strip are at their most spectacular. Typical dinner entrees, such as seared organic salmon or prime rib, cost $40–58; be sure to order the miniature chocolate Strato-sphere Tower for dessert ($14). A five-course tasting menu costs $85.

Downtown

Firefly **The Plaza, 1 Main St** ☎702/380-1352, ⊛firefly lv.com. **Sun–Thurs 5–10pm, Fri & Sat 4.30pm–midnight.** Relishing its splendid location, in the glass dome at the front of the (otherwise virtually defunct) *Plaza* that faces straight down Fremont Street, *Firefly* has quickly established itself as downtown's favourite special-occasion restaurant. Not only does it serve great Spanish tapas, but for once it does so at appropriately low prices; almost everything costs under $10, with gazpacho at just $3.50, calamari for $7.50, and a plate of Manchego cheese and Serrano ham for $9. Larger plates are also available, such as half a roasted chicken for $14 and paella for $15, and with an inexpensive selection of fine wines too, what's not to like?

M&M Soul Food **3923 W Charleston Blvd** ☎702/453-7685. **Daily 7am–8pm.** Serving far and away Las Vegas's best soul food, this small, plain diner lies tucked away in a neglected neighbourhood a few blocks west of downtown. Fried chicken is the obvious dish to go for, though they also offer great short ribs; full dinners, with a couple of sides like collard greens and mac cheese, come to well under $20.

Red Sushi **The Golden Nugget, 129 E Fremont St** ☎702/385-7111. **Daily 4–11pm.** Restaurants come and go at the *Golden Nugget* with alarming rapidity; despite the shortage of genuine fine dining downtown, nothing quite seems to catch on. That this sushi restaurant has managed to last is probably because what you see is exactly what you get – the whole place, including the long sushi bar, lies open to the casino. Besides individual rolls from around $7, there's a short menu of entrees like tempura shrimp for $24, and steak and tempura combos for more like $28.

Second Street Grill **The Fremont Hotel, 200 E Fremont St** ☎702/385-3232. **Mon, Thurs & Sun 5–10pm, Fri & Sat 5–11pm.** Downtown's most original fine-dining option, this contemporary "Pacific Rim" restaurant occupies a disappointingly dull wood-panelled room near the *Fremont*'s front door. The influence of consulting Hawaiian master chef Jean Marie Josselin is apparent throughout the pan-Asian menu, which draws heavily on Chinese, Thai and Japanese traditions. Appetizers, costing $13–15, are largely seafood-oriented, including ahi sashimi and crab cakes; of the meat entrees, there are steaks for $25–33 or Chinese duck with blackberry glaze for $23, while a whole wok-fried snapper with ginger is $28.

The rest of the city

Búzio's **Rio, 3700 W Flamingo Rd** ☎702/777-7923. **Wed–Sun 5–11pm.** This smart, deli-like European seafood restaurant is separated by a long stretch of plate-glass window from the *Rio*'s beach-like Voodoo pool, while its other flank is occupied by an open kitchen with counter seating. There's nothing very fancy about the cooking, but it is consistently good; typical fish entrees, at $26–40, include substantial stews like a $29 bouillabaisse with lobster. A six-course tasting menu costs $75.

Capriotti's Sandwich Shop **322 W Sahara Ave** ☎702/474-0229, ⊛capriottis.com. **Mon–Fri 10am–5pm, Sat 11am–5pm.** For a lunchtime bargain, it's worth straying a short distance west of the Strip to this outlet of the popular chain – one of many in the city – which is renowned for its enormous $8–14 deli subs and sandwiches, prepared using fresh ingredients, like turkey roasted on the premises.

Carluccio's Tivoli Gardens **1775 E Tropicana Ave** ☎702/795-3236, ⊛carlucciosvegas.com. **Daily except Mon 4.30–10pm.** This conventional Italian restaurant has an irresistible angle – it was designed by Liberace himself, whose museum used to stand next door. Hence the mirrored lounge and piano-shaped bar, not to mention the incongruity of the entire English pub he shipped over. The menu is wide ranging and consistently rich, with pizzas and chicken dishes at $13–15, and linguini with mussels for $17, but it's hard to resist Liberace's own personal favourite, the $12 baked lasagne.

Gaylord **Rio, 3700 W Flamingo Rd** ☎702/777-7923, ⊛gaylords.com. **Daily 11.30am–2.30pm & 5–11pm.** With its smart setting, fine silverware and formal service, *Gaylord* is much the classiest Indian restaurant in Las Vegas. That's reflected by a combination of prices that start at $30 for the vegetarian option and range up to the $50 "Grand Mogul". Chicken dishes like tikka masala cost around $23, lamb more like $27, and vegetarian sides such as the deliciously cheesy *mattar paneer* around $17. The $12 set lunch menu, available Mon–Thurs only, amounts to little more than an entrée, but Fri–Sun sees a $20 all-you-can-eat champagne brunch.

Marrakech 3900 Paradise Rd ☏702/737-5611. **Daily 5.30–11pm.** All-you-can-eat banquets of rich Moroccan food, costing $40 per person and eaten with your fingers from low-lying tables around which you sit on scattered cushions. The tasty but very meaty couscous and pastry dishes are complemented by some unexpected seafood alternatives, and followed by heavy desserts. The main reason to come is to enjoy the faux-romantic Middle Eastern atmosphere, belly dancers and all; this is definitely not a place for a quick meal on your own.

Mr Lucky's 24/7 Hard Rock Hotel, 4455 Paradise Rd ☏702/693-5000. **Daily 24hr.** With its open kitchen, faux-fur booths and subdued tan-and-cream paint-job, the *Hard Rock*'s 24hr coffeeshop is actually a pretty classy place, and the food is well above average. As well as all the usual breakfast items, they serve burgers, sandwiches, pizzas and pasta dishes for $10–15, a 12-oz steak for $20, and milkshakes or microbrews for $5.

N9ne Steakhouse The Palms, 4321 W Flamingo Rd ☏702/993-9900, ⓦn9negroup.com. **Sun–Thurs 5–10pm, Fri & Sat 5–11pm.** Las Vegas's first outpost of the Chicago steak specialists is just the place to make you feel pampered and special. Its opulent features include a central champagne and caviar bar, a double-sided water wall, a ceiling that changes colour, and a private celebrity dining area with glass walls so the rest of us can peer in. The menu, naturally, centres on steaks – all, from the 12oz filet mignon to the 24oz bone-in rib eye, cost around $40 – but you can also get a Kobe beef burger with fries for $25, plus assorted seafood appetizers and entrees. Be warned it's not going to be cheap; even the vegetable sides cost $10 a throw.

Nobu Hard Rock Hotel, 4455 Paradise Rd ☏702/693-5090, ⓦnobumatsuhisa.com. **Daily 6–11.15pm.** Thronging with affluent Southern Californian would-be hipsters, the *Hard Rock* makes an appropriate setting for this chic, celebrity-thronged restaurant, run by Japanese-Peruvian chef Nobu Matsuhisa (as seen in New York, LA and London). The decor is supremely tasteful, with individual walls of rounded river rocks and seaweed paper; the crowd is very upmarket; and with the temptation to keep ordering yet another morsel the prices tend to rocket before your eyes. The food, though, is exquisite, whether you simply go for the sushi bar, or select from the "special cold dishes" (three tiny oysters for $14, or salmon tartare with caviar at $26). Sushi or sashimi set dinners start at $30, with a "chef's choice" option for $80, or you can leave the whole thing up to the chef for $100 and up.

Oyster Bar Sunset Station, 1301 W Sunset Rd ☏702/547-7777. **Sun–Thurs 11am–10pm, Fri & Sat 11am–11pm.** Pleasant, spacious casino restaurant, sadly a long way off the Strip, that's encased in an undulating "grotto" complete with cascading waterfalls. Dishing out consistently good seafood, it serves up raw oysters or clams at $8 per half-dozen; steamed with clams or New Zealand mussels at $13; or in an Italian *cioppino* stew, a gumbo or roast, with crab, lobster or shrimp, at around $18. For $13 you can also get six oyster shooters, each with a different spirit.

Paymon's Mediterranean Café and Market 4147 S Maryland Parkway at Flamingo ☏702/731-6030, ⓦpaymons.com. **Mon–Thurs 11am–1am, Fri & Sat 11am–3am, Sun 11am–3pm.** This simple but highly recommended Middle Eastern restaurant – much easier to reach if you're heading south rather than north on Maryland – is Las Vegas's best vegetarian option. In most US cities that might make it an "alternative" hangout; here, despite having the university nearby, *Paymon's* is just a popular and extremely affordable (but not very atmospheric) lunchtime rendezvous. The Cretan murals are attractive, the food is tasty and substantial, the service very friendly, and there's even a "hookah lounge" next door. Salads and pita sandwiches cost $8–10, and spinach pie $12, while dips such as hummus or the eggplant-based *baba ganoush* are $6. If you can't make up your mind, a mountainous best-of-everything combination plate is just $12.50. *Paymon's* has another branch in Summerlin at 8380 W Sahara Ave.

Ping Pang Pong Gold Coast, 4000 W Flamingo Rd, ☎702/367-7111. Daily 10am–3pm & 5pm–3am. Las Vegas does have a small Chinatown, a mile or so west of *Treasure Island*, so it makes sense that its best Chinese restaurant is in the closest casino, the otherwise undistinguished *Gold Coast*, just beyond the *Rio*. *Ping Pang Pong* is packed with Chinese customers pretty much around the clock, thanks to the great selection of inexpensive dim sum on the lunchtime trolleys – try the $9 soft-shell crab, wrapped in rice paper – and a full menu of rice, noodle and meat entrees, few of which cost over $13.

Roy's 620 E Flamingo Rd ☎702/691-2053, ⓦroysrestaurant.com. Mon–Thurs 5.30–9.30pm, Fri 5.30–10pm, Sat 5–10pm, Sun 5–9.30pm. Thanks to its off-Strip location – rare indeed in Las Vegas for a big national name – *Roy's* sees far fewer tourists than locals, but for both food and ambience it's every bit the match of the top casino restaurants, with significantly lower prices to boot. Part of a gourmet Hawaiian chain, it serves Asian-inspired fusion cuisine, specializing in fish. A melt-in-your-mouth miso butterfish appetizer costs $12, while entrees featuring Hawaiian

species ($22–32) include lemongrass *opah*, macadamia-nut-crusted *ono*, and the irresistible whole moi or threadfish. Meat-eaters can get steak, veal or lamb for similar prices, while a set meal with a mixed sampler appetizer, meat or fish entree, and dessert, goes for $35. There's another *Roy's* eight miles west of the Strip in residential Summerlin, at 8701 W Charleston Blvd (☎702/838-3620).

Vintner Grill 10100 W Charleston Blvd ☎702/214-5590, ⓦvglasvegas.com. Mon–Thurs 11am–10pm, Fri–Sun 11am–11pm. Located in Summerlin, ten miles west of the Strip, this deliciously light and airy Modern American bistro – all soothing pistachio, cream and silver decor, with comfortable banquettes and scatter cushions indoors and shady patio seating outside – makes a great stop en route to or from Red Rock Canyon. The menu, which changes daily, offers fresh seasonal produce served with sunny Mediterranean flair: think Moroccan-style spring rolls with braised duck, blood orange and preserved lemons or halibut with couscous, spinach and toasted *orzo*. The white bean hummus and lamb *osso bucco* are outstanding, while the wood-fired flatbread pizzas offer a feast of robust flavours. The wine list is also superb. Expect to pay around $20 at lunch, more like $50 in the evening.

Bars, clubs and live music

A s the perfect fuel to turn a dithering gawker into a diehard gambler, **alcohol** is very easy indeed to come by in Las Vegas. If you want a drink in a casino, there's no need to look for a bar; instead, a tray-toting waitress will come and find you. Beers and cocktails are delivered free of charge to anyone hovering near, let alone seated at, the tables and slot machines, and assuming you keep on tipping the waitress, the supply will keep on going around the clock.

All the casinos have at least one actual **bar** as well, located in the heart of the gaming area and invariably packed with cacophonous slot machines; the ones at *Bellagio*, for example, have video poker screens inlaid into their solid marble counters. Customers who are actively gambling can usually get their drinks free. If you're staying at a major casino on the Strip or downtown, you'll have no difficulty finding a place to drink in your hotel. Neither area, however, holds any significant bars other than those attached to casinos. Elsewhere, neighbourhood bars do exist, where you can drink and eat away from the frenzy of the casinos – the most popular local pub chain, *PT's*, has around thirty locations – but very few tourists bother to seek them out. If you're a beer drinker, you might prefer to seek out the various **brewpubs** to be found both in, and away from, the casinos, but don't expect anything special in terms of food, or imagine that you're going to get away from blaring slot machines.

In terms of enjoying a proper night out, however, ordinary run-of-the-mill bars are just a small part of the picture. In the last few years, Las Vegas has witnessed an explosion of nightlife opportunities. The old-fashioned **Las Vegas lounge** has returned in force, both knowingly retro-styled for twenty-something rockers and lovingly recreated for older visitors looking to recapture the quieter but still deliciously decadent flavour of the Rat-Pack era.

What's even more striking is that Las Vegas has become an international **clubbing** capital. No longer are clubbers considered a breed apart from tourists; instead, after casinos like the *Hard Rock* and *Mandalay Bay* paved the way by opening their own successful nightclubs, all their major rivals have followed suit. All the giants, especially *Caesars*, the *Venetian* and the *Wynn* properties, now hold one or more spectacular state-of-the-art clubs, and there's also been a boom in adult-only **poolside** enclaves that reopen at night as fully-fledged clubs. All that said, and thanks in part to phenomenally high prices, especially for table service, the Las Vegas scene remains somewhat skewed towards older punters.

So many entrepreneurs have so much money to throw around in Las Vegas, aiming to please all of the people all of the time, that it's getting all but impossible to pinpoint the differences between bars, lounges, restaurants and nightclubs. The listings below are divided on the basis that you go to a **bar** to drink, whereas you go to a **club** to dance. We've also listed the city's principal **live music** venues. And as for a **lounge**…well, you go to a lounge because you're in Las Vegas.

Bars and lounges

The Strip

The Bar at Times Square New York-New York, 3790 Las Vegas Blvd S ☎702/740-6466. **Daily 24hr, showtime 8pm–2am, cover $10 standing, reserved seating Sun–Thurs $15, Fri & Sat $25.** This rowdy slice of the Big Apple, set in the heart of Central Park, is dominated nightly by twin duelling pianists, who hammer out showtunes and old hits while the capacity crowd sings along at ear-splitting volume.

BB King's Blues Club The Mirage, 3400 Las Vegas Blvd S ☎702/242-5464, ⓦbbkingclubs .com. **Sun–Wed 6.30am–midnight, Thurs–Sat 6.30am–2am.** Although the man himself turns up to play a couple of nights per year, really BB King's is more of a Southern-tinged bar-cum-American restaurant than a downhome juke joint. It has a supper-club atmosphere in the evening, when the house band has a definite tang of Memphis funk.

Blush Wynn Las Vegas, 3131 Las Vegas Blvd S ☎702/770-3633. **Tues–Sat 9pm–4am.** Ultra-cool, ultra-small ultra-lounge that's a popular rendezvous for *Wynn*'s well-heeled glamour-pusses; it would take a hell of a lot of nerve to commandeer the tiny dance floor.

Caramel Bellagio, 3600 Las Vegas Blvd S ☎702/693-8300, ⓦcaramelbar.com. **Daily 5pm–4am.** Exclusive, expensive and formal bar in the heart of *Bellagio*; perhaps a little too small to count as an ultra-lounge, but its opulent couches, marble tables and pricey martinis offer a hip capsule version of the high-roller lifestyle.

🐆 **Cleopatra's Barge Caesars Palace, 3500 Las Vegas Blvd S** ☎702/967-4000. **Daily 8.30pm–3am.** Proving that there's still a place for camp kitsch in modern Las Vegas, the bar alongside this replica Egyptian ship, fronted by a golden figurehead and genuinely afloat in its own little moat at the front of the Appian Way shops, makes a fun stop-off on a night's bar-hopping. On Friday and Saturday nights, dubbed the "Gossy

Lounge", it plays host to British crooner Matt Goss, formerly of Bros.

Gilley's Saloon TI (Treasure Island), 3300 Las Vegas Blvd S ☎702/894-7111, ⓦgilleys lasvegas.com. **Sun–Thurs 11am–2am, Fri & Sat 11am–4am. $10 cover for live bands.** A defiant bastion of blue-collar values on the oh-so-classy Strip, this beer-and-barbecue honky-tonk, staffed by "Gilley Girls" dressed in black bikinis, black Stetsons and black leather chaps, was transplanted to *Treasure Island* from owner Phil Ruffin's demolished *New Frontier* casino. Lots of live country music, plus mechanical bull-riding, country karaoke and line-dancing.

🐆 **Horse-a-Round Bar Circus Circus, 2880 Las Vegas Blvd S** ☎702/734-0410. **Fri & Sat 5pm–1am.** Tiny but truly bizarre, these days open only irregular hours, this perfect replica of a children's merry-go-round, overlooking the clowns and acrobats of *Circus Circus*'s *Midway*, was immortalized by Hunter S. Thompson in *Fear and Loathing In Las Vegas*.

Japonais The Mirage, 3400 Las Vegas Blvd S ☎702/792-7970. **Sun–Thurs 2pm–midnight, Fri & Sat 2pm–2am.** Right in the centre of the casino floor at the *Mirage*, but screened off behind alluring purple drapery, the Asian-styled *Japonais* lounge is a surprisingly pleasant, sophisticated rendezvous for a drink; they also serve a full Japanese menu.

Liquidity Luxor, 3900 Las Vegas Blvd S ☎702/262-4591. **Sun–Thurs 4pm–3am, Fri & Sat 24hr.** Very blue, very modern, water-themed ultra-lounge in the centre of *Luxor*, with waterfalls both real and virtual cascading from the ceiling, and DJs most nights. As well as beer, wine and cocktails, you can pay $300 to have a bottle of absinthe served at your table.

🐆 **Minus5 Ice Lounge Mandalay Bay, 3950 Las Vegas Blvd S** ☎702/632-7714, ⓦminus5experience.com. **Daily 11am–3am. Cover $25, includes 1 drink.** Oddly enough, there's nothing tricksy about the name here; it's minus 5, and it's an ice lounge. What's an ice lounge? It's a lounge where everything – the seats, the bar, the walls and even the glasses – is made of ice. Customers are kitted out in Eskimo-style parkas and furry hoods, the better to savour frozen margaritas and the like.

Nine Fine Irishmen New York-New York, 3790 Las Vegas Blvd S ☎702/740-6463, ⓦwww .ninefineirishmen.com. Daily 11am–3am. Cover $5 Wed & Thurs, $10 Fri & Sat. The affinity between New York and all things Irish finds expression in this two-storey wood-panelled pub, shipped over from Ireland and featuring live Irish musicians, singers and dancers nightly. There's some outdoor seating – a real rarity – and they serve pretty good pub grub, from Colcannon soup and shepherd's pie to lobster and crab pot pie.

Parasol Up, Parasol Down Wynn Las Vegas, 3131 Las Vegas Blvd S ☎702/770-7000. Sun–Thurs 11am–4am, Fri & Sat 11am–5am. Matching pair of see-and-be-seen bars, decked out in *Wynn's* signature psychedelic palette and facing the Lake of Dreams; *Up* is at the top of the central staircase, while *Down*, at the bottom, offers additional outdoor seating that's very much in demand. Trademark cocktails, including one actually called "Lake of Dreams" (with pear sake and lychee liqueur) cost around $10.

The Pub Monte Carlo, 3770 Las Vegas Blvd S ☎702/730-7777. Sun–Thurs 11am–11pm, Fri & Sat 11am–3am. This massive bar isn't bad for an early-evening drink – even if it has quietly abandoned any pretence of actually making its own beer – but from 9pm onwards it turns into a deafening retro dance club, usually showcasing low-grade rock bands. And even if it is located on the "Street of Dreams", don't even dream of eating here.

Red Square Mandalay Bay, 3950 Las Vegas Blvd S ☎702/632-7407. Sun–Thurs 4pm–1am, Fri & Sat 4pm–2am. Although *Red Square* is a decent fine-dining Russian restaurant – if steaks and Stroganoffs and caviar are your thing – the best way to sample its uniquely post-Communist brand of decadence is to drop in for a drink or two from the world's largest selection of vodkas. The plush velvet booths are lined with peeling propaganda posters, there's a truncated statue of Lenin outside (see if you can find its missing head), and you can even borrow a mink coat to visit the freezing private vodka vault;

best of the lot, the main bar is topped with solid ice, to keep your glass cool.

Revolution Lounge The Mirage, 3400 Las Vegas Blvd S ☎702/692-8300, ⓦthebeatlesrevolutionlounge.com. Daily except Tues 10pm–4am. Cover varies. Of course there's something a bit silly about the claim that this ultra-lounge truly reflects an artistic collaboration between the Beatles and the Cirque du Soleil; get past the pretension, though, and you can enjoy the psychedelic lightshow and fab 1960s decor, with DJ sets most nights, and live music of all kinds. The *Abbey Road Lounge*, separated from the casino only by giant L-O-V-E letters, is open from noon daily.

Seahorse Lounge Caesars Palace, 3500 Las Vegas Blvd S ☎702/731-7110. Daily 8.30pm–3am. A good old-fashioned Las Vegas lounge, decked out with leopard-skin carpeting and statues of mermaids and seahorses, in the heart of *Caesars Palace*.

Smokin' Hot Aces The Venetian, 3355 Las Vegas Blvd S ☎702/541-8700, ⓦsmokinhotaces.com. Daily 5pm–4am. The Gallic element at this French rock'n'roll bar, in prime position on the upper-level walkway from the Strip bridge into the *Venetian*, is thankfully confined to the decadent red-velvet decor, leaving the bar itself to rock out with karaoke, a well-stocked jukebox, pool and regular live bands.

Tabú MGM Grand, 3799 Las Vegas Blvd S ☎702/891-7183. Sun & Mon 10pm–4am, Fri & Sat 10pm–5am. Cover men $20, women $10. In Las Vegas's original ultra-lounge, not only do go-go girls dance on the tables, but the tables themselves respond to touch by dancing with swirling colours. Expert and beautiful staff mix any cocktail, while, despite the lack of a proper dance floor, *Tabù* hosts regular themed DJ nights.

V Bar The Venetian, 3355 Las Vegas Blvd S ☎702/740-6433. Daily 5pm–4am. The minimalist Oriental styling in this understated, grown-up bar, near the restaurants towards the back of the *Venetian*, is tempered with warm auspicious reds, and glamorous waitresses glide around dressed in slinky slips. Happy Hour until 8pm daily; an espresso martini certainly kicks off the evening nicely.

Downtown

Chicago Brewing Co The Four Queens, 202 E Fremont St ☎702/924-5222. Daily 11.30am–1.30pm. The best microbrewed beers in town, from the dark, German-style Old Town Brown to the American Pale Rider, plus deep-dish Chicago pizzas – and, some might say unfortunately, a cigar bar.

Sidebar 201 N Third St ☎702/259-9700, ⓦside barlv.com. Mon–Thurs 3pm–midnight, Fri & Sat 3pm–2am. Where the suave sophisticates of downtown Las Vegas – assuming there are any, maybe it's just visitors who like to play the part – go to unwind over a few leisurely martinis.

Triple 7 Restaurant & MicroBrewery Main Street Station, 200 N Main St ☎702/386-4442. Daily 11am–7am. The service at this roomy, high-ceilinged downtown brewpub can be slow, but the beers are great, the food tasty (as well as pizzas, burgers and ribs, they sell shrimp in vast quantities), and there's often live entertainment as well.

The rest of the city

Crown and Anchor 1350 E Tropicana Ave ☎702/739-8676, ⓦwww.crownandanchorlv .com. Daily 24hr. Counterfeit English pub in the University District, with mock-Tudor decor and an often raucous frat-boy atmosphere. Lots of European beers on draught (Newcastle, Stella, Tetley's, etc), plus a pool table, quiz nights, English soccer games on the TV, and free wifi.

Double Down Saloon 4640 Paradise Rd ☎702/791-5775, ⓦwww.doubledownsaloon .com. Daily 24hr. Cool, dark, post-apocalyptic bar on the edge of the University District; furnished from thrift stores and daubed with psychedelic scrawlings, it's home to the bacon martini. When obscure live bands aren't playing, the fabulously eclectic jukebox surely is.

Gaudí Bar Sunset Station, 1301 W Sunset Rd, Henderson ☎702/547-7777. Daily 24hr. By far the weirdest and most wonderful casino lounge in Las Vegas. *Sunset Station* claims to "have left no tile unbroken" to create this billowing mosaic-encrusted toadstool of a tribute to sublimely surreal Spanish architect Gaudí, complete with faux-sky underbelly and best appreciated with the aid of a $5 speciality martini.

Ghostbar The Palms, 4321 W Flamingo Rd ☎702/942-6832, ⓦghostbar.com. Daily 8pm–dawn. Cover Sun–Thurs $10, Fri & Sat $20. The lack of a dancefloor and the low volume of the (largely hip-hop) music mean that this ultra-lounge on what the *Palms* calls its 55th storey can't quite be considered a nightclub, but it's nevertheless a major celeb hangout. Thirtysomething hipsters wait in line to pay the cover charge, then venture out to enjoy the views from its cantilevered open-air deck, which has a terrifying, vertigo-inducing plexiglass floor.

VooDoo Lounge The Rio, 3700 W Flamingo Rd ☎702/777-8000. Daily 5pm–3am. Cover $10 and up. Though many years have passed since the 51st-floor *VooDoo Lounge* was Las Vegas's hottest bar, tourists and locals alike still happily wait in line to experience its super-cool atmosphere and the amazing Strip views from its outdoor terrace. Inside, the purple-tinted windows make it hard to see out, but most of the self-consciously beautiful crowd prefer to admire their own reflections anyway. The ersatz New Orleans voodoo-themed decor, and the "mixologists" diligently setting cocktails aflame, add to the ambience. There's DJ music most nights, and the food is pretty good too. No T-shirts or sneakers.

Clubs

The **clubbing** scene in Las Vegas is these days very much dominated by the mega-clubs in the giant casinos, with behemoths like the Wynn properties and *Caesars* rivalled only by the *Palms* to the west and the *Hard Rock* to the east. Even along the Strip, many of the biggest and most popular clubs have been developed and run by two main conglomerations: the **Light Group**, whose stable includes *The Bank* in *Bellagio*, *Haze* in *Aria*, and *Jet* in the *Mirage*, and **Pure**, responsible for *Pure* itself in *Caesars Palace* as well as *LAX* in the *Luxor*, and *Christian Audigier* at *TI*.

Although in theory all clubs impose some sort of **cover charge**, as listed below, who exactly pays what on any given evening is all but impossible to unravel. For a start, prices often depend on the whim of the doorman and the level of action inside. In general, all-women parties tend to pay less or nothing at all, while women in mixed groups are often charged the same as men.

That's entertainment

From the very earliest days of the Strip, Las Vegas set out to establish itself as the entertainment capital of the world. In the 1960s, when Frank Sinatra and the Rat Pack shot Ocean's 11 by day before singing the night away at the Sands, it briefly became the hippest city on the planet. Later on it was more of an elephant's graveyard, where declining mega-stars were put out to pasture. Now, in the post-ironic 21st century, the big names are flocking back.

Rat Packers Dean Martin, Joey Bishop and Frank Sinatra ▲

The court jester from Kà ▼

The Rat Pack rule

During the 1950s, the paying power of Las Vegas's Mob-backed casinos was enough to secure the services of all America's leading performers. Beneficiaries included **Liberace**, who received $50,000 to open the *Riviera* in 1955, and **Ronald Reagan**, who graced the *New Frontier* in 1954.

The three pivotal members of the legendary **Rat Pack** were **Frank Sinatra**, who debuted at the *Desert Inn* in 1951; **Sammy Davis Jr**, whose family became the first black audience members on the Strip at the *New Frontier* in 1955; and **Dean Martin**, who first appeared solo at the *Sands* in 1957. After teaming up at the *Sands* in January 1960, during the filming of *Ocean's 11*, they performed together for years to come.

When **Howard Hughes** bought the *Sands* in 1967, Sinatra moved to *Caesars Palace* for a princely $100,000 per week. *Caesars'* heyday as a Rat-Pack hangout ended when Sinatra and the hotel's executive vice president exchanged blows while discussing a baccarat debt, but he was lured back in 1974, under the slogan "The Noblest Roman has returned". Sinatra made his final bow at the *MGM Grand* in 1994.

Today's top 7 shows

▶▶ **Best blue show** *Blue Man Group* p.148
▶▶ **Best Broadway musical** *Jersey Boys* p.149
▶▶ **Best comedy** *Terry Fator* p.151
▶▶ **Best magic show** *Mac King* p.150
▶▶ **Best musical show** *Love* p.150
▶▶ **Best production show** *Kà* p.149
▶▶ **Best showbiz show** *Jubilee!* p.149

Return of the headliner

Performing in Las Vegas had stopped being cool by the time that Elvis died; perhaps artists were earning so much from their recordings that performing night after night didn't seem worth the hassle. A few dependable names have kept going – Tom Jones, Engelbert Humperdinck, Wayne Newton – but the days of the headliner seem to be over.

In any case, it takes more than ticket sales to be a Las Vegas headliner. The bottom line is about who will bring in not just concert crowds, but more importantly, gamblers who will lose big money while they're in town. One statistic that you don't often hear is that the average Las Vegas visitor is **50 years old**. Headliners have to appeal to the older demographic, which is also the segment most likely to be tempted to gamble.

In the last few years – and it does seem to tie in with the global slump in record sales – a new generation of stars has embarked on the kind of marathon Vegas stints thought to be a thing of the past. *Caesars Palace* paved the way in 2003, building the 4000-seat Colosseum theatre for **Celine Dion**, who made around $100 million from her appearances here (and nowhere else) between 2003 and 2007. Divas who subsequently alternated in her place, including **Cher**, **Bette Midler** and **Elton John**, are expected to reappear, while Dion herself has signed up again until 2013. Elsewhere, **Prince** had a long-term gig at the *Rio*, while Steve Wynn lured **Garth Brooks** out of retirement to perform at *Encore*. Neil Diamond is also set to announce a residency in *Caesars Palace*, while rumours as to new acts have centred on Madonna, supposedly offered $1 billion for a five-year stint in 2010.

▲ The Blue Man Group

▼ Tom Jones performing at the *MGM Grand*

▼ Celine Dion live in Vegas

Elvis

More than fifty years after he first appeared in the city, **Elvis Presley** remains synonymous with Las Vegas, his iconic jump-suited, karate-kicking image still a defining presence. The young Elvis made his Vegas debut in 1956, as the "Atomic Powered Singer" at the *New Frontier*. He bombed abysmally. When he returned in 1963, however, to film **Viva Las Vegas**, he gave the city its enduring theme song. On screen, racing driver Elvis married co-star Ann-Margret; in real life, he wed Priscilla at the *Aladdin* in 1967.

When he took to the stage at the new *International Hotel* in July 1969, Elvis had barely performed live since entering the Army in 1958. In his eight-year run at what soon became the *Hilton*, Elvis sold out 837 consecutive shows, appearing in front of 2.5 million people. Typical ticket prices were under $20, though fans tipped hundreds more for front-row seating. A bronze statue in the lobby now commemorates the King's achievement, while his manager **Colonel Tom Parker** continued to live, and lose vast amounts of money thanks to his gambling addiction, at the *Hilton* until 1985.

Elvis weds Priscilla Beaulieu at the *Aladdin* in 1967 ▲

Viva Elvis at Aria ▼

Elvis impersonator at the Imperial Palace ▼

Remembering Elvis

▸▸ **The Cirque du Soleil's** *Viva Elvis* **show at** *Aria* p.151
▸▸ **The King's Ransom Museum in the** *Imperial Palace* p.63
▸▸ **Catch "Big Elvis" in** *Bill's Gamblin' Hall* p.61
▸▸ **Get married at the Graceland wedding chapel** p.168
▸▸ *Legends in Concert* at *Harrah's* p.149

All kinds of free passes, or paid-for **VIP passes** that enable customers to jump queues or reach privileged areas, are given away or sold by the casinos, the clubs themselves, and freelance "promoters", and many end up in the hands of agencies or even on eBay. In addition, you can usually avoid paying the cover charge by agreeing to **bottle service** at your own table – just be warned that a straightforward bottle of vodka can cost up to $1000, so it's hardly a cheap alternative.

The Bank Bellagio, 3600 Las Vegas Blvd S ☎702/693-8300, ⓦlightgroup.com. Thurs–Sun 10.30pm–4am. Cover $30. Enormous, in-your-face *Bellagio* nightclub where "status is everything". Everything is gold and black, and the updating of the former *Light* space resulted in yet more private areas for VIP bottle service, rising in multiple-levels around the dance floor.

Eve Crystals, 3720 Las Vegas Blvd S ☎702/227-3838. ⓦevethenightclub.com. Wed–Sat 10pm–5am. Cover $20–40. This relatively small, chic nightclub, just a step or two up from an ultra lounge, benefits from definite feminine touches, courtesy presumably of nominal host Eva Longoria Parker. It attracts an older crowd, happy to pay premium prices for bottle service. Go-go dancers gyrate at each corner of the dance floor, which has giant video screens all around; the actual music played varies enormously.

Haze Aria, 3730 Las Vegas Blvd S ☎702/693-8300, ⓦlightgroup.com. Thurs–Sat 10.30pm–4am. Cover $20–40. *Aria*'s showpiece nightclub is a colossal, futuristic affair, with a high-tech "light wall" and huge mechanical contraptions dangling above the surprisingly small dance floor.

LAX Luxor, 3900 Las Vegas Blvd S ☎702/262-4529, ⓦlaxthenightclub.com. Wed, Fri & Sat 10pm–5am. Cover men $30, women $20. What better way for *Luxor* to lure in A-listers than to open an outpost of Hollywood's hot *LAX* nightclub? Spread over two storeys, and part-owned by Christina Aguilera, it goes for an opulent, opera-house ambience; with so much attention devoted to the VIP tables, however, ordinary punters can expect both to wait in line a long time, and to feel squashed into random corners, once they do get in.

Pure Caesars Palace, 3570 Las Vegas Blvd S ☎702/731-7873, ⓦpurethe nightclub.com. Tues & Thurs–Sun 10pm–4am. Cover $20–50. Ordinary clubbers can wait three hours or more to get into the massively popular *Pure*, but with four separate clubbing areas, each with its own DJs and dancefloor, there's usually enough space

inside not to feel crowded. Be sure to ride the glass elevator to the top level, for a drink on the huge open-air Strip-view terrace.

Rain The Palms, 4321 W Flamingo Rd ☎702/940-7246, ⓦrainatthepalms.com. Fri & Sat 11pm–4am. Cover $20–50. This glitzy, water-themed dance club has long ranked among the hottest celebrity hangouts in town, thanks to its fabulous decor – fountains of water and fire – huge dancefloor, frequent DJ spots from Paul Oakenfold, and plush, private VIP areas. When it's warm enough, the action spreads into the outdoors area around the pool. Expect to wait an hour or more to be allowed in. No shorts or sneakers.

Studio 54 MGM Grand, 3799 Las Vegas Blvd S ☎702/891-7254, ⓦstudio54lv.com. Tues–Sat 10pm–4am. Cover men $20, women $10–20. This three-storey, four-dancefloor recreation of New York's legendary *Studio 54*, complete with surly doormen, reopened (at least in name) at the *MGM Grand* back in 1997. A separate upstairs locals' room ensures that it's not totally dominated by tourists.

Surrender Encore Beach Club, Encore, 3121 Las Vegas Blvd S ☎702/770-3300, ⓦsurrendernightclub.com. Thurs–Sat 10pm Cover men $30, women $20. They like to think of *Encore*'s adult-only pool as a club all day as well, but it's after dark that things really hot up, with DJs playing poolside, pole dancers cavorting, and drinks prices soaring upwards like skyrockets.

Tao The Venetian, 3355 Las Vegas Blvd S ☎702/388-8588, ⓦtaolasvegas.com. Thurs–Sat 10pm–5am. Cover Thurs & Fri $20, Sat $40. The *Venetian* ran through a quickfire succession of nightclubs before hitting a winning formula with *Tao*, right at the front on the first floor. The decor is extremely opulent, and very Asian-influenced, with lots of glowing golden Buddhas, and it attracts very big names indeed, with Paris Hilton hosting some nights, Mary J Blige performing at parties, and so on. Queues form early at weekends – dominated by very big-spending Californians – and not everyone gets in. A rooftop pool section, *Tao Beach*, opens in summer, only, while the expensive *Tao Asian Bistro*, reviewed on p.136, is next door.

Tryst Wynn Las Vegas, 3131 Las Vegas Blvd S ☎702/770-3375. Thurs–Sun 10pm–4am; cover varies. Very plush, very expensive nightclub

– you won't enjoy it unless you have a private table you can retreat to, and you won't get in at all if you're not dressed up and looking the part – with an indoor/outdoor dancefloor that ranges out onto a patio facing the waterfall of the Lake of Dreams.

Live music

As for **live music** in Las Vegas, a select handful of international names such as **Garth Brooks**, **Celine Dion** and **Elton John** still dip in long-term headliner stints. Casual visitors, however, are much more likely to see whoever happens to be passing through at the time they visit; the city's biggest venues are major stops for touring acts.

Almost all the biggest gigs in town take place in the casino theatres, almost none of which has a particularly consistent booking policy or is worth visiting in its own right. Thus the *MGM Grand* is home to the 750-seat *Hollywood Theatre*, which plays host to a succession of typically one- or two-week engagements by the likes of Tom Jones (tickets usually cost in the region of $70–100), but can also open up the 16,000-seat *Grand Garden* for stars like the Rolling Stones (tickets up to $400). Away from the casinos, a few stadium acts still appear at the University of Nevada's huge, dreary Thomas & Mack Center (☎702/739-3267, ⓦunlvtickets.com),

House of Blues Mandalay Bay, 3950 Las Vegas Blvd S ☎702/632-7600, ⓦhob.com. Happy to play host to this outpost of the national live-music chain, *Mandalay Bay* leaves the *House of Blues* to chart its own voodoo-tinged, folk-art-decorated course. Capable of holding audiences of up to 1800, it has a definite but far from exclusive emphasis toward blues, R&B and the like. Typical prices range from around $35 for B-list names up to $100 for stars like Aretha Franklin. There's also a weekly gospel brunch (Sun 10am & 1pm; $37).

The Joint Hard Rock Hotel, 4455 Paradise Rd ☎702/693-5066, ⓦthejointlasvegas.com. The *Hard Rock* lavished $60 million in 2009 on entirely rebuilding *The Joint* – only the name remains of its predecessor – which now holds four thousand in air-conditioned comfort, with a sloping floor to let everyone see the band. It remains the venue of choice for big-name touring rock acts, not least because its affluent baby-boomer profile enables bands like Aerosmith to charge $200 a throw. Tickets to see the likes of the

Rolling Stones can go for over $1000, but more typical admission for performers such as Carlos Santana ranges between $50 and $150.

Pearl Theater The Palms, 4321 W Flamingo Rd ☎866/942-7777 or 702/942-7777, ⓦpalmspearl.com. Capable of holding 2500, but with a much more intimate feel than that would suggest, and featuring superb acoustics and technology, the *Pearl* has established itself as Las Vegas's best live-rock venue. Typically low ticket prices start at, say, $25 for Vampire Weekend, or $59 for Norah Jones.

The Railhead Boulder Station, 4111 Boulder Hwy ☎702/547-5300, ⓦboulderstation.com. Daily 24hr. Cover typically $25–60 on weekends. Set in an ordinary locals' casino, *The Railhead* is a sizeable and appealing 24hr lounge, where the big stage welcomes not only country names like Merle Haggard, but also soul, R&B and reggae acts, with a cover charge for gigs of anything from $25 to $60.

Shows

L ive entertainment remains a crucial component of the Las Vegas package, and it's nothing like as cheesy and kitsch as first-time visitors might imagine. Only one of the old-style showgirls-and-ostrich-feathers revues is still running – *Jubilee!*, now so outdated it feels like a cherished period-piece – and the scene is dominated instead by the arty Canadian-based circus/theatre troupe, **Cirque du Soleil**. Twenty years since they first overturned Las Vegas attitudes with the stunning *Mystère*, they now have half a dozen major production shows in the city, with more on the way, including a much-vaunted Michael Jackson project. Cirque remains the biggest ticket around; if you leave without seeing them you'll have missed part of what defines modern Vegas.

The success of Cirque marks part of a larger trend, in which big-name stars have been supplanted by ensemble pieces, like Broadway shows (which tend to run for three or four years at most), or the Blue Men, anonymous beneath their latex masks. While a handful of veteran **comedians** still have their own shows, like Rita Rudner, George Wallace and Carrot Top, **magicians** have been vanishing at an alarming rate (recent casualties include Lance Burton and Steve Wyrick) and **singer-impressionists** too now seem to be an endangered species.

For the story of Las Vegas's greatest **headliners**, from Elvis and the Rat Pack to Celine Dion and beyond, plus a rundown of the very best shows currently playing, see the *That's Entertainment* colour insert.

Tickets and discounts

All of Las Vegas's larger shows – including the big-name headliners as well as most of the production shows reviewed here, like the Cirque du Soleil spectaculars and the Broadway musicals – take place in theatres where your ticket is for a specific **numbered seat**. Only the smaller casino showrooms, the kind that may offer several different shows each day, now have un-numbered seats. The old custom of discreetly tipping the *maitre-d* to be given a good seat has all but disappeared.

Across the board, the average **ticket price** is in theory around $74. In practice, everyone seems to be paying different rates, or even not paying at all. Many casinos offer free or discounted show tickets to their guests, most often as two-for-ones or as part of room-and-entertainment packages, and many also give tickets to gamblers who reach a certain level of play. Some simply distribute discount coupons to passers-by.

The only way to be sure of getting tickets for a specific show is to reserve well in advance. If you're happy to take whatever's available, however, head for one of the various **discount ticket outlets** that have proliferated in recent years, which usually offer between 25 and fifty percent off prices for same-day tickets (plus a booking fee). The two main outlets are **Tix4tonight** (☎877/849-4868; Ⓦtix4tonight.com), which has around a dozen locations on the Strip including the Fashion Show Mall, the Showcase Mall, *Bill's Gamblin' Hall* and *Circus Circus*; and the near-namesake **Vegas Tix4less** (☎866/742-0784; Ⓦvegastix4less.com), located in the Showcase Mall, the Harmon Theater at *Planet Hollywood* and *O'Sheas* casino adjoining the *Flamingo*.

As the recession bites ever harder, every single show has had to discount its prices one way or another – look for special deals on the websites.

Shows

Amazing Johnathan Harmon Theater, Miracle Mile Shops, Planet Hollywood, 3667 Las Vegas Blvd S ☎702/836-0833, Ⓦharmontheater.com. Tues–Sat 9pm; $59 & $69. Stressing the Amazing Johnathan's unbridled craziness, the advertising and pre-show build-up here might lead you to expect a crude late-night gross-out. In fact, barring the cartoonish violence he directs against his ditzy blonde assistant "Psychic Tanya," Johnathan's quite a lovable character. He's basically a comedy magician, with the emphasis on the comedy, meaning that he barely completes a trick all evening. That's probably for the best, anyway, as carefully honed patter and skits like "Bad Karate Theater" make this one of Las Vegas's funniest shows.

Blue Man Group The Venetian, 3355 Las Vegas Blvd S ☎1-866/641-7469, Ⓦwww.blueman .com. Daily 7pm & 10pm; $65–149. The Blue Man Group has lasted well over ten years on the Strip where so many other shows – ones with stars, plots and even words – have failed within months. And how have they done it? By the synchronized eating of breakfast cereal; by performing live endoscopies on audience members; by catching marshmallows tossed across the stage in their mouths. In fact, although (very funny) deadpan humour is a major component – and there's little choice but to be deadpan when you're coated in blue latex and don't speak a word – two further elements keep the crowds happy. First is the exhilarating music, which besides pieces set to the Sex Pistols and Jefferson Airplane, also includes lots of meaty drumming on industrial tubing from the Men themselves; and second is some truly stunning digital trickery. Although it's not (quite) for everyone, kids seem to love its essential silliness just as much as adults.

Crazy Horse Paris MGM Grand, 3799 Las Vegas Blvd S ☎866/740-7711, Ⓦwww.mgmgrand .com/crazyhorseparis. Daily except Tues 8pm & 10.30pm, all shows over-21s only. $50.50 & $60.50. Considering that Crazy Horse likes to think of itself as the latest thing in nude cabaret, it feels oddly like a silent movie or Victorian parlour game. The small stage plays host to a succession of static, self-consciously "arty" tableaux, in which not-very-naked women sing breathy songs about "paroxysmes d'érotisme" and the like, to be met by polite applause from an audience who can be heard muttering about the high ticket prices during each plodding scene change. As so often, the best feature is the comedy interlude, in which the Quiddlers present "Micro Jackson."

Gordie Brown The Golden Nugget, 129 E Fremont St ☎866/946-5336, Ⓦgordiebrown .com. Tues–Sat 8pm. $33–71.50. From the moment the curtain rises in the unexciting showroom, revealing a five-piece band ready to follow his every cue, this energetic Canadian singer-comedian-impressionist has the audience roaring. Some of his targets are getting very tired – Forrest Gump, Jimmy Stewart, Neil Diamond – and his intricate mix of script and ad-libs is often lost in the general hullabaloo, but Brown's infectious enthusiasm makes this downtown's best live show. He specializes in quick-fire duos, like a fight between Ozzy Osbourne and Bob Dylan, or Elton John coping with a drunk Billy Joel. And it never hurts to use Elvis to bring things to a crescendo.

Human Nature Human Nature Theater, Imperial Palace, 3535 Las Vegas Blvd S ☎702/794-7361, Ⓦhumannaturelasvegas.com. Daily except Fri 7.30pm, $55 & $66. The full title of this unlikely smash-hit show really does tell it all: "Smokey Robinson Presents Australia's

Human Nature In The Ultimate Celebration Of The Motown Sound". When this Aussie vocal quartet bounds on stage, they acknowledge upfront that you probably won't have heard of them (despite a twenty-year string of their own hits back home), and that four fresh-faced, clean-cut, and above all white Aussies singing Motown in Vegas makes a pretty odd fit. And then, quite simply, they blow your socks off, with good old-fashioned panache and hard work, plus the aid of a hot six-piece band. From fierce stompers to sweet acapella numbers, it's much more than pastiche, and the audience laps it up. Smokey Robinson having lent his name and provided a brief video introduction, the group saves his songs for last, with *Ooh Baby Baby* as a real tour de force.

The Improv Harrah's, 3475 Las Vegas Blvd S ☎702/369-5000, ⊛harrahslasvegas.com. Daily except Mon 8.30pm & 10.30pm. $29 or $45. Chicago's famous Improv has been at *Harrah's* since 1996, just up the stairs inside the main entrance. The formula remains the same, with three polished stand-ups per show rather than free-for-all improvisation. Big-name TV comedians make regular appearances, so the standard of talent is dependably high.

Jersey Boys The Palazzo, 3325 Las Vegas Blvd S ☎702/414-9000, ⊛jerseyboysvegas.com. Mon, Thurs, Fri & Sun 7pm; Tues & Sat 6.30pm & 9.30pm. $72–160. Unusually for a Broadway show, which would normally be truncated to suit restless Las Vegas audiences, Jersey Boys plays its full length at the *Palazzo* – there's simply so much material to cover, in what's a genuine emotional narrative rather than simply a vehicle for the songs of *Frankie Valli and the Four Seasons*. It lasts 2hr 20min (including a "short break", counted down minute by minute on big screens), with each segment featuring a distinct "season" in the band's career, narrated by a different member. The whole thing is hugely enjoyable, with quick-fire wise-guy repartee (along with plenty of what they call "authentic Jersey language") and lightning-fast staging. Above all, the music is irresistible, with an amazing raft of songs like *My Eyes Adored You*, *Sherry*, and *Can't Take My Eyes Off You*.

Jubilee! Bally's, 3645 Las Vegas Blvd S ☎877/374-7469, ⊛ballyslasvegas.com. Daily except Fri 7.30pm & 10.30pm (topless); $73–93. If you've never been to a Las Vegas show, *Jubilee!* is probably what you think they're all like. In fact, it's the only survivor of the old tits'n'tassles tradition left in the city, a lumbering great thing that after its first few jaw-dropping moments – just how bad is this going to be? – can't help but grow on you. The music may be abominable, while the stunts amount either to things rising up from below the stage, or mirrors making it look like there are more things than there really are, but if you're finally tiring of cutting-edge postmodernism, nothing beats the sheer camp of Samson in a studded thong, tearing down a temple or two with his bare hands. Roman soldiers in leather codpieces cavort with Arabian-Nights maidens across the stage, thirty dancing showgirls quick-change from turquoise pantsuits to huge ostrich-feather extravaganzas, and for a finale they even raise the *Titanic*. Diehard devotees who want to see how it's all done can join behind-the-scenes tours on Mon, Wed & Sat at 11am, for $15.

Kà MGM Grand, 3799 Las Vegas Blvd S ☎702/769-9999, ⊛www.cirquedusoleil.com. Tues–Sat 7pm & 9.30pm. $69–150. With so many superb Cirque du Soleil productions running in Las Vegas, it's somehow easy to overlook *Kà*. For anyone interested in theatre, however, it's an absolute must-see. The most expensive theatrical production ever staged, anywhere, it boasts a quite extraordinary set; the stage floor not only rises, but can swivel and pivot in every direction. At one moment, it can turn into a steep cliff-face to which the performers cling for dear life; at the next, they may simply fall, mid-battle, into the abyss below. *Kà* is much more plot-driven than other Cirque shows, telling a complex saga about two Asian twins separated by enemy kidnappers, so although it's still basically a succession of truly breathtaking set-pieces, there's more scope for darkness and emotional impact as opposed to the usual whimsy.

Legends in Concert Harrah's, 3475 Las Vegas Blvd S ☎702/794-3261, ⊛legendsinconcert .com. Mon 6.30pm, Tues & Thurs–Sun 7.30pm & 10pm. $59 and $69, including two drinks. The older of the Strip's two long-running celebrity-tribute shows – the other, *American Superstars*, is at the *Stratosphere* – is also the better, with a changing roster of star impersonators ranging from Christina

Aguilera to Elton John. It's a quick-fire revue in which each cast member performs as just one star, with no lip-synching but plenty of showgirls in flamboyant costumes. Check online to see who exactly is appearing each night – for musical prowess, vocal groups like the Four Tops or Temptations are the best – but you can depend on a tongue-in-cheek Elvis to clown through *Viva Las Vegas* for a fitting finale.

Love The Mirage, 3400 Las Vegas Blvd S ⊤702/792-7777, ⓦcirquedusoleil.com. Daily except Tues & Wed 7pm & 9.30pm. $94–150. In case you missed the headlines when *Love* opened, back in 2006, this is the "Beatles-meets-Cirque du Soleil" show, in which Cirque do their stuff to a soundtrack of remixed Beatles music. Having lost previous headliners Siegfried and Roy to a wayward white tiger, the Mirage gambled $100 million on putting together two more giants of entertainment – and it was money well spent. Performed in an auditorium that's intimate at some moments and exuberantly all-embracing at others, *Love* is nostalgic and visionary in equal measures. It celebrates the Beatles' achievement while skilfully avoiding anything too literal – the actors don't play the roles of specific Beatles, and although characters from their songs appear, they evoke the general mood rather than act out the lyrics. The costumes, lighting and staging are all magnificent, and some of the set-pieces, as you'd expect from Cirque, are astonishing. When all's said and done, it's a dance show more than anything else, but if that might normally put you off, don't let it. For anyone with memories of the music, or the era, or anyone who's been influenced by it – so anyone at all, basically – it's an irresistible evening.

Mac King Harrah's, 3475 Las Vegas Blvd S ⊤702/369-5222, ⓦmackingshow.com. Tues–Sat 1 & 3pm; $25. Magician Mac King's afternoon show represents one of Las Vegas's best entertainment bargains. Hailing from Kentucky (he even has a sponsorship deal with KFC), Mac's an endearingly wide-eyed innocent in a plaid suit, who specializes in good old close-up magic, using ropes, cards, torn-up $20 bills and the like. His corny patter leaves plenty of room for good-natured improvised gags at the expense of those unwary audience members he lures up on stage.

Mystère Treasure Island, 3300 Las Vegas Blvd S ⊤702/894-7722, ⓦwww.cirquedusoleil.com. Sat–Wed 7pm & 9.30pm; $60–109. When it first signed a ten-year contract with *Treasure Island* in 1993, Canada's Cirque du Soleil was widely seen as being too "way-out" for Las Vegas. In fact, *Mystère* proved to be the perfect postmodern product for the Strip; its success redefined the city's approach to entertainment, making Cirque the Las Vegas standard rather than the exception. Almost wordless, *Mystère* is all things to all people, ensuring audience involvement with a clever pre-show and further participation throughout. At base it's a showcase of fabulous circus skills, with tumblers, acrobats, trapeze artists, pole climbers, clowns and a couple of amazing strong men. Unless you read the programme, you might not even realize there's a plot – something about two hungry babies of different species at opposite ends of the universe. Regardless, *Mystère* is such a visual feast – from the gloriously colourful costumes and fantastic animals to the fleeting glimpse of a devil-like creature stalking beneath the stage – with so much more going on than you could ever hope to follow, that it barely matters.

O Bellagio, 3600 Las Vegas Blvd S ⊤702/796-9999, ⓦcirquedusoleil.com. Wed–Sun 7.30pm & 10pm. $94–150. Though in terms of sheer expense and extravagance, this Cirque du Soleil extravaganza has long since been topped by their more recent productions, it remains a remarkable testament to what can be done when cost is barely an issue. The name *O* is a pun on the French for "water," and any part of the stage in this purpose-built theatre can at any time be submerged to any depth; one moment a performer may walk across a particular spot, the next someone may dive headfirst into that same spot from the high wire. With even less of a plot than *Mystère*, *O* is never portentous; from its beaming synchronized swimmers onwards, the cast simply revel in the oppor-tunity to display their magnificent skills to maximum advantage. Highlights include a colossal trapeze frame draped like a pirate ship and crewed by a fearless assortment of acrobats and divers, and footmen flying through the air in swirls of velvet drapery.

Penn & Teller Samba Theatre, The Rio, 3700 W Flamingo Rd ⊤888/746-7784, ⓦpennandteller .com. Nightly except Fri 9pm; $75 & $85.

Having previously established themselves as alternative, even iconoclastic magicians, Penn & Teller are now several years into a *Rio* residency that they "don't like to think of as a typical Las Vegas show." Which begs the question, given that they're charging Las Vegas prices, what is it then? While their habit of deconstructing classic magic tricks to show how they're done is interesting, it's hardly electrifying. They do perform a number of set-piece stunts undeniably well, but the pacing of the show is frankly rather flat, and Penn Jillette's endless patter, when not truculent, seems merely complacent. If you're a fan already, you'll probably love them; if not, don't bother.

Phantom of the Opera The Venetian, 3355 Las Vegas Blvd S ☎702/414-9000, ⊛phantomlasvegas.com. Mon & Sat 7pm & 9.30pm, Tues–Fri 7pm. $69–158. Back in 2006, the *Venetian* spent around $30 million replacing its short-lived Guggenheim Las Vegas museum with an 1800-seat theatre, modelled on the Opera Garnier in Paris, which showcases a shortened (95 minutes, down from the original 150), no-intermission version of Andrew Lloyd Webber's warhorse of a musical. No songs were cut, the special effects outdo anything on Broadway, the show's still going strong – everyone's a winner.

Le Rêve Wynn Las Vegas, 3131 Las Vegas Blvd S ☎888/320-7110, ⊛wynnlasvegas.com. Fri–Tues 7pm & 9.30pm. $99–195. Steve Wynn's eponymous hotel was originally going to be called *Le Rêve*, and this extravagant water-themed show has been integral to the property from the beginning. Focusing on acrobatic stunts and audience intimacy, it was originally put together by former Cirque du Soleil impresario Franco Dragone, and its look and feel will seem familiar to Cirque fans. Even so, *Le Rêve* acquits itself well in comparison to *O*: the staging is even more spectacular, it's funnier and sexier, and it has more of a coherent, and even moving narrative. On the down side, the acrobatic skills aren't quite as breathtaking or the set-pieces as sustained, and there's also that nagging feeling that all that postmodern cavorting looks that bit less original each time around.

Terry Fator & His Cast Of Thousands The Mirage, 3400 Las Vegas Blvd S ☎702/792-7777, ⊛terryfator.com. Tues–Sat 7.30pm; $59–129. If you saw Terry Fator win America's Got

Talent in 2007, you'll know what to expect of this amazing ventriloquist impressionist – and understand how he's so quickly become a major Las Vegas headliner. If you didn't, you're in for a huge and very enjoyable surprise. The man is quite extraordinary; while manipulating animal puppets, he delivers note-perfect imitations of anyone from Marvin Gaye and Roy Orbison to Gary Numan and Gnarls Barkley – without moving his lips. His sheer glee at the recent upturn in his fortunes – prior to his TV success, he was performing in tiny venues and county fairs – gives him a huge rapport with his similarly enthusiastic audiences, and even if his humour is hardly cutting-edge, it is at least funny.

Tournament of Kings Excalibur, 3850 Las Vegas Blvd S ☎702/597-7600, ⊛excalibur.com. Mon, Wed & Fri–Sun 6pm & 8.30pm; Tues & Thurs 8.30pm. $57, including dinner. You can depend on *Excalibur* to know which side its bread is buttered; if the kids are happy, then everyone's happy. This feast of mock-medieval slapstick, centred on a jousting match between a bad black knight and a good white knight, is accompanied by a great deal of tumbling, acrobatics and hell-raising audience participation, plus the chance to devour a Cornish game hen without the benefit of silverware. It's top-notch family fun, though clearly more directed at the younger set.

V – The Ultimate Variety Show Miracle Mile Shops, Planet Hollywood, 3667 Las Vegas Blvd S ☎866/932-1818, ⊛vtheshow.com. Daily 7pm & 8.30pm. $50, or $70 with dinner. This old-fashioned but enjoyable revue show gives half a dozen variety acts – who tend to be comedians, jugglers, strong men and the like, rather than singers – around ten minutes each to prove their worth. Seating is unreserved, so arrive early to get a decent view – you won't want to miss quick-fire Mexican juggler Wally Eastwood playing the piano with his balls, or the hilarious Russ Merlin.

Viva Elvis Aria, 3730 Las Vegas Blvd S ☎877/253-5847, ⊛cirquedusoleil.com. Fri–Tues 7pm & 9.30pm; $99–175. Sadly this Cirque du Soleil take on Las Vegas's greatest-ever box-office draw feels a long way from the triumph that is *Love*. The real drawback is the defining absence at stage centre – Elvis himself. With no single performer ever playing the King – although up to 34 at a time cavort around in his costumes – it can't capture the magic of iconic moments like his triumphant late-career Vegas concerts. Instead we're given frankly bizarre tableaux like giant Elvises at some sort of cowboy cookout in Monument Valley, complete with blazing lassoos; a trapeze act swinging to *Are You Lonesome Tonight?*; and masked superhero acrobats bouncing around to *Gotta Lotta Lovin' To Do*. At least the actual music stands up well, with Elvis's own voice booming out over beefed-up dance tracks, all played live, and it's also wide-ranging, with some great blues and gospel elements.

Zumanity New York–New York, 3790 Las Vegas Blvd S ☎702/740-6815 or 866/606-7111, ⓦzumanity.com. Fri–Tues 7.30pm & 10.30pm; all shows over-18s only; $69–105, or $129 per person for a "duo sofa." If you've ever idly wondered whether everyone's favourite ethereal fantasists, the Cirque du Soleil, would be even better if they took their tops off, here's your answer – no. Almost the first words are "Do you really want to see TITS?" – if you don't, you're in the wrong place. *Zumanity* has sharply divided audiences; some see it as a glorious celebration of human sexuality, others as a vulgar mishmash with only the odd hint of grace and beauty. It's never quite sure if it's trying to be erotic or just camp, and without Cirque's trademark fabulous costumes the performers look pretty much like anyone else. There's certainly less acrobatic skill than in other Cirque shows, and the whole thing is so poorly paced and structured that the audience can't even tell when it's finished. All that said, something here will almost certainly touch your buttons (literally, if you're sitting near the front). Ultimately, it's more accomplished than other topless revues, but if it's the Cirque du Soleil you want to see, catch their other Las Vegas shows first.

13

Gambling

ambling remains the bedrock of the Las Vegas experience. Almost ninety percent of visitors to the city gamble, with an average budget of $550, and in the end, everything else is just frippery; it's the gambling that makes every flourish possible. The shows and restaurants, shark tanks and volcanoes – no matter how profitable any might be – are all just designed to make you stick around longer and spend more money on the slots and tables.

While the casinos prefer to talk about "gaming" rather than gambling, no one plays for fun alone: it's all about the money. Most visitors have their own preferred form of gambling, with the three main choices being **table games** such as blackjack or craps, played in the public gaze and surrounded by glamorous trimmings; **slot machines**, a more private pleasure in which the potential winnings are enormous, and you're spared the fear of not seeming *au fait* with the rules; and **sports betting**, with its hyped-up atmosphere and scope for proving that you know more than the bookies.

The fact that the gambling industry is still booming is a credit to the casinos' ability to change with the times. During the first few decades of Las Vegas's supremacy, the typical gambler was male and likely to be familiar with a wide range of card games thanks to years spent in military service. Slots and other machines, however, overtook the tables during the 1980s, and continue to generate well over half of Nevada's gaming revenue. In the face of the large proportion of modern visitors who see casino games as complicated and intimidating, the casinos are desperate to make gambling as easy, user-friendly and innocuous as possible. All offer free lessons, instructional videos on their in-room TVs, and the like.

All the major casinos operate **players clubs**, which issue you with an electronic ID card that means they can keep track of how much you gamble. As well as rewarding you with points redeemable for discounts and upgrades, show tickets or even cash, they can then target you in future, and potentially lure you back to Las Vegas with special offers on flights and rooms. While the immediate value is never that high, it costs nothing to join, and if you plan to gamble for any length of time there's no reason not to.

Despite Las Vegas's reputation as a stronghold of **crime**, there's no suggestion that gamblers themselves are being cheated. The casinos don't need to cheat; they know they're certain to make money. Yes, the occasional high-roller can seriously damage the corporate balance sheet – the Australian TV magnate Kerry Packer once won twenty consecutive hands of baccarat in twenty minutes at the *Mirage*, at $250,000 per hand. Overall, however, the odds are stacked in the casinos' favour. In the case of table games, as explained in more detail below, each has some combination of a quantifiable "**house edge**" incorporated into its rules. With

All in A player who bets his or her entire available funds in poker, but does not have enough to call, is said to be all in. He or she remains in the pot, but cannot win more than the amount actually wagered from any other player.

Ante A bet that each player is obliged to make to participate in a specific round of a game.

Bank The person responsible for distributing the chips, assessing the winners, and paying them off. In some games this role can be held by one of the players.

Boxman The casino employee in charge of a game of craps.

Buy in To join a game by exchanging your cash for chips.

Cage The cashiers' area in a casino.

Community card A card, as used in certain variations of poker, that's common to all players as an actual or potential component of their hand.

Face cards The Jack, Queen and King.

Flop The act of dealing face-up cards onto the table in poker, and/or the actual cards dealt.

Fold To discard one's hand and thus end one's involvement in the round of a game.

George A player with a reputation for generously tipping – "toking" – dealers.

Hard In blackjack, a total created by counting an ace as worth eleven rather than one.

Hole cards Cards that are dealt face down; especially the dealer's card in blackjack.

House The "house" is synonymous with the "bank" in those games where the bank cannot also be a player; more generically, it's the casino as a whole.

Loose Of slot machines; relatively generous in its payouts.

Natural In blackjack, this is an alternative term for a two-card combination that totals 21.

Nuts In a specific hand of poker, the nuts is the best possible hand that anyone could obtain, given the cards that have been dealt.

Pit boss The casino employee in charge of a group of tables and dealers.

Pot All the chips/money at a stake in a particular round of a game.

Push A hand in which dealer and player have identical cards, and thus neither wins.

Shark A card shark is a professional gambler, who may or may not be concealing that status from other players.

Sharp A card sharp may simply be a card shark, but the term is usually used more pejoratively; a card shark may not be cheating or deceiving other players, a sharp probably is.

Shill A gambler who is in fact a casino employee, taking part to encourage real gamblers to join or stay in the game.

Shoe The rack that holds the cards that have yet to be dealt; shoes most typically hold either six or eight packs of cards.

Soft In blackjack, a total created by counting an ace as worth one rather than eleven.

Stand In blackjack, to decline any further cards and stick with one's existing hand.

Tell An involuntary piece of behaviour by a player that reveals some aspect of his/her attitude or strategy.

Toke A tip to a dealer or other casino employee, usually made after a significant win.

Whale A gambler known for making very high bets.

Wild card A card to which the player is free to assign any value.

slots, it's even more straightforward – they're simply programmed to pay out less than they take in, though only the casinos themselves know just how much less. The average slot machine on the Strip generates almost $200 profit per day; each table game makes in the region of $2000. In the words of Steve Wynn, who should know, "the only way to make money in a casino is to own one".

Gambling is of course supremely **addictive**, and Las Vegas not surprisingly has a higher percentage of problem gamblers than any other city in the world. The generally accepted advice for visitors who want to experience the thrill while minimizing the risk is never to gamble more than you're prepared to lose. In addition, if you want to play for any length of time, don't bet more than around one-fiftieth of your total budget at any one moment. Thus if you've set aside $250 with which to gamble, it makes sense to play $5 slot machines, or bet with $5 roulette chips; if you've got $50, play with $1 stakes. Remember that even if the house edge on your chosen game is as low as two percent, that doesn't mean you'll lose two percent of your money and walk away with the remaining 98 percent. It means that if you play long enough, you'll almost certainly lose it all.

As for **where to gamble**, that really depends on how you see gambling. If you think it's all about fun and glamour, then the **Strip** is the place to be, though the high minimum stakes at the largest casinos can mean you'll lose your money uncomfortably fast. If you feel that an authentic gambling hall should be gritty, grimy and peopled by hard-bitten "characters", you may be happier **downtown**. If you see betting as a business, and want as much bang for your buck as possible, head instead for a **locals' casino** (see p.91), where you'll find more generous odds at video poker and the like.

Table games

Casino "games" are not really games in the same sense as the games you might enjoy at home, where each player has the same chance of winning. They're carefully structured business propositions, in which the casinos know that over time they're certain to end up ahead.

Every casino game has a built-in **house edge**. Imagine taking turns tossing a coin with a friend. If you call it correctly, he gives you $1, while if he calls it correctly you give him $1. Now imagine that he suggests a change in the rules; you still have to give him $1 when he's right, but from now on he'll only pay you 95¢. It's still possible that if you play for a few minutes, you may have a run of luck and win lots of 95¢ pay-outs. If you play all day, however, you're going to lose; if he can persuade millions of others to join in and play all day, every day, he's going to get very rich, very quickly. Thus, for example, the roulette table in most Las Vegas casinos holds 38 squares, numbered 1 to 36 plus "0" and "00." If you bet $1 on the correct number, the casino should in theory recognize that you had a 1-in-38 chance of being right, and pay you $38 (including your original $1 stake). Instead, they pay $36, or 94.74 percent; the $2 they hold back works out at 5.26 percent of the total, and that's the house edge.

Gamblers choose their favourite games to suit their personalities. Devotees of blackjack argue that the house edge is much lower than on other games, and that with enough cool calculation it's even possible to come out ahead. Others are far more drawn to the possibility of a quick big win playing craps and roulette, and say that it's luck that matters, not arithmetic.

Finally, to make it that bit harder to keep your wits about you, all Las Vegas casinos ply gamblers, at both the slot machines and the gaming tables, with **free drinks** – just be sure to tip the waitress.

Baccarat

Despite its sophisticated image – lavishly cultivated by most casinos (not to mention James Bond movies) – the card game **baccarat** is at root a simple game of chance, which requires no skill or judgment from its players. Its name, pronounced *bah-kah-rah* rather than *back-a-rat*, comes from the Italian for "zero," in that all the cards that are worth ten points in other games – 10s, jacks, queens, and kings – are here worth nothing at all. Aces count as one, and other cards are worth their face value.

Even though up to fifteen gamblers can sit around the table, no more than two hands are ever dealt. One is called the "**player**" and the other the "**bank**", but you're free to bet on whichever you choose. Each round starts with a different gambler being invited to deal two cards to each hand. According to a complicated but fixed set of criteria, a third card may then be dealt to either hand or both, starting with the "player." The aim for each hand is to add up to as close to nine as possible; with totals of ten or more, the first digit is always discarded. Thus a 4 and a 3 total seven; a jack and a 3 total three; and a queen, a 9 and a 4 also total three.

Baccarat strategy

To bet on baccarat, you don't need to understand the precise circumstances in which the third card is dealt; the spectacle simply unfolds before you, as often as not in complete silence. All you need to know is that only three bets are possible – "player", "bank" and "tie" – and that although successful "tie" bets pay off at 8 to 1, the house has a 14.4 percent advantage on these, so they're never worth making. "Player" and "bank" both pay back even money, but as "bank" is marginally more likely to win, the casino levies a **commission** on successful "bank" bets.

Betting "bank" is always slightly the better option. When the commission is set at five percent, the most usual amount, the house advantage is 1.06 percent on "bank" bets, and 1.24 percent on "player" bets. You might just see commission levels of four or even three percent, which cut the house edge even lower; commission set at two percent or less would mean you had the edge. Don't fall for those casinos that advertise **no-commission** baccarat; they've simply found some other way to rake back their money, by introducing some such rule as paying lower odds for certain card combinations.

The very narrow house edge on baccarat explains why the game is traditionally reserved for high-rollers, and much more available on the Strip than it is downtown or elsewhere in the city. Strip casinos usually offer it in roped-off enclaves where the minimum stake is at least $100, and a string of bad luck on the baccarat tables can impact severely on a casino's overall profitability. These days, however, you may encounter the all-but-identical, if faster-paced, game of "**mini-baccarat**" being played out on the main casino floor, for lower minimum stakes.

Bingo

It's not easy to find the good old-fashioned game of **bingo** in Las Vegas, but what games there are tend to rank among the city's best deals. That's because, like a cheap buffet restaurant, bingo is seen by lesser casinos as a great way to lure in local customers. The game itself may not even run at a profit; the idea is that with intervals of up to two hours between sessions, bingo buffs will end up playing the slots and other games. While bingo is typically seen as a social game, a moment's reflection will reveal that since you win by completing your card first, it's best to play in a less crowded room.

No Strip casinos currently offer bingo, and only the *Plaza* does downtown; head instead for the various Stations casinos, *Sam's Town* or the *Gold Coast*.

Blackjack is the most popular table game in Las Vegas, probably because many visitors are used to playing similar card games at home, whether that be "21" in North America or "pontoon" in Europe. In any case, it's easy to learn, and although you do have to play against the casino, the dealer is forbidden to exercise any skill or judgment, so there's no danger of being outwitted or cheated. Most tempting of all, not only are the odds relatively good to start with, but there is also a mathematically "correct" way to play blackjack, which may not guarantee success but can cut the house advantage even lower.

Rules of the game

Although blackjack is played with a conventional pack of 52 cards, divided into four suits, the suits play no part in the game. All that matters is the **point value** of each card. The numbered cards, from 2 to 10, are counted at their face value; jacks, queens and kings are worth ten points; and players can choose to count aces as worth either one or eleven. Each player attempts to assemble a hand whose total value adds up as close as possible to, but not more than, **21**; that value must also be higher than, or equal to, the dealer's own hand. Thus a jack, a 3 and an 8 add up to 21, which is good; a 9, a 4, and a 6 add up to 19, which is pretty good; and a king and two 7s add up to 24, which is more than 21 and therefore bad. An ace and a 4 counts as either 5 (the "soft" total) or 15 (the "hard" total). Best of all is an ace and any card worth ten, which adds up to 21, and is known as either a "**natural**" or a "**blackjack**".

In the most usual form of blackjack, each round begins with players placing the chips they wish to stake in their own designated betting area. All are then dealt two cards, traditionally **face down** – in which case you can look at them by raising the edge, but not pick them up – but often these days face up,

in which case you shouldn't touch them at all. The dealer receives one card face down, and one face up. Starting with the player on the dealer's left, each player then plays his or her own hand in its entirety.

On your turn, you repeatedly choose whether to "**hit**" and be dealt another card face up – which you signal by either scratching your fingers toward you on the table or just saying "hit." When you don't want to hit any more, which may well be immediately, signal that you've decided to "**stand**" by pushing your cards, still face down if that's how they were dealt, beneath your stake money. If, after you "hit", your total exceeds 21, you're "**bust**" and you must say so by turning all your cards face up; the dealer will respond by taking your cards and your stake.

Only once all the players have finished does the dealer turn both his or her cards face up and play out his or her own hand. The dealer, however, has no discretion as to how to proceed – the instructions are written on the table for all to see. The most commonly seen system requires the dealer to hit if the total is 16 or lower, and stand as soon it reaches 17 or higher, so he or she has to keep on hitting even when his total of 16 would in theory beat all the players, and stand even in a losing position. In some casinos, however, the dealer is required also to hit on a "soft 17", which slightly increases the house advantage. Either way, when the dealer's final total is settled, all the players' hands are revealed and the bets are paid off; you'll either get your original stake back, plus the same amount again, if you've beaten the dealer; lose your stake if you've been beaten; or simply keep it if you've tied. If the dealer has a "natural," that beats any total of 21 that uses three or more cards.

If, right at the start, you're dealt a "natural," you can immediately turn them over (if face down) to announce this fact. The dealer will then check his or her cards for a natural. If the dealer also has one, it's a tie (and the hand is over for everyone else); otherwise you're paid off at three-to-two odds (or increasingly these days 6:5, a significantly worse deal that's to be avoided if possible).

There are three further standard possibilities. If you're dealt a "pair" – two 3s, two aces, etc – you can "**split**" them and play two separate hands, doubling your original stake so that you have the same bet on each. You can also "**double down**", which means that if your original two cards are such that being dealt one, and only one, more card is likely to give you a winning total, you can double your stake and take that chance. Both those strategies are sound in some circumstances (see below); the third, however, an option called "**insurance**", which is basically a side bet as to whether or not the dealer has a "natural", is said by experts never to be a good idea. Some casinos also allow gamblers to "**surrender**", by folding before you play and losing half your bet rather than the whole thing, which can be convenient if you're dealt a particularly bad hand.

The casinos' built-in advantage at blackjack stems from your having to play your own hand before the dealer plays, and you forfeit your stake if you go "bust" whether or not the dealer subsequently also goes bust.

Card counting

The lure of the game for serious gamblers stems from the work of computer expert Edward Thorp, whose 1962 book *Beat The Dealer* proved that by memorizing the cards as they are dealt, skilled players can consistently beat the house. Panicked Las Vegas casinos responded by banning all "card counters" and set about making things harder, by using several packs of cards at once, and shuffling at random intervals. It soon transpired that in any case hardly anyone can count cards accurately in the noisy, stressful conditions of a modern casino, and most gamblers went on losing at the same rate as ever.

The situation these days is that casinos continue nonetheless to eject suspected card counters – not because counting is illegal, but because they can eject anyone they feel like ejecting, and consistent winners fit firmly into that category. On the other hand, some casinos make a big show of encouraging gamblers by offering "**single-deck**" or "double-deck" blackjack, on which card counting is a much more feasible proposition. The snag is, everywhere on the Strip that does so pays 6:5 odds on a "natural", and thereby takes away the advantage gained by card counting. The *Four Queens* downtown does pay 3:2 on single-deck blackjack, making it the best option in the city, but even there they've changed the rules on doubling down to claw back a small advantage.

Basic strategy

Computer analysis has also shown that if you compare your own cards with the dealer's face-up card, there's a "correct" response to every permutation. Charts displaying this "**basic strategy**", which reduces the house advantage to a mere one percent, are widely available in specialist gambling books; some casinos even distribute them. In essence, if your total is between 12 and 16, you should stand if the dealer's face-up card is between 2 and 6 (with a few exceptions, like if you have 12 and the dealer is showing a 2), and hit if it isn't; if your total is 17, stand (unless you're dealt an ace and a 6); and always stand if your total is 18 or over. On top of that, if your total is 10 or 11, and the dealer has from 2 to 9, you should "double down"; while if you're dealt a pair of 8s, or a pair of aces, you should "split."

The usual **minimum stake** for blackjack games on the Strip is $10, although it tends to rise in the evening at the larger casinos to $25 or more. The *Sahara* is unique on the Strip in guaranteeing $1 tables 24 hours per day, though those tables tend to offer worse odds. Many casinos also offer gimmicky blackjack variations such as "double exposure", in which the dealer's hand is dealt face up, and **Spanish 21**, in which all the 10s are removed from the pack. These feature a host of other minor rule changes, detailed either on the table itself or on leaflets. The odds aren't necessarily any better or worse than usual, but the optimum strategy will differ.

Casino War

Casino War is the easiest, fastest and most banal card game imaginable, introduced to suit an era when fewer and fewer people know any card games at all. Each player, including the dealer, is dealt one card face up. If your card is higher than the dealer's, you win your bet; if it's lower, you lose. If they're the same, you can either "surrender," and lose half your stake, or go to "war," by doubling your stake. You both then get another card; this time if you beat, or tie with, the dealer, you win your original stake only, whereas if you lose the dealer takes both your bets. Assuming you always go to war – the better option – the house advantage is 2.9 percent. The real snag here is that it all happens so fast – you can lose your money very quickly indeed.

Craps

The dice game known as **craps** is the most exciting, frenzied and noisy game on any casino floor, but it's also the most intimidating for novices. It all happens too fast to learn by observation, so prospective players should take a lesson or two first. That said, it's not as hard as it looks, and you don't need to know all the rules to enjoy playing – in fact the easier bets on the table pay much better odds than the more complicated "sucker" ones.

Rules of the game

"Craps" is a noun, the name of the game; "crap" is the matching adjective, as in "crap table." The game is played on a baize table with high, padded and slightly rounded walls. Each game is operated by four casino employees; the "boxman," who's in overall charge; two dealers, to handle the bets at either end of the table; and the "stickman," who uses a stick to recover and distribute the dice. However, it's the players who actually throw the dice, so craps is much more of a participatory experience than other casino games, and a player on a hot streak can take the credit for a table-full of winners.

At the start of each game, the stickman invites a different player to be "**shooter**"; you can decline if you prefer. The shooter then lays a bet, on "**pass**", and makes the "come-out roll" by throwing two dice hard enough to bounce against the end of the table. Meanwhile, the other players have laid any bets they want to make, mainly on either "pass" or "**don't pass**." In effect, they're betting with or against the shooter, although it's the casino that actually pays the bets.

If the come-out roll is 7 or 11, then the shooter, and everyone else who has bet on "pass", wins immediately, while everyone who bet on "don't pass" loses. If, on the other hand, the come-out roll is "craps," meaning 2, 3, or 12, the shooter and all those who bet on "pass" lose; those who bet on "don't pass" win on 2 or 3, or retain their stake on 12.

Any other come-out roll – the possibilities are 4, 5, 6, 8, 9 and 10 – becomes the "**point**" and a marker is placed in the corresponding position on the table. The shooter's sole aim is now to throw the point again before throwing a 7, or "sevening out." If the shooter succeeds, "pass" wins and "don't pass" loses; if not, the reverse is true.

At any point after the come-out roll, anyone – even players who have not bet so far – can also bet on either "**come**" or "**don't come**". These are the same as "pass" and "don't pass", in that the next throw becomes your "come number," and a "come" bet wins if the shooter throws that number again before throwing a 7. If the shooter throws the point before either a 7 or the "come number," then "come" bets stay on the table.

In addition, after a come-out roll that's neither 7, 11 nor "craps", anyone who has bet "pass"/"don't pass" or "come"/"don't come" can make an extra "**odds**" bet on that same bet. This time, you're betting according to the actual odds that the relevant point or come number will or will not be thrown before a 7. To place an odds bet, say "odds" to the dealer and either put your chips behind the pass line if you've already bet "pass", or give them to the dealer to go with your original "come", "don't come" or "don't pass" bet. "Odds" bets are the best-value bets in the casino, in that they pay according to the precise likelihood of throwing that particular dice combination compared to a 7. Some casinos only allow "odds" bets up to double the original stake; others allow them to be as much as a hundred times higher. For serious gamblers, the "odds" bets are the prime reason to play craps at all.

Note, however, that the actual odds for "odds" bets are not marked on the table. All those bets that *are* marked, such as the dice pictured in the middle, are not only harder to understand, but they're also much worse propositions – which is why they're not worth explaining here. If you see "**crapless craps**" advertised, that's a simpler version, developed at the *Stratosphere*, in which every number other than 7 can become the point after the come-out roll; the house edge is much higher.

Though the usual **minimum stake** for craps is $5 or $10 on the Strip, the tiny *Casino Royale*, between *Harrah's* and the *Venetian*, has $3 tables that offer particularly good odds. Come the evening, it can be hard to find a table that accepts stakes of less than $100 at high-roller hang-outs like *Bellagio* or *Caesars*. Downtown, almost all the casinos offer $3 tables.

Keno

By contrast with the superficially similar game of bingo (see p.156), **Keno** is renowned in Las Vegas for offering abysmal odds. The crucial difference is that bingo is played out until someone has circled all the numbers on their score sheet, so there's always a winner. With keno, on the other hand, each player chooses anything up to twenty numbers between 1 and 80, and their choice is then compared with the twenty drawn by the casino. If you achieve five or more matches, you get a pay-off; if all your picks are correct, you'll win a fortune.

Although keno is becoming less ubiquitous these days, most of the major casinos still run a game every half-hour or so. The most usual bet is to pick eight or nine numbers; a typical pay-off for getting all nine right would be 50,000 to one. The average house advantage is reckoned at being around thirty percent – the kind of odds you might expect from a lottery rather than a casino game.

Poker

In its traditional form, **poker** is unique among Las Vegas card games in that gamblers play against each other, not the house. The casinos simply provide a room and a dealer, in return either for a percentage on every hand, which varies from one to ten percent, or, less usually, charging by the hour. Playing poker against a bunch of total strangers is undeniably exciting, but it's not a risk to take lightly.

Casinos generally see traditional poker as a service for guests who will also gamble on other games, though several stage their own poker tournaments, along the lines of the wildly successful **World Series of Poker**, currently held each summer at the *Rio*.

In addition, most casinos offer what are essentially hybrids of poker and blackjack. These new games, played on blackjack-like tables, are designed to pit gamblers directly against the house – and thus seem less intimidating – while also maximizing the house advantage. The usual minimum bet on the Strip is $5, though you might find a $3 table.

Whatever variation of poker you play, hands always consist for ranking purposes of five cards, ranked in the order below.

Within each category, hands are ranked according to **number**, with aces high. Thus a pair of tens ranks higher than a pair of sevens, a flush with a King as its highest member ranks above a flush topped by a Jack, and so on. The one exception is with a straight that runs Ace, 2, 3, 4, 5, in which case the 5 is considered to be the highest card. Even the very lowest combination in each category ranks higher than any possible combination in the category below – thus any straight will always beat three of a kind.

Leftover cards – the fifth card in a hand that contains four of a kind, the two spare cards that don't form part of three of a kind, etc – are known as **kickers**, and are used to rank two otherwise identical hands. Thus if two players have three Kings each – which is possible in games like Texas Hold 'Em – their "kickers" can be used to rank one above the other.

Specific **suits** play no part in the ranking: a flush made of the 3, 4, 8, 10 and Queen of Clubs counts as exactly equal to a flush made up of the same cards in Hearts.

The ranking of poker hands

Royal flush A straight flush from 10 to Ace.

Straight flush Five consecutive cards in the same suit; eg 8, 9, 10, Jack, Queen of Clubs.

Four of a kind Four aces or four 3s, etc.

Full house Three of a kind and a separate pair.

Flush Any five cards in the same suit.

Straight Five consecutive cards not in the same suit. A run of Ace, 2, 3, 4, 5 is permissible, but a straight is not allowed to "wrap around", for example by running Queen, King, Ace, 2, 3.

Three of a kind Three Kings or three 2s, etc.

Two pair Two 3s and two Queens, etc.

One pair Any two cards of matching rank; two 10s, etc.

High card When no player has a pair or better, the winning hand is the one that contains the highest card.

Poker hand slang

American Airlines A pair of Aces as starting cards. Also known as "pocket rockets" or "bullets".

Big lick A starting hand of 6–9. One of the more risqué poker terms.

Canine A starting hand of K–9. Also known as "the dog".

Cowboys A pair of Kings as starting cards.

Dead man's hand A pair of Aces and a pair of 8s. So called because gunfighter Wild Bill Hickok was holding this when he was shot.

Deuces A pair of 2s as starting cards. Also known as "ducks".

Dolly Parton A starting hand of 9–5; named after Dolly's hit song *Working Nine to Five*.

Ladies A pair of Queens as starting cards. Also known as "Siegfried and Roy".

Mommas and papas A starting hand of a Queen and a King.

Snowmen A pair of 8s as starting cards. Also known as an "octopus".

Wheel A straight of Ace-2-3-4-5.

Game variations

The two most widely played variations, both of which offer scope for endless rounds of betting, are **Seven Card Stud**, in which each player is dealt two cards face down, four more face up, and then a final one face down, and **Texas Hold 'Em**, in which each player gets two face-down cards, and then five communal cards are dealt face up on the table. The object in both games is to make the highest hand possible using five of the seven cards, though often how you bet is more crucial than the cards on which you're betting.

In **Caribbean Stud Poker**, originally developed for cruise ships, each player makes a compulsory ante bet, and is dealt five cards face down, while the dealer gets four cards face down and one face up. You can now either "fold" – surrender both hand and bet – or "call", by adding another bet that's double your original ante. Each hand is compared individually with the dealer's. If you beat the dealer, you win your ante bet at even odds, while your call bet might win a bonus of as much as a hundred to one, depending on how high a hand you have. There's an outrageous twist, however; if the dealer has an especially bad hand, of anything less than an ace and a king, it's said not to "qualify," and call bets are returned rather than paid off. As a result, the house edge comes to 5.3 percent. Betting an additional $1 per hand enters you for a progressive jackpot, payable on royal flushes, that can reach over $100,000.

Let It Ride is an unorthodox variation in which you make three separate but equal bets on the three cards you're dealt, but can then withdraw one bet at a time as two further communal cards are revealed. You're not competing against anyone else here, not even the dealer; bets are paid off according to a chart that shows each winning hand and the odds against it. This time the house edge is 3.5 percent.

Pai Gow Poker – as distinct from the Chinese domino game Pai Gow, which you may also encounter – is a slow game that's played with an ordinary pack of cards plus a single joker, which can count as either an ace or a "wild" card to complete a flush or straight. Each player, including the dealer, receives seven cards and has to divide them into one five-card hand and one two-card hand. Although the two-card hand must be worth less than the five-card one, *both* have to defeat *both* the dealer's hands for you to win. If only one beats the dealer, it's a "push," and bets are returned. As any player can choose to be the dealer instead, there is technically no house edge to the game, but instead the house levies a five percent commission on winning bets.

Roulette

Roulette, a game of pure chance, revolves around guessing which of the numbered compartments of a rotating wheel will be the eventual resting place of a ball released by the dealer. Players use the adjoining baize table to bet not only on the precise number, but also on whether it is odd or even, or "black" or "red," or falls within various specified ranges.

The oldest of the regular casino games, roulette was introduced to the casinos of Paris in 1765 with official police blessing, on the grounds that it was impossible to cheat. That doesn't mean, however, that your chances of winning are especially good. *Roulette*, incidentally, means "little wheel" in French.

All roulette wheels hold the numbers 1 to 36, of which half are coloured red and half black, plus a green 0; almost all the wheels in Las Vegas also feature a green 00. On this **"double-zero"** layout, the wheel has 38 compartments, so gamblers have a 1 in 38 chance of choosing the right number (it's possible to bet on 0 or 00, although neither counts as red or black, or odd or even). When there's only one zero, the true odds are 1 in 37. However, the **odds** for successful bets are always the same, set as if there were no zeroes at all. A correct number is paid off at 35 to 1; guessing a pair that includes the winning number pays 17 to 1; a block of three that includes the number pays 11 to 1, and so on.

Thus it's the **zeroes** that give the house its advantage, and the addition of the double zero doubles that advantage from the standard 2.7 percent in Europe to 5.26 percent in Las Vegas. That may sound like a small difference, but it means that you'll lose your money twice as fast on a double-zero table as on a single-zero one, and it explains why only one in fifty of Las Vegas gamblers bothers to play roulette at all.

Strategy

Various **strategies** can improve your chances. Most important of all, play only single-zero tables, and/or those that offer a small variation that's increasingly seen these days, the "**half-back**" or "**en prison**" rule, in which all stakes placed on even-money bets (such as red/black and odd/even) are left on the table if a zero or double-zero comes up, and returned to the gambler if the bet is successful on the next spin.

The ideal combination, a single-zero, half-back table — which has a house advantage of a mere 1.35 percent — can in theory be found on the Strip at *Bellagio*, *Mandalay Bay*, the *MGM Grand*, the *Mirage* and *Wynn*, but they're often reserved for high-stakes gamblers. Straightforward single-zero tables are more common, certainly in the daytime or during quiet periods; strangely enough, single- and double-zero tables can often be found in action side by side, with equal numbers of gamblers at each.

A second worthwhile strategy is to avoid the bet that covers 0, 00, 1, 2, and 3, which pays at 5 to 1 — a house advantage of 7.89 percent — and therefore offers the worst odds on the table. And finally, there's the most boring strategy of all; the fewer spins you take part in, the better, so you should stake all you can afford to risk just once, on one of the (almost) even-money bets – such as red/black, or odd/even – and then walk away, win or lose.

Roulette ranks second only to blackjack for the number of elaborate **systems** devised by hopeful gamblers. Most are variants of the **martingale**, which requires you to keep doubling (or trebling, or whatever) your stake on red or black until your first win, and then stop. The trouble is, you need to have a large reserve of cash to cover even a short sequence of losses, so your initial stake can only be a small proportion of your total cash – and yet all you can ever hope to win is that initial stake. On top of that, each game has a maximum bet, so you can't keep doubling your stake anyway. Other systems, which predict which numbers are "due" to fall, are so sure to fail that most casinos provide electronic boards listing the last twenty or so successful numbers. In a nutshell, in the words of blackjack guru Edward Thorp, "there is no 'mathematical' winning system for roulette and it is impossible ever to discover one."

Finally, don't be tempted by roulette tables that offer "Back to Back" betting. With rewards of 1000 to 1 for naming two consecutive winners, and 10,000 to 1 for three, these give the house an advantage of an abysmal 27 percent and an outrageous eighty percent respectively.

Etiquette

Only players seated at the table are supposed to play, although in practice dealers usually allow passers-by to put a small amount of cash on a straightforward bet. Each player starts by buying a pile of uniquely coloured chips, valid only for roulette, so the dealer can keep track of who owns which chips. After each spin, all losing chips are swept from the table, and the winners are paid off. The actual winning stakes, however, remain in place, so unless you remove successful chips yourself you're betting them again on the next spin.

The value of the chips used at each table varies, and is always displayed together with the size of the minimum bet accepted. These aren't necessarily the same; a table using $1 chips (the typical denomination on the Strip) may well require gamblers to bet at least $5 in total on each spin.

The game variously known as **Wheel of Fortune**, or Big Six, or Money Wheel, is a traditional carnival sideshow that offers some of the worst odds in any casino. Few gamblers play more than once only, on a passing whim; the main appeal is that you can stake cash, not chips.

The dealer spins a rotating pointer on a dartboard-like wheel marked with 54 different dollar amounts, while players place bets on those same dollar amounts on a glass-topped table. If your number matches the pointer, you win that many dollars per dollar staked. As a rule, the house edge is lowest on the 24 or so segments marked with $1, and highest on the two that show a joker or some other house symbol, which pay off at forty to one.

Slot machines

Well over a century since the first "one-armed bandits" appeared in the saloons of San Francisco, **slot machines** are more popular than ever. Thanks to glitzy new technology and highly competitive odds – not to mention some truly huge jackpots – the casinos have largely dispelled the old image of slot arcades as joyless places where tight-lipped seniors pump bucketfuls of small change into unresponsive machines. These days, even the glitziest casinos make twice as much money on slots as they do on the tables, and slot-players are no longer second-class citizens. Note that to play the slots, you must be over 21 and be carrying the ID to prove it; underage winners are not paid off. US citizens must pay tax on wins of $1200 or more.

Traditionally, the house advantage on slot machines used to be around twenty percent, which is to say that for every dollar you gambled, you might win back eighty cents, while the operator kept the other twenty. Those would now be regarded as "tight" odds, as casinos vie to offer "looser" machines – promoted with slogans such as "99% slots guaranteed!" – where the house advantage is as little as five or even one percent. The main reason they can do that is that gamblers these days are prepared to invest much higher stakes, staking $1 or $5 a time rather than the old standard of 25¢. So long as each time you spin the reels, the casino can expect to win 5¢, they're equally happy to achieve that with quarter slots that pay 80 percent, dollar slots that pay 95 percent, or $5 slots set at 99 percent. Insofar as actual figures are available, slot machines in Las Vegas casinos vary between 85 and 95 percent; for them to be set below 75 percent is illegal under Nevada state law.

Modern, computerized slot machines are far more sophisticated than their mechanical forebears. Most still contain giant wheels decorated with different symbols – customers have proved suspicious of machines that just show pictures of those symbols on video screens – but, contrary to appearances, the reels don't simply spin until they stop. Instead, a micro-chip inside each machine generates an unending stream of random numbers. Whenever you set the reels spinning, the current number determines where they will stop. Just because you hit a combination that looks close to a jackpot doesn't mean that you nearly hit the jackpot, and no sequence of combinations, or lack of winners, can ever indicate that a machine is "ready" to hit.

All kinds of new machines are constantly appearing, targeted at different consumers. There are machines that play Elvis or Sinatra tunes, or mimic board games like *Scrabble* or *Monopoly*, or pay homage to favourite TV shows and movies.

Thus the *I Love Lucy* machines, which release a chocolate smell when players hit a bonus round, tend to be positioned to catch the eye of senior gamblers, while the raucous rock-oriented models are found in the hipper, youth-oriented joints.

Beneath all the surface glitter, there are basically two different types of slot machine. "**Non-progressive**" machines have fixed paybacks for every winning combination, and in principle pay lower prizes, more frequently. "**Progressive**" ones, such as *Megabucks* or *Quartermania*, are linked into networks of several similar machines, potentially covering the entire state of Nevada. The longer it takes before someone, somewhere hits the jackpot, the higher that jackpot will be – digital displays show mounting totals that can run into millions of dollars.

It's unusual these days to be able to put coins rather than notes into machines, and all now pay off with **credit slips**, which you have to redeem at the cashier's cage, rather than actual cash. As for **where to play**, the slots are "loosest" (which is good) downtown, and anywhere locals play regularly, and notoriously "tight" at places such as the airport or supermarkets, where most customers are just passing through. Strip options range from the *Riviera*, "where the nickel is king" and you can play for days on end, to the $500 machines in the marble-walled High Limits room at *Bellagio*.

Video poker

The only video game to win widespread acceptance in Las Vegas casinos is **video poker**, a cross between "five-card draw" poker and a conventional slot machine that's addictive enough to be widely known as the "crack cocaine of gambling". Each time you play, five cards are "dealt" onto the screen. You can then, once only, be dealt replacements for as many of those five as you choose not to "hold". While it is a game of skill, you're not required to know the rules of poker; the odds paid for all possible winning hands are listed on the body of the machine.

Apart from sparing you the embarrassment of having to cope with a real live dealer or other players, the appeal of video poker is that the odds can be very good indeed. You can assess just how good a machine is by what it pays for a full house and a flush. There are "progressive" and "non-progressive" video poker machines, just like ordinary slot machines (see above); "loose" progressive machines generally offer eight coins for a full house and five for a flush, while loose non-progressives tend to pay nine and six respectively. On a "nine/six" machine the house edge is a mere half percent or so, but several casinos now offer "ten/six" or "nine/seven" machines on which the advantage is technically slightly in the gambler's favour. The snag is that to have that edge, and win consistently, you have to play perfectly.

Entire books have been written on what constitutes perfect strategy in video poker. It's not the same as in ordinary poker, and it depends on whether the machine you're playing features "wild" cards or not. In brief, because the highest rewards are paid for **royal flushes**, you should almost always play for that at the expense of any other possible – or even certain – win.

Sports betting

Nevada is one of only four states in the US where it's legal to place bets on the outcome of sporting events, and the only one where casinos offer large-scale **sports betting**. The *Plaza* was the first casino to open what's called a **Sports Book** in 1975, and they've only become widespread since changes in federal taxation in the mid-1980s. Now, almost every casino has one, and in most instances it's called a **Race and Sports Book**, meaning that you can bet on horse-racing as well. During major college sports tournaments in particular, Las Vegas throngs with gamblers here specifically to watch, and bet, on all the latest action.

You might imagine that where you do your sports betting would depend on which casino offered the best odds. In fact, although odds do change minute by minute, there's not all that much variation between individual casinos. Until 2008, when the law was deemed impossible to enforce any more, it was illegal to use cell phones or recording devices in Sports Books. You can now compare odds by calling friends in other casinos, but in theory at least it remains illegal to place a bet on someone else's behalf as a result of a phone call, so you have to go to the relevant casino to make your bet.

In practice, the choice centres on what sort of atmosphere you prefer. The range is enormous. Some Sports Books are high-tech extravaganzas, their walls taken up by vast electronic scoreboards interspersed with massive TV screens; during major sporting occasions, they're basically sports bars, filled by shrieking crowds.

Others opt instead for a hushed, reverential ambience, giving each gambler a personal TV monitor to watch their event of choice, and hand-writing the odds with marker pens on white boards. The Race Book at the *Imperial Palace* is an especially irresistible example, rising in tiers above the Strip entrance. There are also those that resemble elegant gentlemen's clubs, like the one at *Bellagio* with its massive padded leatherette armchairs.

As for what you can bet on, the options are nearly limitless; not only can you wager on who will win pretty much any conceivable game, fight or race, you can make more specialized bets, like predicting the combined points total in a game (referred to as the "over-under").

In almost all the casinos, you still can't actually bet on a big game while it's in play. Instead you have to bet either before the start, or during a halftime break that allows the bookmakers enough time to adjust their odds. Three casinos however – the *Venetian*, the *Palazzo* and the off-Strip *M Resort* (see p.94) – now offer a high-tech betting system known as **in-running**, in which gamblers seated at special terminals can bet on games in progress, with constantly changing odds.

One thing all the Sports Books have in common is the provision of **free alcohol** to gamblers; there's usually a snack bar close to hand as well.

Weddings

A round a hundred thousand **marriages** are performed in Las Vegas each year. Having a Vegas wedding has become a byword for tongue-in-cheek chic, and there are drive-through chapels where bride and groom do no more than roll down their car windows before being serenaded on their way by Elvis himself. Especially busy days include New Year's Eve, which gives American couples the right to file a joint tax return for the preceding year, and Valentine's Day.

What's more surprising, however, is that most marriages in the city seem to be deeply **formal affairs** (think Elvis himself, when he married Priscilla at the *Aladdin* in 1967). Both the casinos and a horde of independent wedding chapels compete to offer elaborate and expensive ceremonies with all the traditional trimmings, from white gowns and black limousines to garters and buttonholes. The happy couples are more likely to have saved and planned long in advance than to have succumbed to a spur-of-the-moment impulse.

You don't have to be a local resident or take a blood test to get wed in Las Vegas. Assuming you're both at least 18 years old, carrying **picture ID**, and not already married – US citizens are also expected to know their Social Security Numbers – you can simply turn up at the Clark County Marriage Bureau, downtown at 201 E Clark Ave (daily 8am–midnight; ☎702/671-0600; ⓦwww.accessclarkcounty .com), and buy a **marriage licence** for $60 cash, or $65 with a credit card; you can speed things up a little by completing the application form online on the Bureau's website. With no waiting period required, the cheapest option once you have your licence is then to walk one block to the office of the Commissioner of Civil Marriages, at 309 S Third St (daily 8am–10pm; ☎702/455-3774; same website), and pay another $50 cash to have a civil wedding performed.

If you want a little more ceremony than that, **wedding chapels** claim to charge as little as $60 for basic ceremonies, but at that sort of rate even the minister is an "extra" costing an additional $50. Reckon on paying at least $200 for the bare minimum, which is liable to be as romantic a process as checking in at a hotel, and to take about as long. The full deluxe service ranges up to whatever you can afford. **Photography** in particular can be expensive; many chapels won't even let you bring a camera. When you pay for the services of their own photographers, you're not usually buying the right to keep the originals, and may have to pay exorbitant rates for each individual print.

As well as the chapels listed below, all the **casinos** offer weddings in their own chapels; you can find full details on each casino's website. It's only common sense to take a look at the actual chapel before you commit yourself to the ceremony; many are simply small office-like rooms off the main casino floor. If you really want to get hitched in style, the sky is literally the limit. **Novelty options** include getting hitched as you float on a gondola in the *Venetian's* Grand Canal, or beside your helicopter at the bottom of the Grand Canyon (Papillon; ☎702/736-7243, ⓦwww.papillon.com).

Full lists of all chapels and wedding organizers can be found on the official Las Vegas CVB website, ⓦ www.lasvegas24hours.com. Note that many chapels, both independent and in the casinos, also offer **gay or lesbian "weddings"**, which lack any legal force.

Wedding chapels

Chapel of the Bells 2233 Las Vegas Blvd S ☏702/735-6803 or 1-800/233-2391, ⓦ www .chapelofthebellslasvegas.com. **Sun–Thurs 9am–10pm, Fri & Sat 9am–1am.** Belying the giant neon sign outside, this small chapel, across from the *Sahara*, is surprisingly traditional (ie white and silky) inside, and has been satisfying customers from Pele to Micky Rooney since 1957. Packages range from $135 to $500; the latter includes a bottle of non-alcoholic "champagne".

Chapel of the Flowers 1717 Las Vegas Blvd S ☏702/735-4331 or 1-800/843-2410, ⓦ www .littlechapel.com. **Mon–Thurs 7am–8pm, Fri 7am–9pm, Sat 6am–9pm.** Rather traditional, not to say twee, establishment with two antique-furnished chapels off the same lobby, that's most notorious for being the site where Dennis Rodman and Carmen Electra were briefly hitched. Until recently this was the Little Chapel of the Flowers, but the addition of a garden complete with waterfall and gazebo necessitated the name change. Weddings range upwards from $195; for $4150 you can be married on a yacht on Lake Mead; and for $3750 you can fly by helicopter to the floor of the Grand Canyon and get married there.

Graceland Wedding Chapel 619 S Las Vegas Blvd ☏702/382-0091 or 1-800/824-5732, ⓦ www.gracelandchapel.com. **Daily 9am–11pm.** This comparatively tasteful white-painted church, close to downtown and complete with stained-glass windows, offers conventional ceremonies for $199–499, not

including the minister's fees. Elvis will act as best man, give the bride away, or serenade you, but unfortunately he can't perform the service.

The Little Church of the West 4617 Las Vegas Blvd S ☏702/739-7971 or 1-800/821-2452, ⓦ www.littlechurchlv.com. **Daily 8am–midnight.** Built in 1942 and originally part of the *Last Frontier* casino, this wedding chapel is now on the National Register of Historic Places and has moved progressively down the Strip over the years to its current site, south of *Mandalay Bay*. Among the more peaceful and quiet places to exchange your Vegas vows – if that's really what you want. Packages start with the $199 "Let's Elope".

A Little White Chapel 1301 Las Vegas Blvd S ☏702/382-5943 or 1-800/545-8111, ⓦ www .alittlewhitechapel.com. **Daily 24hr.** The chapel where Bruce Willis and Demi Moore married each other, and Michael Jordan and Joan Collins (whose names are on the sign out front) married other people, and Britney Spears married Jason Alexander in 2004. The chapel that pioneered the "24-hr Drive-Up Wedding Window" has refined the concept by roofing over the driveway as the "Tunnel of Love," and painting naked cherubs on its blue-sky ceiling. Staffed by fifteen ministers, it can provide tasteful black baseball caps embroidered for "Bride" and "Groom". Packages start at $229 and range upwards to include Hawaiian, Elvis and even Michael Jordan options, as well as helicopter trips.

Shopping

S

hopping has become one of Las Vegas's biggest attractions. Until the Forum first boggled minds at *Caesars Palace* in 1992, none of the casinos had its own shopping mall, and the city's stores catered almost exclusively to locals. Since then, however, malls and arcades have proliferated all along the Strip, and for many visitors the chance to do some serious shopping is a prime reason to visit the city.

Not that Las Vegas is a great destination for **bargain hunters**; apart from the odd souvenir store, it's not tacky, and it's not cheap. Broadly speaking, there's no budget shopping along the Strip itself; the one distinction that can be drawn lies between the large and undeniably spectacular showpiece malls like the Forum itself, and the Grand Canal at the *Venetian*, each of which holds much the same assortment of jazzed-up outlets of the best-known US chains, leavened by a few high-end international names, and the smaller enclaves of ludicrously expensive and "exclusive" stores contained in places like *Wynn Las Vegas*, *Bellagio*, the *Palazzo* and the new *Crystals* mall.

Not every casino has succumbed to the mall-building craze, however. Of the Harrah's properties, only *Caesars Palace* and *Planet Hollywood* hold stores of any interest, while from the MGM roster both the *MGM Grand* and the *Mirage* devote a tiny proportion of their space to shopping. There's also almost no shopping to speak of Downtown.

As for the rest of the city, a short drive or bus ride from the Strip can take you to a more ordinary kind of mall, including a couple of cut-price "outlet centers", but it's still hard to find anything particularly unusual or unexpected, and there are no shopping neighbourhoods where you can simply walk from store to store.

One welcome aspect of Las Vegas's shopping scene is a general lack of the **snootiness** so often associated with big-name stores. Whatever store you walk into, you'll be greeted with deference – presumably because they're never quite sure who might just be a successful gambler keen to flaunt his or her new-found wealth.

In truth, though, the reason the malls of Las Vegas are the **most profitable** in the nation is probably because visitors find themselves losing so much on the tables and slots, with nothing to show for it, that getting something in return for their money – however expensive – suddenly seems like a miraculous alternative.

The Strip malls

Appian Way Caesars Palace, 3500 Las Vegas Blvd S ☎702/731-7222. Individual store hours vary. It's the Forum shops that garner most of the attention at *Caesars Palace*, but the casino's other mall, the Appian Way, has occupied a couple of hallways behind the lobby and central casino area since 1978. Its upscale stores – including Cartier jewellers and the Italian clothing specialist Bernini Couture – radiate out from a domed

The major Strip malls are so skewed towards a specific clientele – affluent adult visitors making expensive impulse purchases – that several categories of shopping are almost entirely absent.

Perhaps the most surprising is **consumer electronics**. Apple has stores in both the Forum and the Fashion Show Mall, but otherwise the Strip holds no **computer** stores. Fry's Electronics (Ⓦwww.frys.com) in Town Square (see p.175) is the nearest comprehensive source for most consumer devices. There's a Sony Style store in the Forum, but that's more concerned with promoting upcoming products than actually selling anything.

Similarly there are no real **camera** stores, though Futuretronics in the Fashion Show Mall stocks a small selection of new digital cameras. Otherwise, off-Strip options include Fry's (as above); the Sahara Camera Center, at 2600 W Sahara Ave (Ⓣ702/457-3333, Ⓦwww.saharacameracenter.com); Casey's Cameras, at 1550 E Tropicana Ave (Ⓣ702/736-0890, Ⓦwww.caseyscamera.com); and the Ritz Camera outlets (Ⓦwww.ritzcamera.com) in the Outlet and the Galleria at Sunset.

There isn't a single full-sized **bookstore** along the Strip, just one small Borders Express in the Fashion Show Mall. If that doesn't have what you want, head to one of the four larger Borders (Ⓦwww.borders.com) in the metropolitan area, of which the closest is at Town Square (see p.175), or the four Barnes and Noble outlets (Ⓦwww.barnesandnoble.com), with the nearest at 3860 Maryland Parkway.

Neither will you find many **CDs** or **DVDs** along the Strip; elsewhere, Borders and Barnes and Nobles are once again the main sources, though Zia Records Exchange sells new and used CDs and DVDs, plus vinyl and even VHS, all day every day at both 4503 W Sahara Ave and 4225 S Eastern Ave.

Finally, the Strip holds no significant **supermarket** or **grocery**. Every casino has its own little store selling things like toothbrushes and water, but otherwise for all-purpose everyday shopping the best places are the 24hr CVS Pharmacy, next to the *Monte Carlo* at 3758 Las Vegas Blvd S (Ⓣ702/262-9284), and the Walgreens adjoining the *Palazzo* at 3339 Las Vegas Blvd S (Ⓣ702/369-8166). The Hawaiian chain ABC Stores (Ⓦwww.abcstores.com) has outlets in the Miracle Mile; the Fashion Show Mall; the small Showcase Mall next to the *MGM Grand*; and the *Riviera* casino.

---

area that holds an 18ft marble replica of Michelangelo's *David*, identical to the original in every respect except for remaining uncircumcised.

Crystals 3720 Las Vegas Blvd S Ⓣ702/590-5299, Ⓦcrystalsatcitycenter.com. Daily 10am–midnight. The flamboyant Crystals mall is the one part of the CityCenter complex that truly catches the eye as you pass by along the Strip. As a spectacle, it's not to be missed, but its dazzlingly white stores are pitched way beyond the pockets of most visitors. Thus while the Paul Smith clothing boutique holds some ravishing displays, you'd be hard pushed to find a price ticket under $500 inside. Other marquee attractions include the Tom Ford store, while the biggest of the lot is the huge Tiffany jewellery outlet.

The Fashion Show Mall 3200 Las Vegas Blvd S Ⓣ702/369-8382, Ⓦwww.thefashionshow.com.

Mon–Sat 10am–9pm, Sun 11am–7pm. The Fashion Show Mall caused a sensation when it opened in 1981, as the first significant shopping mall to appear on the Strip. Thirty years on, it has grown out of all proportion, and it's now ensconced behind a glittering frontage and topped by the bizarre 300ft disc-shaped "Cloud". Strangely enough, it's still the only mall on the Strip that's not attached to a casino, which is both a strength and a weakness. While it's certainly not a must-see attraction like the Forum or Grand Canal Shoppes, it surpasses both by offering full-sized department stores, and if you just want to shop quickly and efficiently, this is the place to come.

Away from the department stores – Nordstrom, Bloomingdale's, Neiman Marcus, Saks Fifth Avenue, Dillard's and

Strip Malls At A Glance

	Crystals	Fashion Show	Forum	Grand Canal*	Miracle Mile	Via Bellagio	Wynn/ Encore
Agent Provocateur			X				
Alexander McQueen							X
American Apparel					X		
Ann Taylor		X	X	X	X		
Apple		X	X				
Armani§			X			X	
Banana Republic		X	X	X			
bebe		X		X	X		
Ben Sherman					X		
Betsey Johnson		X			X		
Bettie Page		X			X		
Bulgari	X		X				
Burberry			X	X			
Cartier	X		X				
Chanel						X	X
Chloé				X			
Diesel		X					
Dior	X		X			X	X
DKNY			X				
Dolce & Gabbana			X				
Fendi	X		X	X		X	
Fossil		X					
Fred Leighton						X	
Fredericks		X			X		
French Connection		X			X		
Gap		X			X		
Gucci			X			X	
H&M			X		X		
Hermès	X						X
Jean-Paul Gaultier							X
Jimmy Choo			X	X			
Kenneth Cole		X		X			
L'Occitane		X			X		
Louis Vuitton	X	X	X				X
Manolo Blahnik							X
Niketown			X				
Paul Smith	X						
Prada						X	
Quiksilver/Roxy		X			X		
Sephora				X	X		
Swarovski		X	X				
Ted Baker			X				
Tiffany & Co	X		X			X	
Tom Ford	X						
Tommy Bahama		X	X		X		
Urban Outfitters					X		
Versace	X		X				
Victoria's Secret		X	X	X	X		
Yves St Laurent						X	

* Grand Canal includes Shoppes at Palazzo
§ Armani includes Armani Exchange, Georgio Armani, etc

Macy's – the emphasis here is somewhat more mid-range than in the high-end casino malls. Z Gallerie, near the back, ranks among the best home furnishings stores in the city, while speciality outlets to look out for include the funky Betsey Johnson; Boot Star, which has a sensational selection of colourful cowboy boots; Paul Frank's out front; and an Apple store.

The Tix 4 Tonight outlet beside the main Strip entrance is a good place to pick up cut-price show tickets (see p.148). There's also a large but rather poor fast-food court upstairs, with a view of the Strip as well as several proper restaurants. And in case you're wondering about the name, the mall does actually put on fashion shows, usually hourly on the hour at weekends.

Forum Shops Caesars Palace, 3500 Las Vegas Blvd S ☎702/893-3807, ⓦ www.forumshops.com. Sun–Thurs 10am–11pm, Fri & Sat 10am–midnight. The mall that kick-started Las Vegas's shopping boom, back in 1992, the Forum continues to be the most profitable in the United States, generating around four times the national average income per square foot. It continues to grow ever larger, and its Strip entrance now soars three storeys high, negotiated by a breathtaking spiral escalator (albeit with a maddening habit of never quite leading where you want it to).

With new rivals appearing all the time, it would be hard to claim that the Forum any longer offers an exceptional array of stores. However, the basic concept remains irresistible, with faux-Roman columns and fountains everywhere, animatronic "statues" that come alive, and an artificial sky that wheels each hour between dawn and dusk. Among the 160-plus stores, clothing choices range from Gap and Banana Republic, through to Diesel, Ted Baker and Agent Provocateur, while there's also a Niketown and an Apple Store. The Forum doesn't have a food court as such – there's one not far away in the casino proper – but it does hold some fine restaurants, including *The Palm* (see p.135).

The Grand Canal Shoppes and the Shoppes at the Palazzo The Venetian, 3355 Las Vegas Blvd S ☎702/414-4500, ⓦ www.thegrandcanal shoppes.com and ⓦ www.theshoppesatthe palazzo.com. Sun–Thurs 10am–11pm, Fri & Sat 10am–midnight. Naturally enough, the shopping mall at the Venetian claims to draw its inspiration from Venice itself, but its true

model is rather closer to hand. From its false Italian sky (here set permanently to early evening) down to many of the actual stores, the Grand Canal Shoppes slavishly imitates the most effective elements of the Forum across the street, and in many respects surpasses it. The Grand Canal itself is cheekily impressive, not least for the sheer chutzpah of locating a full-blown waterway (complete with working gondolas; see p.70) on the second storey of the building, while with its "open-air" restaurants, St Mark's Square skilfully echoes the feel of a vibrant city square, and features on-the-hour musical performances plus living statues and the like.

In terms of shopping, there's a definite Italian flavour to many of the stores – those making their first appearance outside Venice include Il Prato, selling carnival masks and paper goods, and Ripa de Monti, which specializes in bold Venetian glass – while the overall emphasis is somewhat more upscale than at the Forum, with jewellery specialists such as Ca' D'Oro (gold) and Simayof (diamonds). Several big international clothing brands are also represented, such as Ann Taylor and Banana Republic, though you'll find more "exclusive" stores like Burberry and Chloé in the nominally distinct Shoppes at the Palazzo, at the far end of the Grand Canal, which is basically a rather dull extension of the Shoppes, redeemed by the presence of Annie Creamcheese (see opposite) and a branch of Barney's of New York.

Mandalay Place Mandalay Bay, 3930 Las Vegas Blvd S ☎702/632-9333. Sun–Thurs 10am–11pm, Fri & Sat 10am–midnight. At heart, Mandalay Place is not so much a mall as a corridor; it's certainly not on the scale of the Forum or the Grand Canal. Thanks to the constant pedestrian traffic it receives as the main walkway between *Mandalay Bay* and *Luxor* next door, however, and a reasonable array of restaurants (including *Hussong's*, see p.131) and bars (such as *Minus5 Ice Lounge*, p.142), it just about ranks as a destination its own right, rather than simply a corridor. Its most significant retailers are the hipster clothing and lifestyle store Urban Outfitters; Frederick's of Hollywood; and the first-ever Nike Golf store.

Miracle Mile Shops Planet Hollywood, 3663 Las Vegas Blvd S ☎702/866-0703, ⓦ www.miracle mileshopslv.com. Sun–Thurs 10am–11pm, Fri & Sat 10am–midnight. Walking through the

Miracle Mile Shops – the most affordable of the Strip malls – can be a disorienting experience. Not only does its figure-of-eight floor plan, wrapped around and through the casino at *Planet Hollywood*, make it easy to lose your bearings, but it has never quite managed to shed its previous identity as the "Desert Passage", when this used to be the *Aladdin*. Left-over Arabian Nights theming is everywhere interspersed with tacky, dispiriting "updates".

The whole place is much more of a mixed bag than its rivals, and its restaurants and bars tend to be poor, but several of the stores are still worth visiting. Highlights include the big Urban Outfitters at the front; Wild Pair, which stocks some great, inexpensive Las Vegas shoes; and the quirky Bettie Page Store, which has some great 1950s' dresses and accessories (@www.bettiepageclothing.com). Look out too for a pair of fabulously tasteless art galleries facing each other at the far end of the mall, Oh My Godard with its acrylic strawberries bathing in champagne, and the

Wyland Gallery, which specializes in space-travelling humpback whales.

Via Bellagio Bellagio, 3600 Las Vegas Blvd S ☏702/693-7111. Daily 10am–midnight. While Via Bellagio consists of just ten stores, set along the plushly carpeted passageway that leads to the heart of *Bellagio* from the Strip-corner entrance nearest *Caesars Palace*, its single-minded focus on the very top end of the spectrum makes this one of the chic-est places to shop in Las Vegas. For window-shoppers, the most distinctive feature is the antique jewellery at Fred Leighton, which ranges from the Indian Raj to prized Art Deco and Art Nouveau pieces. The rest of the array is a little more predictable – Gucci, Prada, Georgio Armani, Chanel, Dior, Bottega Veneta, Fendi, Tiffany & Co and Yves St Laurent.

Wynn and Encore Esplanades Wynn Las Vegas, 3131 Las Vegas Blvd S ☏702/770-7000, @www.wynnlasvegas.com. Sun–Thurs 10am–11pm, Fri & Sat 10am–midnight. While it's not always easy to tell where *Wynn* ends and *Encore* begins, or to distinguish the

Vintage Las Vegas

Las Vegas's main sources of genuine vintage clothing are located well away from the Strip.

The much-loved **Attic** (☏702/388-4088, @www.atticvintage.com), a glorious emporium of vintage Americana both chic and kitsch, is in an insalubrious part of downtown, at ten blocks south of Fremont – way too far to reach on foot. A July 2010 gas explosion forced it to move into temporary premises at 1025 S Main St, with only a small proportion of its stock on display, and reduced opening hours (Tues–Sat 10am–6pm). However, it may have moved again by the time you read this, either back to 1018 S Main St, or on to a new home that can do justice to its fine array of clothes, costumes, shoes, hats, accessories and even furniture.

As part of a nationwide chain, **Buffalo Exchange**, a couple of miles east along Flamingo Rd from the Strip at 4110 S Maryland Parkway (Mon–Sat 10am–8pm, Sun 11am–7pm; ☏702/791-3960, @www.buffaloexchange.com), is much less characterful. If you're looking for anything specific, however, like a party costume, classic shoes, or simply cheap threads, it's a more dependable source of inexpensive retro items.

If your interests are a little more specialized, it's also well worth checking out **Valentino's Zoot Suit Connection**, at 107 E Charleston Blvd (daily 11am–5pm; ☏702/383-9555), which has a phenomenal array of zoot suits, fedoras and Forties fashions in general. Also try **Serge's Showgirl Wigs**, at 953 E Sahara Ave (Mon–Sat 10am–5.30pm; ☏702/732-1015, @www.showgirlwigs.com), where the showgirl is queen, and her hair is...artificial.

The one vintage outlet on the Strip itself is a very different kettle of fish. **Annie Creamcheese Designer Vintage**, in the Shoppes at the Palazzo (☏702/452-9600, @www.anniecreamcheese.com), sells fabulous designer creations dating as far back as the 1920s alongside brand-new stuff. It's a great place to browse, but the prices mean you're unlikely to leave with your arms full.

Las Vegas souvenirs

Perhaps because its must-see attractions change one year to the next, Las Vegas has never quite hit on a definitive sum-it-all-up souvenir to take back home. Each casino sells its own wide range of logo items, and T-shirts with the latest marketing slogans are everywhere you look, but otherwise the biggest-selling items these days seem to be miniature replicas of the "Welcome To Las Vegas" sign, squeezed if you're lucky into a snowglobe.

The single best outlet for Las Vegas tack has to be the **Bonanza Gift Shop**, at the north end of the Strip at 2460 Las Vegas Blvd S (℡702/385-7359, ⓦwww.worldslargestgiftshop.com; daily 8am–midnight). Across from the *Sahara* and just south of the *Stratosphere*, the "World's Largest Gift Store" is not as big as it likes to pretend, but it's still bursting with fuzzy dice, whoopee cushions, fart candy, used playing cards from all the casinos, gaming boards, postcards, Elvis clocks and nudie ballpoint pens.

For a truly authentic Las Vegas souvenir, you can also head to the **Gamblers General Store**, a few blocks south of downtown at 800 S Main St (℡702/382-9903, ⓦwww.gamblersgeneralstore.com; daily 9am–6pm). As well as old slot machines and full-sized craps tables, they sell felt mats with roulette, blackjack and craps layouts starting at around $30, and playing cards from each casino for $1.99. There's also a large library of books on gambling, detailing techniques for blackjack, craps, horses and even slots – assuming you don't mind paying $20 for a photocopied pamphlet that explains why you'll never win.

shopping areas from the rest of the complex as a whole, each nominally holds its own "Esplanade" of extremely exclusive stores. The Wynn Esplanade is the walkway that curves into the property from its northwest entrance, closest to *Palazzo* and the Fashion Show Mall. Standouts along the way include the only Manolo Blahnik shoe store outside New York, plus designer outlets bearing such names as Oscar de la Renta and Jean-Paul Gaultier. The shorter

Encore Esplanade is a fancy name for the main passageway that connects the two properties; besides Chanel and Hermès stores, it holds outlets that sell the linens used in the hotels' guest rooms, and the cookware used in their kitchens.

Nearby, the Penske-Wynn car dealership sells only Ferraris and Maseratis (ⓦwww.penskewynn.com) – and largely red ones at that, to match the prevailing decor – and there's also a Ferrari logo shop.

The rest of the city

Galleria at Sunset 1300 W Sunset Rd, Henderson ℡702/434-0202, ⓦwww.galleriaatsunset.com. Mon–Sat 10am–9pm, Sun 11am–6pm. This suburban mall (anchored by Dillard's, Macy's and JC Penney, and featuring many of the usual chain suspects in between) stands at the heart of a busy shopping district – eight miles southeast of the Strip, opposite *Sunset Station* – with neighbours including a Borders and a Barnes & Noble.
Las Vegas Premium Outlets 875 S Grand Central Parkway ℡702/474-7500, ⓦwww.premiumoutlets.com. Mon–Sat 10am–9pm, Sun 10am–8pm. This large and predominantly open-air mall, on the Gold Line CAT bus route (see p.24), a mile southwest of central

downtown or two miles north of the *Stratosphere*, holds a comprehensive selection of major international brands. Big fashion and footwear names include American Apparel, Calvin Klein, Levi's, Ted Baker and Tommy Hilfiger. Some outlets are wholly or partly devoted to discounted or discontinued lines from their parent stores; some, such as Ann Taylor, Banana Republic, Brook Brothers and Nike, are specifically sub-branded as being "Factory Stores"; and some are much the same as you'd find elsewhere. While it's not an exciting place to spend any time, it's your best and most convenient bet for finding bargain prices. It has a food court but no real restaurants.

Las Vegas Outlet Center **7400 Las Vegas Blvd S**
☎ 702/896-5599, ⓦ www.lasvegasoutletcenter
.com. Mon–Sat 10am–9pm, Sun 10am–8pm.
Though this ever-expanding, aesthetically
challenged mall – located around three
miles south of *Mandalay Bay* on the east
side of Las Vegas Boulevard – started life as
a discount shopping centre, its prices these
days seem no cheaper than anywhere else,
and it has been somewhat overshadowed
by the same owners' Premium Outlets (see
above). It is, however, easily accessible by
car, and hosts over 150 stores, mostly
clothing and footwear retailers like Levi's,
Dress Barn, OshKosh B'Gosh, Nike Factory
Store and Reebok, plus the odd specialist
store like Bose and Ritz Camera.
Town Square **6605 Las Vegas Blvd S,** ⓦ www
.townsquarelasvegas.com. Individual stores set
own hours. The open-air Town Square mall
is very easy to reach from the southern end
of the Strip – just head three miles straight
down Las Vegas Boulevard from *Mandalay
Bay*, on a Gold Line CAT bus (see p.24) if

you're not driving, to the intersection of the
I-15 and I-245 interstates. Intended to
resemble a "European village", Town
Square is a bigger hit with locals than
visitors. Its various stores and amenities are
laid out along streets and open squares, to
create an artificial shopping neighbourhood
of the kind Las Vegas otherwise lacks.
However, there's a very good reason why
the city's other malls are indoors and
air-conditioned; in the merciless summer
sun, walking around Town Square can be a
real trial. Big-name attractions include a
large Whole Foods supermarket; Fry's
Electronics, selling anything from computers
to cameras; and the biggest bookstore
anywhere near the Strip, Borders.
Otherwise there's a standard roster of mall
stores – Apple, Banana Republic, Fossil,
Gap, H&M, etc – plus a Tix 4 Tonight
cut-price ticket outlet and an eighteen-
screen cinema. There are also plenty of
restaurants, though none is worth making a
special trip for.

SHOPPING | The rest of the city

Gay Las Vegas

While Las Vegas is by and large a gay-friendly city, that's much truer of the Strip than of its often-conservative residential neighbourhoods. That said, the casinos make few special efforts towards attracting gay visitors, and there's only one specifically gay club on the Strip, *Krave*. Otherwise, as far as gay **nightlife** is concerned, it's largely a question of joining in with the local scene. There's a scattering of gay bars and clubs throughout the city, but the main concentrations are in what's affectionately known as the "**Fruit Loop**", around the intersection of **Paradise Road** and **Naples Drive**, a mile east of the Strip and just south of the *Hard Rock Casino*, and in the Commercial Center on **Sahara Avenue**, not far east of the Strip. None of the bars is exclusively devoted to women.

By far the biggest event in the local gay calendar is **Las Vegas Pride**, in the middle weekend of September (☎702/615-9249, ⓦwww.lasvegaspride.org). Friday night sees a parade thorough downtown, followed by an open-air festival on Saturday in the grounds of the Clark County Government Center, a few blocks southwest. In addition, the Nevada Gay Rodeo Association (ⓦwww.ngra.com), stages the annual BigHorn Rodeo at Horseman's Park, 5800 E Flamingo Rd, in late May.

Although Nevada state law does not recognize gay or lesbian **weddings**, many of Las Vegas's wedding chapels offer commitment ceremonies. The Gay Chapel of Las Vegas, at 1205 Las Vegas Blvd S (☎702/384-0771 or 1-800/574-4450, ⓦwww.gaychapeloflasvegas.com), regularly hosts such ceremonies, though it doubles as the traditional Viva Las Vegas Wedding Chapel as well, while the major casino chapels at *Paris*, *Luxor*, *Bellagio* and *Mandalay Bay* are all known to have hosted them.

Information and resources

For up-to-date information on events and happenings in Las Vegas's gay community, look at the print or online versions of the free monthly magazine *QVegas* (ⓦqvegas.com), or visit ⓦwww.gayvegas.com. Get Booked is a gay and lesbian **bookstore**, in the Fruit Loop at 4640 S Paradise Rd (Sun–Thurs 10am–midnight, Fri & Sat 10am–2am; ☎702737-7780, ⓦwww.getbooked.com), one block north of Tropicana Ave.

The **Gay and Lesbian Center of Las Vegas**, at 953 E Sahara Ave (Mon–Fri 11am–7pm; ☎702/733-9800, ⓦwww.thecenterlv.com), is a drop-in centre that provides information on community resources, social clubs and health-related issues.

Accommodation

Blue Moon Resort 2651 Westwood Drive
T 1-866/798-9194 or 702/361-9110, W blue
moonlv.com. Not so much a "resort" as a
tastefully converted motel, the *Blue Moon*,
off Sahara Ave about a mile west of the
Strip, is the only Las Vegas hotel exclusively
devoted to gay male travellers, and has
quite a cruisy atmosphere. The actual
accommodation is OK, and there's a jacuzzi
and pool, but the noise of the nearby interstate can be disturbing. Sun–Thurs $75, Fri
& Sat $140.

Bars

8½ Ultra Lounge 4633 Paradise Rd T 702/791-
0100, W www.piranhavegas.com. Daily
10pm–5am. Fruit Loop lounge/bar, belonging
to the same owners as the neighbouring
Gipsy, and run in conjunction with the
Piranha nightclub (see p.178), which
occupies the other half of what from the
outside seems an unremarkable building.
Inside, this is a welcoming, earth-toned and
very contemporary bar, equipped with
comfortable sofas and curtained-off booths,
as well as its own small dance floor and a
pool table.

The Buffalo 4640 Paradise Rd T 702/733-8355.
Daily 24hr. This lively Levi's-and-leathers bar,
a long-standing bear hangout in the heart of
the main gay district, is also the headquarters for local gay motorcycle clubs; there's
good music but no dancefloor. $5 all
you-can-drink beer busts on Tuesday and
Friday nights.

Charlie's Las Vegas 5012 S Arville St
T 702/876-1844, W www.charlieslasvegas.com.
Daily 24hr. Formerly the *Backstreet Bar*, this
very friendly, gay-oriented country bar still
has a strong Western vibe, catering to both
men and women with free dance lessons on
Monday evenings, and line dancing on both
Thursday and Friday, plus almighty $5 beer
busts on Saturday and Sunday afternoons.

Escape Lounge 4213 W Sahara Ave T 702/364-
1167, W www.escapeloungelv.com. Daily 24hr.
A sister property to *Goodtimes* across the
valley, the *Escape Lounge* is basically a
quiet, neighbourhood gay bar, with pool
tables and sports TV. Twice-daily happy
hours, from 3am to 5am and 5pm to 7pm.

Goodtimes Bar 1775 E Tropicana Ave T 702/736-
9494, W www.goodtimeslv.com. Daily 24hr.
Welcoming neighbourhood gay bar with
happy hours from 5am to 7am and
5pm to 7pm on Tuesday, Thursday &
Sunday, plus a hectic beer bust on Monday
from 11pm–3am, and the Goth/darkwave
"Carpe Noctem" on Wednesday night.

Las Vegas Eagle 3430 E Tropicana Ave
T 702/458-8662. Daily 24hr. Dimly lit gay bar,
roughly four miles east of the Strip, which
has a small dancefloor and a pool table,
and hosts underwear nights every
Wednesday and Friday. Not a desperately
beautiful joint, it attracts a primarily older
male crowd.

Spotlight Lounge 957 E Sahara Ave T 702/696-
0202. Daily 24hr. Large, unglamorous but
very friendly gay bar in the Commercial
Center. Friday and Saturday nights count as
"underwear weekends", with free drinks for
men in their underwear, and there are beer
or liquor busts every other day.

Clubs

Flex Cocktail Lounge 4371 W Charleston Blvd
T 702/385-3539, W www.flexlasvegas.com.
Daily 24hr. No cover. Flamboyant gay club
where the emphasis is on music and
dancing as opposed to drinking, and
occasional strip shows. Beer flows freely all
week, with DJs most nights; Monday is set
aside for karaoke.

Freezone 610 E Naples Drive T 702/794-2300,
W www.freezonelv.com. Daily 24hr. Busy
gay-district bar/club, popular with women
and men alike, two blocks south of the *Hard
Rock*. In the absence of an exclusively
lesbian club in the city, Freezone's specifically lesbian night on Tuesday is as close as
the city comes. Besides the weekend's drag
acts (Fri & Sat 10pm), it also features an
all-male revue every Thursday, while its
restaurant serves good food daily
6pm–2am.

Krave Miracle Mile Shops, Planet Hollywood, 3667 Las Vegas Blvd S ☎702/836-0830, ⓦwww.kravelasvegas.com. Daily from 10.30pm. Cover varies, up to $20. As the first full-scale gay club ever to thrive on the Strip, this hybrid of lounge, theatre and nightclub not surprisingly claims to be the hottest gay nightclub in the US. That's an overstatement, particularly because the Strip location ensures it's usually as much straight as gay, but it's still a spectacular, flamboyant experience. Officially the *Krave* club operates on Fridays and Saturdays only, but the same enormous space is used every night of the week, with a different theme nightly, currently ranging from the unabashed, locals-dominated "Meat Market" on Mondays to "Superheroes and Villains" on Saturday.

Piranha 4633 Paradise Rd ☎702/791-0100, ⓦwww.piranhavegas.com. Daily 10pm–5am. Cover varies; typically $20. To enter the nightclub half of the complex that's also home to *8½ Ultra Lounge* (see p.177), you have first to brave a wraparound piranha-filled aquarium. Beyond lies the frenetic dance floor, with a plush bar alongside and an exclusive VIP section, featuring private "skyboxes", upstairs. There's also a fabulous outdoor patio, with individual fireplaces. Drag shows Fri & Sat 11.30pm.

⑰

Sports, activities and spas

as Vegas is not exactly renowned for its healthy lifestyle, but if you start to feel the need for exercise, opportunities do exist. For visitors, the highest profile activity these days is **golf**, with almost fifty courses scattered around the city. All the casinos do at least have a **swimming pool**, and the larger ones on the Strip offer full-service **spas** as well. Locals' casinos, on the other hand, usually out in more residential neighbourhoods, specialize in offering popular year-round indoor pursuits such as **bowling**.

As for **spectator sports**, despite the best efforts of Mayor Goodman – who's on record as saying that "until you have major-league sports, you'll always be thought of as a minor-league town" – Las Vegas lacks high-profile professional teams. Although tourists flock from all over the nation to watch events like the Super Bowl on giant-screen TVs – and of course, bet on them – the only sport to draw sizeable crowds for live action is championship **boxing**.

Indoor sports and activities

Bowling

Gold Coast 4000 W Flamingo Rd ☎702/367-7111, ⓦgoldcoastcasino.com. Daily 24hr. The usual low rates at the Gold Coast's superbly equipped 70-lane bowling centre drop even lower after midnight on weekdays, or 2.30am at weekends. Kids bowl free on Tuesdays.

Orleans 4500 W Tropicana Ave ☎702/365-7111, ⓦorleanscasino.com. Daily 24hr. Adults pay around $3 per game at the Orleans' 70-lane upstairs bowling arcade.

Sam's Town 5111 Boulder Hwy ☎702/454-8022, ⓦwww.samstownlv.com. Daily 24hr. This bright 56-lane downstairs bowling centre plays host on Friday and Saturday nights (from midnight until 4am) to "extreme bowling"; basically, it becomes a nightclub,

with music, lights, dry ice, and, of course, bowling. For the rest of the week, rates drop between midnight and 8am.

Gyms and fitness facilities

Every casino offers **fitness facilities** of some kind. Access to a small room filled with standard exercise machines is usually reserved for hotel guests only, and is often either free, or included in the "resort fee". More elaborate complexes generally form part of each hotel's spa, open for a daily fee to guests and visitors alike.

Otherwise, the city's largest health-club chain is the **Las Vegas Athletic Club**. The closest to the Strip of its six valley locations, most of which remain

179

The Best Spas in Las Vegas

Almost all the major casinos offer their own luxurious **spa** facilities, open as a rule to guests and non-guests alike, but occasionally restricted to guests only at weekends.

Typical rates for a single day's access start at around $25, though some charge less if you only use the fitness equipment rather than the full range of hot and cold pools, steam rooms and so on. Beyond that, a vast range of more expensive treatments is available, ranging from massage of all kinds (typically costing from $90 for 25min and $135 for 50min) to beauty treatments, facials and waxings.

The list below includes the finest spas Las Vegas has to offer. The top three are generally acknowledged to be those at *Encore* and the *Venetian*, run by the renowned *Canyon Ranch* group, and *Qua*, in the Augustus Tower at *Caesars Palace*, which evokes the decadence and luxury of ancient Rome.

Aria	**The Spa** ☏702/590-9600; daily 6am–8pm
Bellagio	**Spa Bellagio** ☏702/693-7472; daily 6am–8pm
Caesars Palace	**Qua** ☏1-866/782-0655; daily 6am–8pm
Encore	**Spa** ☏702/770-4772; daily 7am–9pm
Golden Nugget	**Spa** ☏702/386-8186; daily 6am–8pm
Hard Rock	**Reliquary** ☏702/693-5520; daily 8am–8pm
Mandalay Bay	**Spa Mandalay** ☏702/632-7777; daily 6am–8.30pm
MGM Grand	**Grand Spa** ☏702/891-3077; daily 6am–8pm
Planet Hollywood	**Mandara** ☏702/785-5772; daily 6am–7pm
The Mirage	**Spa** ☏702/791-7472; daily 6.30am–7pm
Venetian	**Canyon Ranch** ☏702/414-3600; daily 6am–8pm

open around the clock, is at 2655 S Maryland Pkwy (☏702/734-5822; ⓦ www.lvac.com). All feature indoor and outdoor pools, exercise equipment and classes, saunas and spas, and other sports facilities.

Outdoor sports and activities

Golf

Only one Las Vegas casino now has its own **golf course**. You can walk right out of **Wynn Las Vegas** onto the relandscaped version of the former *Desert Inn* course; the snag is, only guests at the resort can play, and even they have to pay $500 each for the privilege.

There is another course very close to the Strip, however. Not far south of *Mandalay Bay*, the extraordinarily lavish water-themed **Bali Hai** course at 5160 Las Vegas Blvd S (☏1-888/427-6678, ⓦ balihaigolfclub.com) charges a standard green fee of $245. Each golf cart has its own GPS system, while Wolfgang Puck's *Cili* is the clubhouse restaurant.

The best and most affordable **public courses** are the **Las Vegas Golf Club**, at 4300 W Washington Ave (non-residents $49 Mon–Thurs, $59 Fri–Sun; ☏702/646-3003, ⓦ las vegasgc.com); the **Craig Ranch Golf Course**, **at** 628 W Craig Rd ($30; ☏702/642-9700, no website); and the **Desert Pines Golf Club**, **at** 3415 E Bonanza Rd ($49 Mon–Thurs, $59 Fri–Sun; ☏702/366-1616, ⓦ desert pinesgolfclub.com).

For a complete list of courses, plus discount reservations, visit ⓦ lasvegas golf.com or ⓦ golfvegas.com.

Horseriding

Cowboy Trail Rides ☏702/387-2457, ⓦ www .cowboytrailrides.com. Hours vary. Riding expeditions in the Spring Mountains, in the vicinity of Red Rock Canyon, from $99 for 90min up to $329 for five hours.

Rafting

Black Canyon River Adventures Boulder City
☎1-800/455-3490, Ⓦwww.rafts.com. One-day
rafting trips downriver from Hoover Dam as
far as Willow Beach, for $86 per person if
you make your own way to Boulder City, or
$130 with hotel pickup.

Skiing

Las Vegas Ski and Snowboard Resort Hwy-156,
Mt Charleston ☎702/385-2754, Ⓦwww.ski
lasvegas.com. Late Nov to early April only. Lifts
operate daily 9am–4pm. Las Vegas's only ski
slopes are almost fifty miles from the Strip
(see p.103). Four chair lifts lead to eleven
different slopes, graded from novice to
advanced; lift passes cost $50 for a full day
(daily 9am–4pm), or $45 for half a day (daily
noon–4pm). The resort holds a coffee shop,
ski school and equipment-rental shop, but
no accommodation.

Skydiving

Skydive Las Vegas 1401 Airport Rd, Boulder City
☎702/759-3483 or 1-800/875-9348, Ⓦwww
.skydivelasvegas.com. By reservation. Leap
from an airplane 12,500ft over the Nevada
desert, strapped to an instructor, then
free-fall and parachute for a total of well
over five minutes, for $199, including free
shuttle service from the Strip to and from
the Boulder City airport.

Tennis

Only two Strip casinos still have their
own **tennis** courts. Fees at both *Bally's*

(☎702/967-4598), which has eight
indoor night-lit hard courts, and the
Flamingo (☎702/733-3444), where the
four outdoor hard courts are only open
in daytime, start at $20 per hour for
guests, and $25 for non-guests. Both
have pro shops and offer lessons.

Elsewhere, the *Hilton*, at 3000
Paradise Rd (☎702/732-5009), has a
fully fledged tennis club charging
similar rates.

Watersports

Renting water craft of all kinds for use
on Lake Mead has long been a popular
summer activity for Las Vegas visitors.
Water levels have been dropping in
recent years, however, forcing some
marinas to move to new locations, and
others to close altogether. Currently the
closest marinas to the city, not far from
Hoover Dam a thirty-mile drive
southeast of the Strip, are **Las Vegas
Boat Harbor** (☎702/293-1191, Ⓦboat
inglakemead.com) and **Lake Mead
Marina** (☎702/293-3484, Ⓦriverlakes
.com). Typical rental rates start at $50 per
hour for a small powerboat, and $70 per
hour for a two-person waverunner.

Larger craft are available at **Callville
Bay** (☎1-800/255-5561, Ⓦcallville
bay.com), forty miles east of Las Vegas
on the north shore of the lake, including
fishing boats for $40 per hour or $215
per day, and houseboats for overnight
cruises.

Spectator sports

Baseball

The **Las Vegas 51s**, a class AAA team
affiliated to the Toronto Blue Jays, play
in baseball's Pacific Coast League.
Named in honour of Area 51, Nevada's
legendary UFO epicentre, they host
around seventy home games between
April and Labor Day each year at
Cashman Field, 850 Las Vegas Blvd N
(☎702/386-7200; Ⓦwww.lv51.com).
General admission prices start at $9.

Boxing

Las Vegas remains the world capital of
boxing. A heavyweight title fight brings
so many high-rollers into town that the
major casinos will pay almost any purse
to the boxers concerned (even upwards
of $20 million). The three principal
venues these days are *Caesars Palace*, the
MGM Grand and *Mandalay Bay*. Ticket
prices depend completely on demand
and can range up to thousands of dollars.

College sports

The men's **basketball** team of the University of Nevada, Las Vegas, the Runnin' Rebels (@unlvrebels.cstv.com), plays its home games at the Thomas & Mack Center, 4505 S Maryland Pkwy at Tropicana and Swenson (@unlvtickets.com; ☎702/739-3267), between November and March; the Lady Rebels are based next door at the Cox Pavilion (same websites and phone).

The University's (American) **football** team, the UNLV Rebels, play at Sam Boyd Stadium, on Russell Rd in Henderson (@unlvtickets.com; ☎702/739-3267), between September and December.

Motor sports

The **Las Vegas Motor Speedway**, just off I-15 well northeast of downtown at 7000 Las Vegas Blvd N (☎702/644-4443, @www.lvms.com), puts on an extensive programme of racing year-round. The highlight of the calendar is the three-day **NASCAR Weekend** in early March.

Contexts

Contexts

History

Still no older than a single human lifetime, Las Vegas has been forced for almost its entire existence to live with the consequences of its dependence on **casino gambling**. No other industry has gained a serious foothold, while the desire – and power – of casino owners to keep city government as weak as possible has allowed Las Vegas to become a hideous sprawl, with an infrastructure that is at best haphazard and at worst downright inadequate.

Despite it all, however, Las Vegas has grown to become an astonishing and in many ways irresistible city. Some twists in the tale have been thanks to its being utterly in tune with its times, others can be put down to pure luck, but it's been an extraordinary journey, and you can but wonder what its second century will bring.

A valley without a city

Little trace remains of the earliest inhabitants of the Las Vegas Valley. Until around 1150 AD, the region lay on the extreme western periphery of the domains of the **Ancestral Puebloans**, the Native American people also known as the Anasazi. The ruins of their dramatic "cliff dwellings" are scattered throughout the Colorado Plateau to the east, but the only significant Ancestral Puebloan relics in Nevada are preserved in the Lost City Museum near Overton, sixty miles northeast of Las Vegas (see p.106). In more recent times, the valley was roamed by the nomadic **Paiute**, whose descendants still occupy a small reservation northwest of the city.

Although what's now southern Nevada was claimed for Spain in 1598, as part of the Spanish colony of New Mexico, no outsiders are known to have passed this way before 1829, by which time it belonged to the newly independent nation of Mexico. These first explorers were members of an expedition led by Antonio Armejo, seeking to extend the **Old Spanish Trail** from Santa Fe all the way to California. Encountering an unexpected oasis of grasslands fed by underground springs, they named it **Las Vegas** – "The Meadows."

Significant traffic along the Old Spanish Trail only began to appear in the late 1840s. In 1847, **Mormon** refugees established Salt Lake City beyond the western frontier of the United States, and proclaimed it the capital of the promised land of **Deseret**, which supposedly included much of Nevada and California. That same year, however, the US acquired New Mexico from Mexico. The Mormons were granted the smaller Territory of Utah, while Nevada achieved statehood in its own right in 1864.

The Las Vegas Valley became a crucial staging post on the route between Utah and California, now known as the **Mormon Trail**. In 1855, Mormon leader Brigham Young decided to establish a colony here, known as **Bringhurst**, because there was already a town of Las Vegas, New Mexico. Centred on a small adobe fort, it lasted a mere three years.

Thanks to the discovery of silver in southern Nevada in 1859, however, Las Vegas survived as a supply centre serving miners and prospectors. The former Mormon fort became the hub of the **Las Vegas Ranch**, which was run by Octavio Gass between 1865 and 1882, and then by Helen Stewart. Even in 1900, the census for the whole valley took up only half a sheet of paper; you can see it in the Nevada State Museum (see p.97), listing just seven families and a total of eighteen people.

The founding of Las Vegas

In 1903, Helen Stewart sold the Las Vegas Ranch to Montana railroad proprietor **William Clark**, for $55,000. Not only did the valley stand roughly halfway between Salt Lake City and Los Angeles, it also offered the only dependable water supply for hundreds of miles. Newly constructed railroad tracks were approaching Las Vegas from both directions, and they finally met near what's now Jean, 23 miles southwest, on January 30, 1905.

By then, freebooters had set up a speculative townsite west of the tracks near modern Las Vegas, but the official birth of **"Clark's Las Vegas Townsite"** came a few months later, on May 15. At the corner of Fremont and Main streets downtown, forty blocks, each divided into 32 lots, were auctioned off. Soon the nascent businesses and residences of a typical small western town occupied the space. The sale of liquor was confined to **Block 16**, bounded by First, Second, Ogden and Stewart streets, which quickly gained a reputation for raucous saloons and gambling dens.

Las Vegas was very much a railroad town in its early years. In 1909, the southern portion of Lincoln County, in which it originally stood, became **Clark County** in its own right, and, ironically enough, Nevada became the first state in the US to **outlaw gambling**.

A boost from the Feds

When Nevada relegalized gambling in 1931, the *Las Vegas Review-Journal* commented that "People should not get overly excited over the effects of the new gambling bill – conditions will be little different than they are at the present time." The measure was a response to the recent experience of Prohibition, when "speakeasies" serving bootleg liquor had proved a major source of political corruption across the nation. Rather than go through the same problems with the then-burgeoning illegal casinos, Nevada's legislators decided to keep them above board, and gain a little tax revenue in the process. What they hadn't anticipated, however, was that every other state in the country would decide to tackle the situation differently, and crack down on gambling instead.

Reno was the first city to benefit from Nevada's new renown as a haven for gamblers, and Las Vegas might never have amounted to anything had Congress not decided to dam nearby Boulder Canyon. The aim was to harness the Colorado River to provide cheap electricity and water for the entire southwest, but from the very start, the **Hoover Dam** project amounted to a massive federal subsidy for the infant city.

The government deliberately housed the dam workers in purpose-built **Boulder City** – "a wholesome American community" in which gambling remains banned to this day – rather than the "boisterous frontier town" of Las Vegas. Not only did that fail to deter them from frittering away their pay-packets on Fremont Street, but they were immediately joined by a vast influx of **tourists**. In 1932 alone, the first year of the dam's construction, over a hundred thousand visitors came to admire the new "World Wonder".

Las Vegas had first attempted to encourage tourism during the 1920s, opening a dude ranch and even a golf course. Its first out-of-town casino, the *Meadows*, opened in 1931 on Boulder Highway – not that it lasted long – while its first luxury hotel, the *Apache*, followed a year later. Las Vegas played host to its first **convention** in 1935, when the arrival of five thousand Shriners from California briefly doubled the local population.

By the time the dam builders left town in 1937, Las Vegas had grown used to the tourist dollar (and also to its first taste of **air-conditioning**, thanks to dam-powered "swamp coolers"). While it vigorously promoted such events as its "Helldorado" rodeo, and an annual regatta on Lake Mead (then known as Boulder Lake), its continuing appeal depended on two mighty pillars: legalized gambling and easy **divorce**. Then as now, any American citizen had only to spend six weeks in Nevada to take advantage of the state's liberal divorce laws. Glamorous movie depictions of desert-ranch sojourns, and real-life cases like the separation of Clark Gable and Ria Longham in March 1939, publicized Las Vegas across the nation.

The emergence of the Strip

While Las Vegas's destiny as a resort was already becoming clear in 1940, its population was still a mere eight thousand. Like Phoenix and Albuquerque, however, it prospered mightily during World War II. Las Vegas itself swiftly acquired a large air force base, while what's now **Henderson** started out in 1941 as Basic Town Site, built to house the ten thousand employees of the huge Basic magnesium plant.

Inevitably, gambling also boomed during the war. Thus far, the casino industry had been almost exclusively concentrated along Fremont Street downtown, well away from residential neighbourhoods. However, as the illegal casinos of California were forced out of business, a new breed of entrepreneur began to show up in Las Vegas. Although **Guy McAfee**, a former chief of LA's vice squad, opened the *Pair-O-Dice* in 1938, the first fully fledged resort to appear on the Strip was *El Rancho*, in 1941. Its location just outside the city line (on what's now an empty lot opposite the *Sahara*) enabled its owner, California hotelier Thomas Hull, to benefit from lower taxes and cheaper real estate prices. The original *Rancho* only had fifty rooms, but its lawns, palm trees, swimming pool and central windmill tower came as a revelation. One impressed guest, William Moore, followed suit by opening the *Last Frontier* a mile south in 1942, and the career of the Strip as a "casino suburb" was launched.

As described on p.62, mobster **Benjamin "Bugsy" Siegel** was the powerhouse behind the early Strip's definitive occupant, the seven-million-dollar *Flamingo*. Shortly after its premature opening night in December 1946, heavy losses forced him to shut up shop. The *Flamingo* was back on its feet by March 1947, but Siegel's erstwhile partners were dissatisfied enough to have him murdered in LA in June. If anything, such murky goings-on merely added to the allure of Las Vegas for visitors who were drawn to the city precisely because of, rather than despite, its "Sin City" image.

The heyday of the Mob

With downtown Las Vegas becoming increasingly out-Stripped, in 1950 Las Vegas's city authorities made a last great effort to annex the Strip. The attempt was thwarted when a consortium of casino owners and Clark County officials declared the Strip area to be the unincorporated township of **Paradise City** instead. That unholy alliance lay behind the Strip's developing status as the barely concealed playground and cash cow for the criminal underworld of the entire United States.

The flow of new resorts in the 1950s seemed all but unstoppable. The luxurious *Desert Inn*, which opened in 1950, was the cream of the crop, featuring a chef imported from the *Ritz* in Paris and a guest list that included the Duke and Duchess of Windsor and John F Kennedy. Next came the *Sands* in 1952, the *Riviera* in 1955 (which finally proved it was possible to build high-rise hotels in the desert), the *Dunes* later that year, and the *Hacienda* in 1957. However, sinister figures lurked in the shadows. To complete the *Desert Inn*, nominal owner Wilbur Clark had been obliged to sell a 75 percent stake to a Detroit syndicate led by Moe Dalitz, while when East Coast gangster Frank Costello was shot in New York in 1957, the monthly profit figures from the new *Tropicana* were found in his pocket.

In 1950, the **Kefauver Committee on Organized Crime**, set up by the US Senate, held hearings in Las Vegas to investigate links between casinos and the Mafia, and established that licenses had been granted to known criminals. In belated response, Nevada established its Gaming Control Board in 1955, with the aim of vetting potential casino owners. In 1960, the board went further by issuing the legendary **Black Book**, listing underworld figures who were barred from even entering any casino in the state.

Meanwhile, Las Vegas was establishing itself as the **entertainment** centre of the world. Frank Sinatra debuted at the *Desert Inn* in 1951, and Liberace received $50,000 to open the *Riviera* in 1955. The *New Frontier* played host to Ronald Reagan with the Adorabelles in 1954; Sammy Davis Jr in 1955; and the young Elvis Presley, who bombed abysmally, in 1956.

The opening of the city's **Convention Center** in 1959, on Paradise Road, was yet another factor that boosted the Strip at the expense of downtown; conventioneers stayed almost exclusively in the nearby Strip hotels. At first, almost all came from the western states, but with the advent of jet planes in 1960 they began to arrive from all over the country, and not for the last time the **airport** had to expand. California's ever-growing car culture made road links increasingly important too, and construction began on the I-15 freeway.

Las Vegas and the bomb

In 1950 the Atomic Energy Commission decided that a remote area of Nellis Air Force Base, sixty miles northwest of Las Vegas, would be ideal for testing atomic bombs, and designated it the **Nevada Test Site**. Publicly, the citizens of Las Vegas were assured that they were in no danger, as they'd be shielded by the Spring Mountains. Behind closed doors in the White House, more sanguine assessments concluded that the potential price, of perhaps a few thousand victims of radiation poisoning, was worth paying.

Las Vegas embraced the bomb, turning it into another show for tourists. The first explosion, at Frenchmans Flat on January 26, 1951, was close enough to shatter windows in the city, though it took seven minutes for the shock wave to arrive. While the **mushroom cloud** was visible from the city, sightseers began to drive out to get a better look. Soon, traffic on test days out to the best viewpoints on Mount Charleston (see p.103) was bumper to bumper.

Blasts continued above ground until 1958 (indeed tests were conducted underground until 1992), with unfailing popularity. Schedules were released months in advance, so tourists could time their vacations to join in the fun. The *Sands* ran a "Miss Atomic Bomb" contest in May 1957, and the Atomic Energy Commission even encouraged the Boy Scouts to have an atomic energy merit badge.

Las Vegas was spared the worst of the fallout; prevailing winds blew east instead, to St George, Utah, where the John Wayne movie *The Conqueror* was being filmed in 1954. Radiation is thought to have contributed to the cancer-related deaths of almost half the cast and crew, including Wayne himself and producer Howard Hughes.

Nevada's nuclear connection continues to this day. In 2002, the Bush administration gave the green light to a plan to store nuclear waste from across the nation on the Test Site, beneath **Yucca Mountain**. Despite endless controversy, inquiries and political wrangling ever since, the scheme has neither been shelved nor implemented.

Howard Hughes and the new Las Vegas

At the start of the 1960s, Las Vegas was the epitome of cool. Even the glamorous young John F Kennedy, as both senator and President-elect, beat a path to the *Sands* to be brushed by the magic of the legendary **Rat Pack** – Frank Sinatra, Dean Martin, Sammy Davis Jr, Peter Lawford and Joey Bishop.

As President, on the other hand, Kennedy stopped taking Sinatra's calls. His brother Robert, the new US Attorney General, went further, castigating Las Vegas as "the bank of America's organized crime." RFK had long loathed Jimmy Hoffa, the president of the International Brotherhood of Teamsters, whose pension fund was the principal investor in several Strip casinos. Both Las Vegas and the Teamsters were forced to clean up their act, though not before the Teamsters achieved their last and greatest gasp, financing the construction in 1966 of *Caesars Palace*, the first of the great themed casinos.

Although *Godfather* author Mario Puzo visited a Hell-themed casino in Reno as early as 1939, *Caesars* was something very new for Las Vegas. Its original owner **Jay Sarno**, who lives on as the plump little bald cartoon "Caesar" in the casino's logo, swiftly followed up by building *Circus Circus*. His most crucial legacy, however, was to set *Caesars* up on an expanse of land – originally rented from **Kirk Kerkorian** (see p.41), who remains a major Las Vegas player to this day – that has so far proved big enough to hold every enlargement architects have been able to imagine.

The beginning of the end for Mob rule in Vegas was signalled by the arrival of reclusive airline tycoon **Howard Hughes** at the *Desert Inn* in late 1966, having just sold TWA for $546 million. When the owners tired of his stingy – specifically, non-gambling – ways, he simply bought the hotel. Hughes went on to buy the *Sands*, the *Silver Slipper* and the *New Frontier*, together with vast tracts of real estate throughout the city, but more important still was his sheer example. Personally he's a candidate for the weirdest human being in history – see p.76 – but financially he was regarded as utterly beyond reproach, and individual entrepreneurs and Wall Street corporations alike soon followed in his wake.

Kirk Kerkorian went on to open the world's largest hotel in Las Vegas on three separate occasions. The first was the *International* in 1969, which witnessed the second coming of **Elvis Presley** as a karate-kicking lounge lizard, and became the *Las Vegas Hilton* within a year; the second was the original *MGM Grand* in 1973, now *Bally's*; and the third was the current *MGM Grand*.

The defining figure of modern Las Vegas, **Steve Wynn**, made his debut on the scene in the early 1970s. He somehow parlayed ownership of a small piece of the parking lot at *Caesars Palace* – acquired by Howard Hughes as part of a bid to buy *Caesars*, then sold to Wynn for no obvious reason – into gaining control of downtown's *Golden Nugget* in 1973. His success in reinventing the *Nugget* as a glittering glamour joint, coupled with a stain-free image, swiftly turned him into a major player.

Hard times

Throughout the 1970s, Las Vegas continued to struggle free from the Mob. Almost every veteran casino went through its own catharsis, as endless federal swoops and stings uncovered "skimming" operations in one after another. Just as the worst seemed finally to be over, however, the city took its biggest blow yet, with the opening of legal casinos in **Atlantic City** in 1978.

In its early years, the growth of gambling on the East Coast hit Las Vegas very hard, with tourists and investors alike flocking to New Jersey rather than Nevada.

Following notorious fires at the *MGM Grand* in 1980, which killed 84 people, and the *Las Vegas Hilton* in 1981, things reached the stage where the last direct flight service between New York and Las Vegas was discontinued in 1983.

And yet Las Vegas survived, and went on to survive the explosion of gambling to cover almost all the United States. Atlantic City found itself on the ropes instead, having served simply to prepare novice gamblers for the sophisticated pleasures of Las Vegas. Donald Trump's much-vaunted *Taj Mahal* in Atlantic City was originally regarded as the trump card that defeated Steve Wynn, who had opened *Golden Nugget Atlantic City* in 1980. In retrospect, however, Wynn can be seen to have won that particular battle by opting to lose the battle over Atlantic City and turn his attention back to Las Vegas.

The development boom

When Steve Wynn opened the *Mirage* in 1989, backed by junk-bond mega-dollars raised in conjunction with the soon-to-be-disgraced financier Michael Milken, he appeared to be taking a breathtaking risk. The first top-flight casino to be built for sixteen years, it required a daily profit of one million dollars from its gaming tables just to stay open, much less be in the black. The *Mirage* was however an instant smash, and its success launched Las Vegas on its biggest boom yet.

The long-established Circus Circus crew swiftly opened *Excalibur*, then leapfrogged to *Luxor* and *Mandalay Bay*. Wynn himself went from *Treasure Island* by way of the *Monte Carlo* to the sumptuous *Bellagio*, Kerkorian constructed his latest *MGM Grand*, and a succession of miniature cities sprang up along the Strip – New York, Venice and Paris. Even downtown got into the act, throwing a roof over its head and calling itself the **Fremont Street Experience**.

The 1990s also saw Las Vegas succeed in adding world-class dining, shopping and clubbing to its bedrock appeal of casino gambling. The one false step along the way was the widely publicized assertion in mid-decade that the city was now a **family destination**. Everyone knows that in fact it's a place to get away from the kids and behave irresponsibly, not to bring them along, and the casinos these days deny they ever suggested anything else.

As the millennium approached, Las Vegas's self-confidence as the world's pre-eminent adult resort seemed unshakeable.

The 21st century

The **21st century** has so far been a thrilling but uncomfortable ride for Las Vegas. It began with a tremendous shock in 2000, when out of the blue Steve Wynn sold the Mirage organization to MGM, and thus lost control of his beloved *Bellagio*. By most accounts other than his own, Wynn was forced to sell, following a disastrous attempt to replicate *Bellagio* in Mississippi. In the wake of the *Venetian's* struggles to establish itself (see p.70) and the foundering of the new *Aladdin* (see p.56), the downturn in tourism that followed 9/11 seemed to sound the death knell for the mega-casino boom.

Soon, however, Las Vegas seemed to be thriving again. Visitor numbers soared once more, thanks in part to a new American preference for domestic travel. The *Venetian* went from strength to strength, and Steve Wynn bounced back in style, unveiling yet another showpiece, *Wynn Las Vegas*, on the site of the old *Desert Inn* in 2005.

The biggest change of all was that the gaming industry was finally seen as respectable enough to attract investment from America's leading banks and financial institutions. Two huge and largely contiguous blocks of Strip casinos became consolidated into the hands of giant **corporations**. In 2005, **MGM–Mirage** bought the Mandalay Resort Group, and thus added *Luxor*, *Excalibur*, *Circus Circus* and *Mandalay Bay* itself to its own already extensive roster. Step by step, the previously unsung **Harrah's** group acquired a number of properties at the heart of the Strip, culminating with the great prize of *Caesars Palace*. A certain excitement drained from the Strip now that each individual casino no longer had to fight all its neighbours, but with revenues at an all-time high their owners grew more ambitious than ever. MGM set about building **CityCenter**, the largest private construction project ever seen.

And then, in 2008, it turned out that the banks had after all been no more reliable or respectable than the old-style casinos. Always especially vulnerable in times of recession, as its fortunes depend on gamblers having money to burn, Las Vegas was suffering as this book went to press. Visitor numbers were down, and casino revenue more so. For MGM to cancel CityCenter would have been a disaster – see p.45 – but completing it in 2009 gave the city thousands more high-end rooms it really didn't need, and depressed the market even further. For the moment, the city is more affordable for visitors than it has been for many years; unless the economy improves soon, however, the big players may start to go broke, in which case it's hard to imagine what the future might hold.

Books

Most of the books listed below are in print and in paperback – those that are out of print are marked o/p. Titles marked with the ✹ symbol are particularly recommended. Las Vegas changes so fast that although exposés of the city's early rise to fame abound, there's currently no up-to-date history that covers the boom of the last decade.

Architecture

Alan Hess *Viva Las Vegas* (o/p). This comprehensive, lovingly illustrated survey of Las Vegas's architectural history up to the early 1990s throws fascinating sidelights on the development of the city.

✹ **Robert Venturi, Denise Scott Brown and Steve Izenour** *Learning From Las Vegas*. Seminal architectural treatise that was in 1972 the first work to hail the Strip as something new and intriguing, and introduced the great debate between "ducks" and "decorated sheds" to the aesthetics of Las Vegas.

History

✹ **Christina Binkley** *Winner Takes All*. Written by a *Wall Street Journal* reporter, this is the only book – so far – to reveal the inside story of how MGM and Harrah's carved up Las Vegas from the mid-2000s onwards.

Jeff Burbank *Las Vegas Babylon*. Breathless romp through Las Vegas scandals old and new, with some entertaining stories about Steve Wynn and Sheldon Adelson to go with the usual Bugsy material.

Deke Castleman *Whale Hunt In The Desert*. A Vegas veteran lifts the lid on the little-known world of how casino "hosts" entice and ensnare big-time gamblers (the "whales" in question) into gambling at their properties.

Dennis Griffin *The Battle For Las Vegas*. Meticulous unpicking of how the Mob finally lost its hold on Las Vegas in the mid-1980s, based on the stories of the law enforcement agents responsible.

Shawn Levy *Rat Pack Confidential*. Enjoyable hymn to the "last great showbiz party", when Las Vegas

prostrated itself at the feet of Frank Sinatra and the boys.

Eugene P Moehring *Resort City In The Sunbelt; Las Vegas 1930–2000*. A dry but very detailed history that aims to show how much Las Vegas has in common with other western cities, as well as what makes it unique.

Nicholas Pileggi *Casino*. The mind-boggling true-life story of Frank "Lefty" Rosenthal and the "skimming" of the *Stardust* by organized crime during the 1970s, which became the basis of Martin Scorsese's movie.

Ed Reid and Ovid Demaris *The Green Felt Jungle*. This classic journalistic exposé from 1963 of Las Vegas's seamy underbelly did nothing whatsoever to dent the city's growth; murders, the Mob, prostitution, it's all here.

Jack Sheehan (ed) *The Players: The Men Who Made Las Vegas*. Very readable warts'n'all biographies of the major figures in Las Vegas's casino history.

John L Smith *No Limit*. An entertaining chronicle of the genesis of Bob Stupak's folly, the *Stratosphere*.

John L Smith *Running Scared: The Life and Treacherous Times of Las Vegas Casino King Steve Wynn*. Comprehensive but now dated biography, in which it turns out, despite Smith's best efforts, that there's not much more to Steve Wynn than meets the eye.

Mike Weatherford *Cult Vegas*. The *Las Vegas-Review Journal*'s entertainment columnist runs a loving eye over the city's music and movie scene, with separate chapters devoted to Frank Sinatra and Elvis Presley, and a fascinating survey of lounges both past and present.

Gambling

Edward Thorp *Beat The Dealer*. The card-counter's bible; mathematical proof that it is possible to win at blackjack if you're equipped with the perfect brain. The casinos soon learned not to fear those who attempted to follow this first of many fiendishly complicated systems.

Barney Vinson *Ask Barney*. Casino insider Vinson, the gaming instructor at *Caesars Palace*, gives the low-down on the gambling business and all that goes with it; fascinating reading, even if it makes you want to give up for good.

Literature

Andres Martinez *24/7: Living It Up and Doubling Down in the New Las Vegas* (o/p). A journalist's non-fiction account of how he took his $50,000 book advance and put it on the line at Vegas's gambling tables.

Robert B Parker *Chance*. Fictional detective Spenser keeps his head above the murky waters of Las Vegas as he delves into some very dirty business indeed.

Mario Puzo *Fools Die*. No, it's not *The Godfather*, and not especially well written either, but this tale of high-stakes gambling, casino cons, Mafioso

and the like manages to be diverting enough.

Hunter S Thompson *Fear and Loathing in Las Vegas*. Classic account of the drug-propelled "gonzo" journalist's lost weekend in early 1970s Las Vegas. What's really striking is how much further over the top the place has gone since then.

Mike Tronnes (ed) *Literary Las Vegas* (o/p). Superb collection of book extracts and magazine articles, which provides the full flavour of the changing city.

Films

With its glittering signs and glamorous casinos, tantalizing hints of menace and decay, and general over-the-top flamboyance, Las Vegas has long been a favourite location for **movie-makers**. The following list highlights films that have used the city to best – or most ludicrous – advantage.

Bugsy *(1991)*. Warren Beatty serves up a larger-than-life version of the *Flamingo*'s Founding Father; he subsequently married co-star Annette Bening.

Casino *(1995)*. Robert de Niro stars as Frank Rosenthal, and Joe Pesci as Antony Spilotro, in Martin Scorsese's gripping account of the dying days of organized crime in 1970s' Las Vegas; the *Tangiers* casino may not exist, but the story's true enough.

Diamonds Are Forever *(1971)*. In his final appearance as James Bond, Sean Connery pursues smuggled diamonds via the fictitious *Whyte House* casino to the all-too-real *Circus Circus*.

Fear and Loathing in Las Vegas *(1998)*. Though Hunter S Thompson's 1971 classic was renowned as the book they couldn't film, Terry Gilliam made a pretty decent stab of it. Johnny Depp is a memorable Thompson, and Benicio del Toro a great Gonzo.

Honeymoon In Vegas *(1992)*. Nicolas Cage is the would-be-groom who loses his intended, Sarah Jessica Parker, to crooked gambler James Caan, then wins her back by parachuting into *Bally's* with the Flying Elvises.

Indecent Proposal *(1993)*. Much the same plot as *Honeymoon In Vegas*, though this time no one, from billionaire Robert Redford to the bewildered Demi Moore or the hapless Woody Harrelson, is playing it for laughs.

Leaving Las Vegas *(1995)*. This time Nicolas Cage is in Las Vegas to drink himself to death. Despite the best Elisabeth Shue can do, as the proverbial hooker with a heart of gold, he succeeds – and wins an Oscar and a Golden Globe for his pains.

Mars Attacks *(1996)*. Tim Burton's playful sci-fi fantasy captures all the exuberance and absurdity of Las Vegas, incorporating the real-life destruction of the *Landmark* casino before Tom Jones finally saves the day.

Ocean's 11 *(1960/2001)*. The definitive oh-so-cool original saw Frank, Dino, Sammy and the rest of the Rat Pack rob five casinos in the same night; George Clooney, Brad Pitt and a new gang pulled off the same stunt against a thinly-veiled Steve Wynn forty years later.

Showgirls *(1995)*. Paul Verhoeven's sexploitation saga lingers lovingly on young Elizabeth Berkley, struggling to make it big as a Las Vegas dancer. A flop in cinemas, it sold millions on DVD; now why would that be?

The Hangover *(2009)*. The biggest Las Vegas hit for many years makes great play out of its *Caesars Palace* setting; Mike Tyson steals the show in an unforgettable cameo.

Viva Las Vegas *(1964)*. Elvis as a hotshot racing driver Lucky Jackson, Ann Margret as the teacher he woos and wins; what's not to like?

What Happens in Vegas *(2008)*. Making a hit romantic comedy out of a marketing slogan was never really going to work, but Cameron Diaz and Ashton Kutcher squeeze a little mileage from their ill-fated meeting at *Planet Hollywood*.

FAIR FARES from
NORTH SOUTH TRAVEL

Our great-value air fares cover the world, from Abuja to Zanzibar and from Zurich to Anchorage. North South Travel is a fund-raising travel agency, owned by the NST Development Trust.

ALL our profits go to development organisations.

Call 01245 608 291 (or +44 1245 608 291 if outside UK) to speak to a friendly advisor. Your money is safe (ATOL 5401). For more information, visit northsouthtravel.co.uk. Free Rough Guide of your choice for every booking over £500.

EVERY FLIGHT A FIGHT AGAINST POVERTY

Small print and

Index

A Rough Guide to Rough Guides

Published in 1982, the first Rough Guide – to Greece – was a student scheme that became a publishing phenomenon. Mark Ellingham, a recent graduate in English from Bristol University, had been travelling in Greece the previous summer and couldn't find the right guidebook. With a small group of friends he wrote his own guide, combining a highly contemporary, journalistic style with a thoroughly practical approach to travellers' needs.

The immediate success of the book spawned a series that rapidly covered dozens of destinations. And, in addition to impecunious backpackers, Rough Guides soon acquired a much broader and older readership that relished the guides' wit and inquisitiveness as much as their enthusiastic, critical approach and value-for-money ethos.

These days, Rough Guides include recommendations from shoestring to luxury and cover more than 200 destinations around the globe, including almost every country in the Americas and Europe, more than half of Africa and most of Asia and Australasia. Our ever-growing team of authors and photographers is spread all over the world, particularly in Europe, the US and Australia.

In the early 1990s, Rough Guides branched out of travel, with the publication of Rough Guides to World Music, Classical Music and the Internet. All three have become benchmark titles in their fields, spearheading the publication of a wide range of books under the Rough Guide name.

Including the travel series, Rough Guides now number more than 350 titles, covering: phrasebooks, waterproof maps, music guides from Opera to Heavy Metal, reference works as diverse as Conspiracy Theories and Shakespeare, and popular culture books from iPods to Poker. Rough Guides also produce a series of more than 120 World Music CDs in partnership with World Music Network.

Visit www.roughguides.com to see our latest publications.

Rough Guide credits

Text editor: James Rice
Layout: Umesh Aggarwal
Cartography: Ed Wright, Katie Lloyd-Jones
Picture editor: Sarah Cummins
Production: Erika Pepe
Proofreader: Stewart Wild
Cover design: Nicole Newman, Dan May,
Chloë Roberts
Photographers: Greg Roden and Greg Ward
Editorial: London Andy Turner, Keith Drew,
Edward Aves, Alice Park, Lucy White, Jo Kirby,
James Smart, Natasha Foges, Róisín Cameron,
Emma Beatson, Emma Gibbs, Kathryn Lane,
Monica Woods, Mani Ramaswamy, Harry Wilson,
Lucy Cowie, Alison Roberts, Lara Kavanagh,
Eleanor Aldridge, Ian Blenkinsop, Joe Staines,
Matthew Milton, Tracy Hopkins; **Delhi** Madhavi
Singh, Jalpreen Kaur Chhatwal, Jubbi Francis
Design & Pictures: London Scott Stickland,
Dan May, Diana Jarvis, Mark Thomas, Nicole

Newman, Emily Taylor; **Delhi** Ajay Verma, Jessica
Subramanian, Ankur Guha, Pradeep Thapliyal,
Sachin Tanwar, Anita Singh, Nikhil Agarwal,
Sachin Gupta
Production: Rebecca Short, Liz Cherry,
Louise Daly
Cartography: Delhi Rajesh Chhibber, Ashutosh
Bharti, Rajesh Mishra, Animesh Pathak, Jasbir
Sandhu, Swati Handoo, Deshpal Dabas,
Lokamata Sahu
Marketing, Publicity & roughguides.com:
Liz Statham
Digital Travel Publisher: Peter Buckley
Reference Director: Andrew Lockett
Operations Assistant: Becky Doyle
Operations Manager: Helen Atkinson
Publishing Director (Travel): Clare Currie
Commercial Manager: Gino Magnotta
Managing Director: John Duhigg

Publishing information

This first edition published April 2011 by
Rough Guides Ltd,
80 Strand, London WC2R 0RL
11, Community Centre, Panchsheel Park,
New Delhi 110017, India

Distributed by the Penguin Group

Penguin Books Ltd,
80 Strand, London WC2R 0RL

Penguin Group (USA)
375 Hudson Street, NY 10014, USA

Penguin Group (Australia)
250 Camberwell Road, Camberwell,
Victoria 3124, Australia

Penguin Group (NZ)
67 Apollo Drive, Mairangi Bay, Auckland 1310,
New Zealand

Rough Guides is represented in Canada by
Tourmaline Editions Inc. 662 King Street West,
Suite 304, Toronto, Ontario M5V 1M7

Cover concept by Peter Dyer.

Typeset in Bembo and Helvetica to an original
design by Henry Iles.

Printed in Singapore
© Greg Ward 2011
Maps © Rough Guides
No part of this book may be reproduced in any
form without permission from the publisher except
for the quotation of brief passages in reviews.
208pp includes index
A catalogue record for this book is available from
the British Library
ISBN: 978-1-84836-566-7

The publishers and authors have done their best
to ensure the accuracy and currency of all the
information in **The Rough Guide to Las Vegas**,
however, they can accept no responsibility for
any loss, injury, or inconvenience sustained by
any traveller as a result of information or advice
contained in the guide.

1   3   5   7   9   8   6   4   2

Help us update

We've gone to a lot of effort to ensure that the
first edition of **The Rough Guide to Las Vegas**
is accurate and up-to-date. However, things
change – places get "discovered", opening hours
are notoriously fickle, restaurants and rooms raise
prices or lower standards. If you feel we've got it
wrong or left something out, we'd like to know,
and if you can remember the address, the price,
the hours, the phone number, so much the better.

Please send your comments with the subject
line "**Rough Guide Las Vegas Update**" to ©mail
@uk.roughguides.com. We'll credit all
contributions and send a copy of the next edition
(or any other Rough Guide if you prefer) for the
very best emails.

Find more travel information, connect with
fellow travellers and book your trip on ®www
.roughguides.com

Acknowledgements

Greg Ward Thanks as so often before to my dear wife Sam, for all her support, encouragement and positive input. At Rough Guides, thanks to James Rice for his insightful and constructive editing, and Katie and Ed for producing such great maps. Thanks also to everyone who helped me to find and enjoy the very best of Las Vegas, including Cara Abrahams, Hannah Allen, Claudia Balfe-Taylor, Emily Burton, Stephanie Capellas, Stephanie Chavez, Katie Conway, Jerry Digney, Maggie Feldman, David Gonzalez, Robert Graff, Sara Gorgon, Kimberly Juday, Alison Monaghan, Marina Nicola, Ann Paladie, Lindsey Rathjen, Rochelle Samilin-Jurani, Brad Seidel, Mandi Walsh, Ziva Werber and Wendy Zamaripa.

Index

Map entries are in colour.

So now we've told you about the things not to miss, the best places to stay, the top restaurants, the liveliest bars and the most spectacular sights, it only seems fair to tell you about the best travel insurance around

WorldNomads.com
keep travelling safely

Recommended by Rough Guides

Map symbols

maps are listed in the full index using coloured text

▬ ▬ · ▬ ▬	State border
▬⟨17⟩▬	Interstate highway
═⟨89⟩═ ·	US highway
═⟨12⟩═	State highway
═ ═ ═ ═ ═ ═	Unpaved road
}═ ═ ═ {	Tunnel
▬▬●▬▬	Railway
▬ ▬ ▬ ▬ ▬	Private railway
─ ─ ─ ─ ─	Footpath/trail
·······●·······	Monorail/tram route & station
⊞⊞⊞⊞⊞	Escalator/steps
───────	Coastline/river
▭	Water
⊏⊐	Bridge
▲	Peak
◆	Point of interest

ⓘ	Visitor center/ tourist information
🅿	Parking
☀	Viewpoint/overlook
◉	Accommodation
🛆	Campsite
♟	Museum
🎿	Ski area
👥	Racing circuit
⛳	Golf course
✈	Major airport
✈	Minor airport/airfield
▬	Building
⊞	Church
▦	Park/gardens/ national monument
▨	Indian reservation

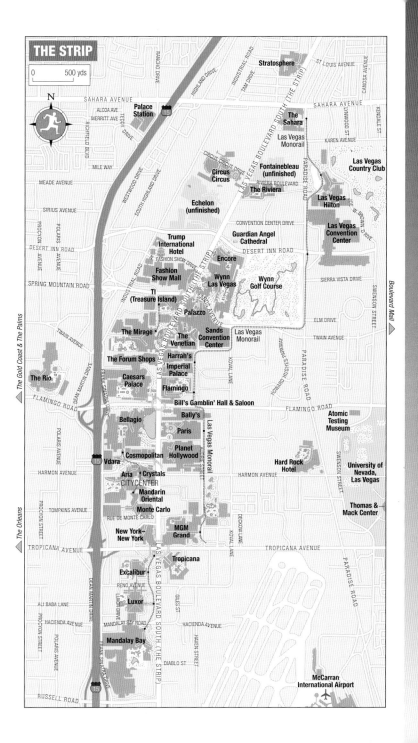

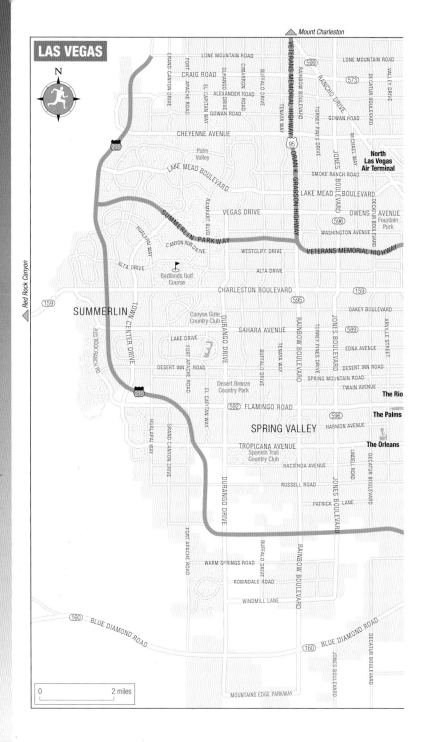

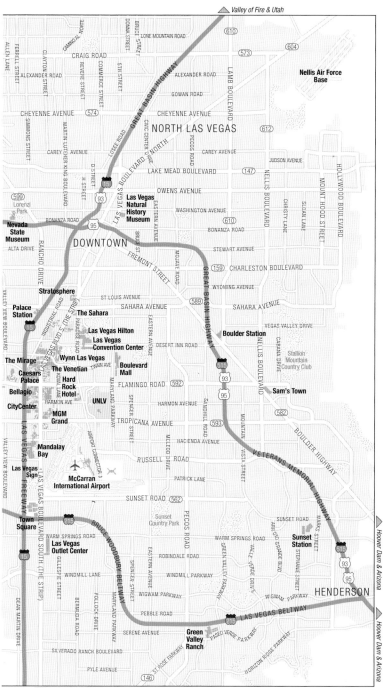

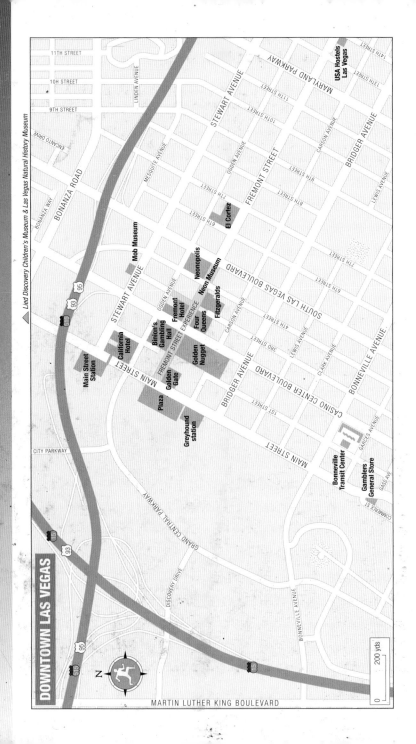

▲ Lied Discovery Children's Museum & Las Vegas Natural History Museum

DOWNTOWN LAS VEGAS

N

0 : 200 yds

MARTIN LUTHER KING BOULEVARD

CITY PARKWAY

11TH STREET
10H STREET
9TH STREET

LINDEN AVENUE

ENCANTO DRIVE

BONANZA ROAD

BONANZA WAY

MESQUITE AVENUE

STEWART AVENUE

Mob Museum

Main Street Station

California Hotel

OGDEN AVENUE

Binion's Gambling Hall

FREMONT STREET EXPERIENCE

Fremont Hotel

Four Queens

Neonopolis

Neon Museum

Fitzgeralds

El Cortez

Golden Gate

Plaza

Golden Nugget

Greyhound station

MAIN STREET

STEWART AVENUE

GRAND CENTRAL PARKWAY

DISCOVERY DRIVE

STEWART AVENUE

MARYLAND PARKWAY

USA Hostels Las Vegas

14TH STREET
13TH STREET

FREMONT STREET

OGDEN AVENUE

7TH STREET
8TH STREET
9TH STREET
10TH STREET
11TH STREET

CARSON AVENUE

BRIDGER AVENUE

LEWIS AVENUE

SOUTH LAS VEGAS BOULEVARD

6TH STREET
7TH STREET

CARSON AVENUE

4TH STREET

3RD STREET

BRIDGER AVENUE

CASINO CENTER BOULEVARD

LEWIS AVENUE

CLARK AVENUE

1ST STREET

BONNEVILLE AVENUE

BONNEVILLE AVENUE

MAIN STREET

GARCES AVENUE

Bonneville Transit Center

Gamblers General Store

GASS AVE

COMMERCE ST

BONNEVILLE AVENUE